NICE IS JUST A PLACE IN FRANCE

NICE IS JUST A PLACE IN FRANCE

HOW TO WIN AT BASICALLY EVERYTHING

The Betches

G

GALLERY BOOKS

New York London Toronto Sydney New Delhi

Disclaimer: Before writing this book we spoke to our lawyer (obvi one our dads recommended). We told him that even though there are some jokes about shit like not eating and blacking out daily, we'd feel really bad if someone actually took our advice and like died. We kind of feel bad for anyone who takes our advice in general. Just like you should never copy a betch's notes or test answers (the first don't exist, and the second are probably just copied from someone else), you should be careful before you copy a betch's lifestyle. Okay, that's enough niceness for one book. And if you try to sue us because you thought you followed our advice and acted like a fucking idiot, we will just follow in Cher's footsteps: call our father, tell him the problem, and he'll figure out how to argue it.

G

Gallery Books
A Division of Simon & Schuster, Inc.
1230 Avenue of the Americas
New York, NY 10020

First Gallery Books trade paperback edition March 2013

GALLERY BOOKS and colophon are registered trademarks of Simon & Schuster, Inc.

For information about special discounts for bulk purchases, please contact Simon & Schuster Special Sales at 1-866-506-1949 or business@simonandschuster.com.

The Simon & Schuster Speakers Bureau can bring authors to your live event.
For more information or to book an event contact the Simon & Schuster Speakers Bureau at 1-866-248-3049 or visit our website at www.simonspeakers.com.

Designed by Jaime Putorti

Manufactured in the United States of America

20 19 18

Library of Congress Cataloging-in-Publication Data is available

ISBN 978-1-4516-8776-7
ISBN 978-1-4516-8777-4 (e-book)

Thank you to Xanax, for getting us through those anxiety-ridden meetings with publishers.

Thank you to Adderall, without which we'd probably still be trying to figure out how to make a website.

Contents

Image: How to Appear
Unapproachable and Hot ✦ 67

Social Life: People Who ~~You Like~~ Are
Worthy of Your Friendship— ✦ 111

College: Using Higher Education to Get Ahead ✦ *149*

"Career": A Word We Use Loosely ✦ *183*

Sex: Keep Your Legs Closed and You Too Can Rule the World ✦ *203*

NICE IS JUST A PLACE IN FRANCE

Introduction to the Best Book You'll Ever Read

Dear Reader,

Jambo! If you're anything like us, and we'll assume you are because you're reading our book, you probably have a very short attention span, so we'll keep this introduction brief. But first we must commend you on already making it farther into a book than Helen Keller ever could. Nice.

Apologies if that last comment was insensitive. Relax, it's not like she can see it anyway. That, however, was a test, and if we've already offended your sensibilities, we advise you to walk away. The ride toward enlightenment on which you're about to embark is not going to get any smoother.

So what is this book? It's like a guide to everything, but really it's just all the shit that no one will say out loud. A collection of truths, if you will. As you read on, you'll find yourself agreeing that, in most cases, conventional wisdom can and should go fuck itself. For

> "*I succeeded by saying what everyone else is thinking.*"
> —Joan Rivers

example, life is not a box of chocolates. Instead, you should give that box of chocolates to someone else to eat, learn from their expanding ass what happens to people who sample chocolates as a hobby, and remain a size 2. Or a personal favorite of ours: A watched pot never boils. . . . Really? Um, yeah, we're fairly sure it does boil, at the exact same rate, regardless of whether you're watching. We know this because we once boiled water to clean our bong.

But the most important thing this book will teach you is in the title, *Nice Is Just a Place in France*. What does it mean, exactly? Simply put, niceness is boring and overrated. Girls who think that being "nice" is something to aspire to are most likely setting themselves up for a life of mediocrity, boredom, and cats.

We're not saying you should be a huge bitch and never give a shit about anyone. Having friends is definitely encouraged; we even devote a whole chapter to them. We're simply cautioning you against becoming what we've dubbed the "nicegirl."

WHAT IS THE NICEGIRL?

The nicegirl plays by the rules without ever questioning them. She's dull, lacks depth, lets people walk all over her, yet brings nothing to the table. If she disappeared, you wouldn't even notice. She's the girl who rarely colors outside the lines of her life, and even then only in baby pink. She's the kind of girl who uses a real bookmark. In other words, she's boring as fuck.

What's so bad about being nice? Nothing. We have no problem with girls who are nice people, though we personally know only one or two. All we're saying is that you should learn to be a girl who looks out for herself first and does not allow others to take advantage of her. Ideally, you should be doing the advantage-taking. Think about it, if you were ever describing someone you really respected or admired, would you ever describe this person as "nice"? No way. You would have a list of fifty other interesting things to say about that person before you would ever resort to that word. "Nice" is what you'd call someone who's so melba you can't even take the time to think of why you don't like them. To call them dry toast would be generous, because even dry toast has flavor, whereas nicegirls do not.

The way we see it, nicegirls are a problem for the whole female gender. They perpetuate the stereotypes that women are inferior, that we're not smart or funny, and that we should stay in the kitchen while men continue running things. Sometimes this works to our advantage. For instance, we definitely don't want to work. However, not on the basis that we're too stupid to do so; it's simply because we want rich husbands who would make that pointless.

So what does not being a nicegirl have to do with winning? The underlying principle of winning is understanding why and when you don't need to be nice, which is most of the time (unless you're talking to your dog). The reality of being a nicegirl is that you'll be pushed over, looked down upon, and considered boring. Think Anne Hathaway in *The Devil Wears Prada*. Actually, think Anne Hathaway period. Women can't win by accommodating people; we need to be decisive and know what we want and achieve it in a smart way, while putting forth minimal effort for optimal results. And that's what this book is about.

We're also not writing about the Charlie Sheen version of #winning, which is the alpha-

HISTORICAL BLIND ITEM

A not-so-attractive betch once said: "~~Well-behaved women~~ Nicegirls seldom make history."

male idea of winning, also known as acting like a massive dickshit. We're talking about the female version of succeeding at life, which contrary to traditional feminist propaganda isn't necessarily synonymous with becoming your company's first female CEO. We're talking about getting what you want and coming out on top of any situation: relationships, career, friends, enemies, and all the acquaintances in between. And, of course, choosing the right Facebook profile picture.

So who's the girl who's always winning? She, my frenemies, is the betch.

SO WTF IS A BETCH?

You may not know the word, but you definitely know the girl. She's the girl who has guys wrapped around her finger, whose outfit is always perfectly conceived, and who magically accomplishes whatever she wants, whether it's getting an amazing job at twenty-two or engaged at twenty-five, and she does it effortlessly. She may seem unapproachable, but those who are lucky enough to know her are likely to claim that she's "really great if you're friends with her, but she can be a *huge* bitch."

But unlike those girls who peak in high school, the betch is the one who always has (mostly) everything figured out, minus maybe a stomach pump or two. Everything she associates with is trendy, every guy wants to date her, and every girl wants to be her friend, but not because she's, like, kind or anything. She's edgy, speaks her mind, and commands a room just by being in it.

If you find yourself smiling right now, it's either because you think you're this girl or you want to be her. And who better to tell you how than the people who like invented her?

It's easy to confuse the word "betch" with "bitch," but make no mistake, they're vastly different. It's like how nicegirls read magazines, but you can be a not-nicegirl and read magazines. Bitches are not automatically betches. No girl wants to be called a bitch, even though she most definitely acts like one; that is, girls want to be strong, confident, not

> *"Men are not the enemy, but the fellow victims. The real enemy is women's denigration of themselves."*
> —Betty Friedan

care what people say about them, and not take shit from anyone. But there has never been a word that embodies this girl. Guys are bros; they do bro-y things. Until we popularized the term "betch," girls never had a name—and no, we don't think slampiece or cum-dumpster qualify. Regardless of what she says, every girl wants to be a betch, because a betch gets what she wants.

Betchiness is a way to succeed in the world, with a vagina, in a real way. Who are we to know anything about this? We're just a few girls who realized that there's more to life than being really, really ridiculously good-looking. (But not that much.)

TENETS OF BETCHINESS

Betchiness is not what you have or where you're from. It's an attitude. It's a lifestyle. It's a state of mind. Betchiness comes from the inside, unlike beauty. These tenets are the major points that underlie the entire theory of winning at life. Follow them and you will achieve ~~Zen~~ power.

Tenet 1: Don't Do Work—The Threshold Theory

As females, we've accepted that for the vast majority of history, society's list of expectations for our gender read as such: Reproduce. Check baby for penis. If none, reproduce again. Repeat.

Obviously, things are different now that women sometimes get jobs or like get elected prime minister or whatever. Go ahead and do those things if you so desire, we're clearly supportive of power.

However, it's important to realize that as a woman, you have the special privilege of not *needing* to work as hard as men do—in the general sense—unless you want to. The truth is that men pretty much gave up their right to demand we do anything, if you consider that for most of human existence, society ran pretty smoothly without our involvement. We don't have to be the breadwinning gender if we don't want to be, and we are fucking happy about that.

> "If you always do what interests you, at least one person is pleased."
> —Katharine Hepburn

Don't get us wrong, we're definitely progressive and want our shit-talking voice to be heard. We're just saying it's perfectly okay to let men believe they are superior beings without whom civilization would crumble. Regardless of whether you agree, this ego boost is exactly what they need to do things for you (e.g., pay for dinner, overachieve on work projects, propose marriage).

When it comes to most things, it's okay to let other people, especially men, do things that you are too lazy to do for yourself. This leaves you with more time and options to choose what you *want* to do. That's the freedom in being female.

> "The English language is all about subliminal domination . . . semen to ovaries. That's why I'm petitioning to have next term be referred to as winter o-ves-ter."
> —That lesbian from *Legally Blonde*

So how do you determine the right balance of effort to put forth to get what you want? The Threshold Theory, obvs. We fortuitously arrived at this theory as a result of being high in Barnes & Noble one time, when we accidentally skimmed through *The Tao of Pooh,* and holy shit, did we see the light. The Taoists say (or at least from what we remember) that inaction is the best form of action. It's called wu wei. Look it up. Anyway, we decided to apply this philosophy to our lives. From that point forward, whoever was

> "Govern a great nation as you would cook a small fish. Do not overdo it."
> —Lao Tze

the most bothered by the weed ashes and sticky shot glasses on our kitchen counter would be the one to clean it up. Unfortunately, this was none of us. Moral of the story: Call a cleaning lady.

The Threshold Theory essentially means that the person who most wants the metaphorical apartment to be clean will clean it up. Think of life as an ongoing auction, and whoever wants something most desperately will be the one who puts forth the effort to get it.

Why is this meaningful? Because the key to getting people to do shit for you is to care less (or appear to care less) than others.[1] If you find yourself caring about something, just remind yourself that you don't need to give a fuck. Caring is for nicegirls.

For example, if you want to hang out with a guy, let him contact you. If you want to get an A on your group project, be in the group with the bitch who turned down Princeton. If you want an iced coffee, order delivery.

> "Generally speaking, anybody is more interesting doing nothing than doing anything."
> —Gertrude Stein

Point-blank, chill out. Don't be too aggressive about things unless they're *really* meaningful to you, and don't be afraid to let other people do shit for you. You don't even need to worry that you're taking advantage. Phoebe Buffay taught us that there's no such thing as a selfless good deed, so anyone who's helping you is most likely help-

---

1   Unless you're talking about charities or causes. How else would people recognize you for having the most money to donate?

ing themselves in some way, whether or not this is clear to you. Just go with it and let the chips fall ~~where they may~~ into your handbag. Your goal should always be to achieve the maximum result with the least effort; whether it's through manipulation or taking advantage of an opportunity. (See: sex tapes, Kardashian.)

Always remember that less is more, unless you're talking about shots.

Tenet 2: Don't Be Weak

Perhaps the biggest generalizations that people make about the female gender are that women are weak and can't make decisions and cry too much.

We'll start off this tenet with a true story. While sitting in a class about diversity in college, the Japanese-American-MeltingPotOfRaces professor proclaimed that at the current rate, it would take two hundred years for there to be an equal ratio of male and female CEOs in the workforce. Upon hearing this, some bitch sitting next to us burst into tears. The worst part was that Melting Pot was all, *I completely understand why you're crying over this.* But we were just like, U mad?

This story demonstrates the very essence of why two hundred years is too soon. Granted, the girl was probably on her period, but the fact that she was moved to tears by data she didn't like is the precise reason why it will take at least two centuries for an equal number of women to finally get the chance to write one of those cute little IPO letters. Women who whine about the glass ceiling are not just part of the problem, they are the problem. Any time an aspiring female CEO cries, an actual female CEO gets hit by a

> "Any woman who understands the problems of running a home will be nearer to understanding the problems of running a country."
> —Margaret Thatcher

bus. Tears are like lies. The more you use them, the less they're worth. The moral of the story is: STOP FUCKING CRYING.

Here's why: weakness = death. The weaker you are, the less likely you are to get where you want to be. Whether it's in a relationship or career, the amount of abuse you will or won't take from other people will have a direct effect on your success in anything. If you take shit from a guy you're hooking up with, you're never going to date him. If you take shit from your coworkers,

> "*You want some respect? Go out there and get it for yourself.*" —Don Draper

you're never going to get promoted. If you take shit from your parents, your sibling will get the better half of the estate.

Tenet 3: Image Matters

We'll keep this one short because we dedicate an entire chapter to image, but for now we'll say that the Spice Girls are the perfect model for the importance of image. By the time of their tragic breakup in 2001, they were all huge celebrities who could've made themselves into anything. Sporty could've been a spokeswoman for Nike. Ginger, who was all bulimic and shit, could've been a spokeswoman for L'Oréal DIY highlights or like done porn. Baby could've been in *Rugrats on Ice,* and Scary could've been the next Foxxy Cleopatra. But the only one who actually made a name for herself post–girl band era was Victoria Beckham.

Why? Because she was hot, skinny, never seemed to give a shit, and her alias, Posh, didn't suggest that she was a monster, a toddler, or an Asian seasoning.

The reason why Victoria Beckham became an icon is proof enough that the image you make for yourself means everything. Sure her cheat days consist of a fish egg and two strawberries, but if that's what it takes to be married to David Beckham and produce a litter of Anne Geddes models while never gaining a pound, so be it.

The underlying reason that this all matters is that it's every woman's goal in life to have healthy and good-looking children. If you're a fat bitch with high cholesterol, do you think your husband is going to be a man with chiseled abs and the metabolism of a professional athlete? And without the sperm of said athlete, there's no chance you're going to reproduce these golden children. Moral of the story: Don't fuck the goalie.

Tenet 4: Work with What You Have

Let's say your image isn't up to societal par. Perhaps you're plagued with a semiannual goiter or whatever. In your case, the limit exists. The key here is to understand the cards you've been dealt and how far you can go with them. Assess the distance you can really "travel" in life with your goiter in tow. What can you do to make your life better? Do you get surgery? The woman who understands her limitations and asks herself these honest questions is already five steps ahead of the girl who's still wallowing in self-pity over her stage-4 rosacea.

The solution is to face the reality of who you are and how you look, take the opportunities you discover, and understand how to manipulate the system.

Tenet 5: Face Reality and Take Opportunity

Here's the thing about Snooki: She might be the weirdest-looking human you've ever seen, but she's debatably one of the most cunning opportunists of the past ten years, after Kris Jenner of course. We're not calling Snooki a betch necessarily, but think about this, where was Snooki going if she hadn't been on *Jersey Shore*? She's an adopted Chilean girl who's not even five feet tall, from a trashy place, and yet every single person in America knows her name. The bitch branded herself as the little meatball that could. And that's why no other cast member on that show is paid more than she is.

You may laugh that we're seriously using Snooki as an example, but just because her goals are not the same as your own, the lesson lies in what she did with the image she had. Like, if you were a Jersey Guido, wouldn't you want to be the best and richest fucking Jersey Guido ever? Moral of the story: If you're uneducated, look out for MTV casting calls.

Tenet 6: Manipulate the System

Make fun of the Kardashians all you want, but Kris Jenner has essentially manipulated the entire world into becoming obsessed with her family's every move. Armed with only a sex tape and a marital bond to a tight-faced Olympian, the family used what they had to become an American dynasty.

When the Kardashians became a sensation, Kris Jenner was already well past her prime, but she clearly realized that by using her Armenian offspring as pawns in her family drama, she could create an empire.

You may protest that Kris Jenner singlehandedly caused America's demise and her family embodies everything that's wrong with our generation, but you're not going to improve your own life with that attitude. Think about it, you're complaining about America, but you're still living here and that's not going to change. If you hate it so much, then leave. Oh, wait, you probably can't, because you don't have enough money or employment mobility or general options to go elsewhere. But guess who does: the fucking Kardashians.

You can argue that it's only because they're privileged rich kids whose mom got them a reality show, and that's true. But had they not handled their situation so well, they could've easily gone down the well-blazed trail of Lindsay Lohan, Courtney Love, and countless other celebrities who wasted their money on drug addictions that rendered them talentless. Instead, the Kardashians garnered all the stupidity they could muster, took their one show and made themselves into caricatures of humans to each get their own shows, and then took advantage of America's fascination to sell us shit we don't need.

The point is that people need to stop bitching about how things should be and learn to live with how they are. Once you accept this you can spin things to your advantage. The difference between you and the Kardashians is that they took an opportunity to work within the system, depraved as it may be, instead of trying to hate on it. No matter where you are in life, you can always figure out how to use a situation to your advantage, but first you have to accept it for what it is. Moral of the story: The Kardashians get paid for breathing.

SO YOUR INTRO WAS LIKE REALLY PRETTY . . . WHAT ELSE IS THIS BOOK ABOUT?

Chill the fuck out. This book isn't self-help. Self-help is for fat people and divorcées. If you're looking for a book on how to deal with being alone, go elsewhere. This book is the betchy girl's bible, guiding her through situations a betch might encounter, such as: what to do if you find yourself being drawn to act like a nicegirl, what to do when your pot dealer doesn't answer, and is it okay to give head on the first date?

This is how to deal with your problems when you have no problems.

Glossary

BBB: Back-Burner Bro. The back-burner bro is technically great: He's perfect on paper so you *should* like him but for some reason you just don't. Like most guys, he's into you, so you keep him around for purposes of making the guy you actually like jealous or as someone to make out with whenever you're drunk and bored.

BSCB: Bat Shit Crazy Betch. Every bestie group should have one of these people. She is the token crazy friend. In addition to providing entertainment, the BSCB serves to make the rest of us feel like we are normal. The BSCB persona can take many forms but typically possesses the following qualities: compulsive need to rage, psycho breakdowns/tantrums, and sociopathic tendencies.

GBFF: The Gay BFF. Gay best friends are both total fucking experts in how to behave and completely emotionally removed from whatever questionable behavior we confess to them. Kind of like the kid with Asperger's who, when the professor asked what you thought your team's project grade should be, gave his group a D. They're the referees of the betch life, objective bystanders who you can trust because they have no (fore)skin in the game.

JPB: Jealous Pasty Betch. When tanning, the JPB is the one who gets sunburned in less time than it takes to get through an *Us Weekly* article. She'll go on and on about how unhealthy it is to tan, simultaneously applying SPF 70 and smoking a cigarette.

Lucky-Sperm Club. The Lucky-Sperm Club is used to describe talentless celebrities and rich people who were born into wealthy or famous families. We love these people because their lack of talent makes them very entertaining, and everyone secretly wishes to have been born into one of these families and be famous for no reason. Classic examples include Prince William, Kim Kardashian, and Nicole Richie.

MGB: Maybe Gay Bro. The maybe gay bro is someone many people suspect is gay due to his keen fashion sense and appreciation for the finer things in life. However, no one is positive if he is gay, and he still hooks up with girls, although he has many female friends. Occasionally a betch may date the MGB, if only for his perfect features, amazing style, and taste for restaurants that serve tiny portions of extremely expensive food.

Mupload. Mobile upload. *Fucking duh.*

Pros. Bros in the future or former nice guys turned rich and asshole-ish. These guys make a lot of money and are not afraid to spend it on you. As a betch gets older, she moves from liking bros to liking pros, because she's tired of dealing with shadiness.

SAB: Shady Asshole Bro. The bro who is regularly fucking five girls at a time, of whom betches should steer clear. This bro can and will string you along for anywhere from two weeks to ten years, depending on how long you're willing to put up with his shady shit.

TGF: Trying to Get Fucked. Much like being DTF, only much more pathetic. This girl is actively desperate for any guy to have sex with her. TGF can also be a vibe you get from a girl, like when she's standing on a street corner visibly trying to display her cleavage and pop her ass while engaging in serious close-talking with any bro she sees. It sometimes reminds us of the prostitutes we saw in the red-light district in Amsterdam. It's like so sad.

VIP: Very Important Penis. This is basically another term for a fuck buddy. One usually has about two of these to ensure no attachments and that one gets laid on a regular basis. They are "friends" in theory, but really they just use each other for sex.

WGA: (The Guy Who) Won't Go Away. The WGA is the guy with whom you feel you have a "special connection" and who you've been seeing for a while, and yet he's never actually dated you consistently. He lingers around your life like a dementor and tends to check in periodically, swooping in whenever it seems like you're happy, only to fuck shit up. Best to get rid of him to make room for guys who are into you.

WYDEL: The Wish You Didn't Exist List. Being a member of this list is harmful to your physical and mental health because it means you are a betch's arch nemesis and you can expect a drunken brawl to come your way very soon.

Lifestyle

How to Live Like a Betch

The betch's lifestyle is chic and carefree and involves a lifelong pattern of being given everything we deserve. *I mean, I was born with perfect symmetry of the face, so of course I deserve a horse at age four.* Who cares if times are tough, we've always gotten what we wanted, let's keep things consistent. Like, I didn't ask to be born in the booming '90s when everyone was rich as fuck, and I didn't ask for my closet to be half the size of my bedroom, nor did I ask you to fill my closet . . . well, maybe I did, but it's whatever, you didn't say no!

Above all things, it was fucked up of our parents to even birth us into this world and then suddenly expect us to fend for ourselves in our midtwenties. Do you realize how much richer we'll have to marry in order to keep up our streak of never flying commercial?

But as we all know, life isn't about arriving at your destination, it's about how many shots you take on the plane. Your goal should always be to enjoy the ride as much as you can. We know whoever coined the term "lifestyle" must've been a betch, because that's exactly what you want: a life of style.

While our lives may appear to be perfect, to quote my anorexic friend's therapist, there's no such thing as perfection. To say we exist in a state of endless bliss is an exaggeration. Our lives are nothing like Precious's or anything, but it's all relative. We have plenty of problems and issues to address, like imperfect gel manicures or how we wish the gardener would muffle his fucking leaf blower in the morning. So how does one solve these problems? The only way we know how: by talking shit about them.

TALKING SHIT: EMBRACING THE END OF NICEGIRLS

Be it gossiping among your friends, writing an angry letter to the editor, making snarky comments during a graduation speech, whatever—talking shit is the reason we get up every afternoon.

Whether it's about other girls, guys, our besties, celebrities, professors, poor people . . . if you have a flaw, we will find a way to talk shit about it. At first glance, the act of saying negative things about someone can seem catty and mean. But we're just being honest. Being critical gives us edge in a world of fluff and incessant, undeserved flattery. The nicegirl in the room may urge you, "*Stop! These are real people we're talking about!*" But we know the truth: If you're not hot, fucking hilarious, and/or rich, you're not a real person.

> "*Why can't you just be happy for me and then go home and talk behind my back later like a normal person!?*"
> —*Bridesmaids*

Some may call talking shit "giving our insecurities a voice," but in actuality, it's just a natural facet of being a female—kind of like wearing makeup or not knowing how to drive.

As seen from any TV show that calls itself "reality," from *Laguna Beach* to the entire *Real Housewives* franchise, the plot of each episode never fails to focus on one betch meeting another betch at an outdoor restaurant patio to have a drink and talk about their other ~~friends~~ cast members. You think Lisa Vanderpump actually wants to invite tacky Adrienne Maloof over for tea? Fuck no! They just need an excuse to discuss the claustrophobic issues of Bravo Andy's clubhouse or debate which of the housewives was the most airbrushed on her book cover.

But talking shit isn't just something betches do to counteract boredom and show people how funny we are; though these are indeed added benefits, it's also fundamental to getting our fix of manipulating others. How do you expect your coworker to help you sabotage the office overachiever's plan to steal your promotion if you don't first express your mutual dislike of her? Now you've not only bonded with a colleague and found a way to entertain yourself at work, but you've also been promoted.

> **CAVEAT:** We should warn you that men have no interest in talking shit and doing so in front of them will make you appear foolish and petty. It's important to remember that talking shit is a feminine instinct, and this ritual governs female lives in a way that males could never understand. While men generally get along as long as they can talk about sports and play beer pong, women tend to dislike one another for whatever shallow reason they can find. This is evolutionary and has to do with the fact that women naturally compete for the best resources, probs.

For those who continue to doubt the historical significance and evolutionary need for shit-talking, we offer you a history.

A History of Talking Shit

Talking shit is a basic human right. It says so in the First Amendment. Entire countries have fallen apart due to the inability of citizens to openly bash people they hate. Though some may say it was because Soviets couldn't voice their opinions about the government, we're willing to bet Communism fell because Russian betches were sick of having no outlet to make fun of Gorbachev's male-pattern baldness.

For an overwhelming majority of history, talking shit had to be done behind closed doors and out loud. For example, in order to discuss Alice's shitty butter-churning skills, Mary and Ethel had to physically meet up somewhere and trade livestock stories. *My cow did the funniest thing yesterday!* No wonder everyone thinks the Amish are so polite and proper: they can't just bitch to their friends at the push of a SEND button.

We're pretty much convinced that sororities were created as part of a revolutionary movement that gave college women what they had been demanding for years: a communal house in which to talk shit. It was only a matter of time before ladies got together and decided that if we were smart enough to create a legitimate institution that revolves around shit-talking, we wanted our right to vote to talk shit about the first lady to be expressed on the ballot.

Now that we've entered the modern era, you no longer need to ever physically interact with someone to talk about them. Let's take a look at how technology has transformed our shit-talking habits.

The telephone: We imagine telegrams at the turn of the twentieth century looking like this: ASHLEY WEDDING DRESS FUGLY. STOP. Obviously leaving something to be desired in the details department. Thank God for the telephone. Who doesn't remember her mother ignoring her in the kitchen all throughout her childhood while talking to an endless array of besties on the wall-mounted phone while twirling the cord? How else was the news going to get around about other women in the neighborhood and why they sucked? The phone made shit-talking way more detailed.

GOSSIP VS. TALKING SHIT

Many people are confused by the distinction between talking shit and gossip. We'll clear this up for you.

✦ Gossip is like the headline of a news story. *OMG, did you hear Julie fucked a seventeen-year-old prefrosh last week?*

✦ Talking shit is usually less specific and merely involves offering your analysis about gossip like *Ewww . . . can we afford to be friends with a statutory rapist!?*

Cell phone: Cut to seventh grade, when you got your bedazzled Nokia so all the bros-in-training could text you. Welcome to the greatest phenomenon not only for shit-talking but also the Game. *You can bawl Sarah out on her own phone line! Alexa's mom doesn't have to interfere on our three-way call detailing our takedown of that slut in homeroom!*

The cell phone also facilitated the onset of shit-texting, which has pretty much continued to dominate our lives to this day. Now we can talk shit without ever having to talk out loud! I mean, can you imagine how the Potsdam Conference might have gone differently if Winston Churchill and Harry Truman were able to text under the table about what an idiot douchebag Joseph Stalin was?

The group text chat/Facebook/Twitter/AIM/Gchat: The modern age of shit-talking has been a revolution that we are taking advantage of to the fullest extent. Now there's an entire array of Facebook statuses and ironic hashtags to make fun of. Now I can send all my besties the gross picture that Jenna decided to make her FB default in our group thread . . . *so efficient!* Seriously, our biggest fear at the death of Steve Jobs was that shit-talking might never become holographic. Can you imagine how much fun that's going to be? We can't fucking wait.

You might be thinking, *but I haven't done anything to offend anyone!* Well, if that's what you're thinking, it means that you're either (A) a nicegirl or (B) wrong, because it doesn't matter if you've done anything to offend anyone. People, especially girls, will *always* find a reason to talk shit. The best thing you can do is to talk shit right back to make sure no one fucks with you, and that's why being nice is soooo over.

So, like they say, there are three lies that you can be certain of: I'll pay you back, I won't come in your mouth, and I never talk shit about you.

ABBREVIATIONS AND LINGUISTICS: THE LANGUAGE OF EFFICIENCY AND HUMOR

While our shit-talking tendencies may be obvious to outsiders, the language in which we do so is more elusive. Enter Abbrevs, the chicest new dialect since the Tower of Babel.

You might wonder how learning to speak in abbreviations will help you win at anything other than pissing off the village grammar Nazi. Fuck this fascist. If you already know how to speak in Abbrevs, you can skip this chapter. That is unless you have friends who mock your modern words and you're looking for something to prove that they're the arcane weirdos. Learning Abbrevs isn't so much about winning; it's more about the fact that if you want to speak in accordance with the social norm, you have to understand this language. Abbrevs is to English as English is to Olde English.

We're not even pulling this out of our asses; there's science to back it up. Somewhere, someday, someone wrote something that ended up in the *New York Times* (ever heard of it?) and we read it, and it said that young women actually set the linguistic trends that everyone else follows later. If you take this historical evidence to the furthest logical conclusion, you could even say that we invented words. Now that's LOL. But this isn't the first time that the fairer gender has set an example for others. I mean if it weren't for us, men wouldn't ever have thought to wear tight jeans or get breast cancer.

> "As Paris is to fashion, the thinking goes, so are young women to linguistic innovation."
> —*New York Times*, 2.27.2012

But we digress. To all those who are unfamiliar with the language of Abbrevs, try not to dismiss it as just another example of stupid girls being complacent with their own stupidity. Au contraire, loser, we're not dumb, we're efficient. We're very busy people and it saves us a lot of time when we abbreviate words. Every time you say "definitely" instead of "def," or "totally" instead of "totes," you're wasting half a second of your precious life.

How to Speak like a Betch

Abbrevs: The standard abbreviations that everyone uses are pretty straightforward, but every once in a while you may come across a girl who speaks in her own special tongue. Her entire life sounds like one huge instant message from 2001. *TTYL! BRB! OMG!* She will actually say these letters in conversation, and usually no one will acknowledge how weird it is. (See: Shoshanna from *Girls* for a real-world example.)

A common habit is the highly necessary addition of "Z" to the end of any word, or to replace "S" at the end of something that's pluralized. While betch-haters and old people might need a second to register what it means when we ask our parents for some *dollaz to go to PV for SB, where I'll finally get to cash in my V! . . .* every betch knows exactly what was just said. *Triz story.*

Anything can be abbreviated. Just when you thought certain words couldn't be abbreviated any more, we will easily prove you wrong.

For example: *FYI, I'm going to the VS to get some more Ty-Ty PM. Need anything?*

After this, even her bestie might be confused. *What the FUCK are you talking about?*

Obvi, I'm just saying that I need to go to CVS to get more Tylenol PM! Get with it, betch!

Side note: Sometimes abbreviations become a hybrid between a nickname and an abbreviation. See what we did there with CVS? The most quick-witted among us will know how to cleverly abbreviate things that are already abbreviated.

Last but not least, there is always a caveat. Using Abbrevs bonds us with others of our kind; however, if you find yourself telling your great-aunt that you're D to go to lunch, or your boss that you probz won't make it to the offi on Fri, beware that some people might not take you seriously. Like all historical injustices that take time to correct, such as segregation and Don't Ask Don't Tell, we're still fighting for the Right to Abbrev. But when betches take over the Supreme C. and the House of Reps, our first law will be to implement Abbrevs as Second Language. *Adios, ESL!*

Nicknames: Why put forth the effort to give people a second name when they already have one? Simple answer: we're always looking for new ways to showcase our creativity and talk shit without people finding out. However, nicknames have another practical usage. If somebody's worth talking about, it's likely you're going to talk about them often, and it gives your friends context while maintaining a sense of discretion.

Say you have a crush on a guy in your English class named Nick. If one day you started talking about a random guy named Nick but no one knows who he is, you will leave your friends baffled. *Nick who?!?* That's why it's utterly necessary that you and your friends call him English Nick. Here's why: you can't expect everyone to waste their coveted time thinking about the guy in your English class, so by calling him English Nick, you not only let your friends have more time to think about themselves, but it also saves you the trouble of having to explain that it's this guy Nick who you're trying to fuck . . . from your English class.

> **INSPIRATIONAL SCENE FROM**
> ***BRIDESMAIDS***
>
> FLIGHT ATTENDANT STEVE: You have three seconds to get back to your seat.
>
> ANNIE: Oh, you can't get anywhere in three seconds!
>
> FLIGHT ATTENDANT STEVE: Well, you better try.
>
> ANNIE: You're setting me up for a loss already.
>
> FLIGHT ATTENDANT STEVE: Okay, thank you.
>
> ANNIE: [pointing to his name badge] Whatever you say, Stove!
>
> FLIGHT ATTENDANT STEVE: It's Steve.
>
> ANNIE: Stove! What kind of a name is that?
>
> FLIGHT ATTENDANT STEVE: Well, that's not my name. My name is Steve.
>
> ANNIE: Are you an appliance?
>
> FLIGHT ATTENDANT STEVE: No. I'm a man, and my name is Steve.

Take, for instance, how we nickname other girls. Think of the girl who suffers under the delusion that she can pull off curly hair, but everyone else thinks her fro resembles an unkempt vagina . . . or Bush, as we like to call her.

Naming girls is obvious, but when it comes to guys, nicknames tend to be less derived from their appearance and more based on experiences. The guy you hooked up with who had an unusually small penis? Baby Dick.

Put it this way, if you're cool enough to be talked about or lame enough that we just can't look away, you probably have a nickname. Just watch out, because it only takes one faux pas to be permanently branded with not only an embarrassing nickname but also a tagline like "Remember the time you wore that hat?"

DIETS: TALKING SHIT WAS NEVER SO TOPICAL

Everyone knows obesity is a huge problem in America, but there's no reason you should be part of it. We don't see these obese people too often, so it's hard to know for sure, but Jared from Subway doesn't seem like a liar. Regardless, all betches know that nutrition is important. And by nutrition, we mean looking like we're in dire need of some. Why does this matter, you ask? Because no one likes fat people. Looking skinny is a basic requirement if you want to be a person who other people want to associate with.

Being thin is crucial to your attractiveness and has a profound impact on how others perceive and

> "I've really been eating, just not like a crazy person. . . . Taste everything, eat nothing."
> —Bethenny Frankel, author of Naturally Thin

treat you, even if you don't realize it. We aren't saying this to encourage an unrealistic body image. Looking hot is something to do for yourself, and anyone who's lost substantial weight will tell you that their life changed dramatically because of it. But if you prefer the taste of a glazed doughnut to a long life full of good sex and the admiration of strangers, then by all means, enjoy your days among the overweight.

Even if you've attempted to diet, if you think that Weight Watchers/South Beach/Atkins/Nutrisystem will ever work for you, let's take a look at basic reality. The fact that dieting is an industry is the problem, because if they actually wanted people to lose weight, their business would have no purpose, and there's no money in being obsolete. Here's the truth: commercial diets aren't the answer; not eating shit is. It's simple as fuck: the fewer calories you consume, the fewer pounds you will weigh. Seriously, we can't just sit back and let all these obese monsters exist in the same country as us any longer. *Schindler's List* taught us nothing if not that bystanders are guilty just like criminals and also they never get movies made about them.

It's clear that the only thing that should be going down your throat is vodka, and maybe semen, but only if your boyfriend got you a really expensive birthday present. But we thought we'd weigh in on some of the mainstream diets that Jennifer Hudson and other former celebri-fatties are trying to push down our throats and why they're a waste of your time and money.

> "I used to starve, then binge, and I was twenty-five pounds heavier. I tried every diet from Beverly Hills to South Beach. Any diet that says to limit eating watermelon but processed protein bars are good means we've become stupid. Now I eat what I crave and make sure I'm having a balanced variety."
>
> —Bethenny Frankel, *Self* magazine

Weight Watchers: This is generally viewed as the healthy, nonextreme way to lose weight. Fuck that. It's way too slow and involves math. If we wanted to spend our afternoons listening to the feelings of old fat women, we would attend a PTA meeting.

South Beach: All we know about this diet is that you're not allowed to eat carbs for the first two weeks but like no one will stay on it long enough to know what happens after that. Every betch has claimed to be "on South Beach" at some point because it's the closest thing there is to physician-approved anorexia. Plus it reminds us of Miami.

Atkins: Hahaha, what a j! What kind of serious diet actually allows you to eat things like sausages and cheese and encourages you to eat full-fat whipped cream while forbidding light cream? Robert Atkins died for a reason.[2]

The Zone/Nutrisystem: This involves ~~three meals~~ four ounces of turd disguised as food being delivered to your house every day. Pause for reflection: Isn't it great to see a meal plan that encourages people to think critically about their food choices? Like, you want me to wait around for a deliveryman to bring me the magical string beans and salmon that I couldn't possibly ask my chef to make? Wait, you're right, you can't make their meals at home because the ones they send are probably carefully cooked with carbon monoxide. Unless you're a sad middle-aged woman trying to fit into your less-huge mom jeans, the only zone you should care about is the one around your refrigerator, and we mean not go fucking near it.

---

2   Supposedly he slipped on ice on his way to work. Or was he just distracted by the deliciousness of the Atkins-approved beef jerky that he was dipping into cream cheese on the go?

The Dukan Diet: We heard Kate Middleton did it, but honestly, if it doesn't have an app, why bother?

The *Skinny Bitch* Diet: Though betches may not read books, we definitely read *Skinny Bitch*. *Skinny Bitch* was great because it taught us valuable lessons like "never eat again." But more important, it exposed all the nasty things, like floor polish and rat livers, that are key ingredients in any food that's not organic and expensive. These revelations were really good evidence that rich people do everything better than poor people, even grocery shop.

> **INSPIRATIONAL SCENE FROM
> *BILLY MADISON***
>
> BILLY MADISON: Where's my Snack Pack!?
> JUANITA: You got a banana, you don't need no snack pack.

Being "vegetarian": Since betches don't eat carbs, if you claim that you're a "vegetarian," you might as well just come out and say that you don't eat anything, and then when you feel like you're about to faint, you eat a cube of cheese. But as a vegetarian, at least you can reap the benefits of talking about yourself and how much you care about the environment and aren't carnivores such a fucking menace to society? *I mean, I saw* The Lion King, *okay!?*

Jenny Craig: Kirstie Alley, ever heard of her?

The New Food Pyramid: Let Them Eat Nothing

Now that we've thoroughly talked shit about the diet industry, it's time to impart our own methods. When it comes to food, we prefer to pretend it doesn't exist.

Before all the fat girls and self-righteous former anos start bitching that we promote an unhealthy body image, we're just saying that the best diet is to keep your fucking mouth shut. Like it is to life, the key to dieting is simple: inaction over action.

THINSPIRATIONAL QUOTE FROM ON-SITE NUTRITIONIST KATE MOSS

"Nothing tastes as good as skinny feels."

Okay, so we don't mean you should literally starve yourself. But truthfully, if you aren't feeling hungry for like at least 75 percent of the day, you're not doing it right.

We're going to show you the food pyramid that the FDA and Michelle Obama have been hiding from you. These are the main food groups that are key to any successful diet.

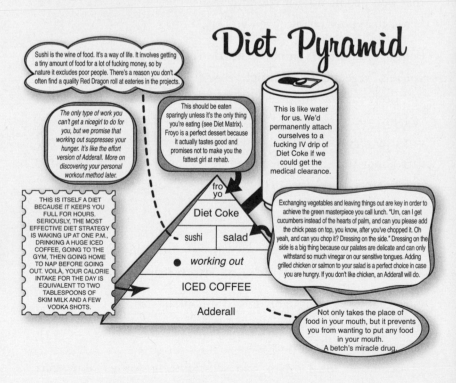

The Betch's Diet Matrix: One for Every Lifestyle

Once you know which foods are safe to eat, it's important to understand how these fit into your well-rounded lifestyle. Not everyone has the same habits, so it's important to find the diet plan that works for you. Now, there are some diets in this book you won't read about anywhere else, but they are the most effective. You can count on us to let you in on our secret to shedding those lbs. one bite at a time . . . literally, one bite.

Follow this matrix and uncover the secret to skeletal living. First, you must understand where you lie on the self control/laziness spectrum.

✦ Self control is essential to winning, whether it's refusing the urge to eat late-night pizza or refusing the equally strong urge to text a guy who's not that into you. If you can't control yourself, you most certainly cannot fucking control others, so lock it down.

✦ Most of us are lazy, but the extent to which you just "don't have enough time for the gym today" defines where you stand on this spectrum. We all know the girl who's so lazy she'd rather pay for the entire eighth than physically go get it.

The relationship between eating and working out is as follows: The less you eat, the less necessary it is to work out. We must note, however, that exercise has added physical benefits that eating fewer than one thousand calories a day will never account for—muscle tone, flexibility, and the ability to walk up a flight of stairs without an inhaler.

The Betch's Diet Matrix
There's one for every betch's lifestyle

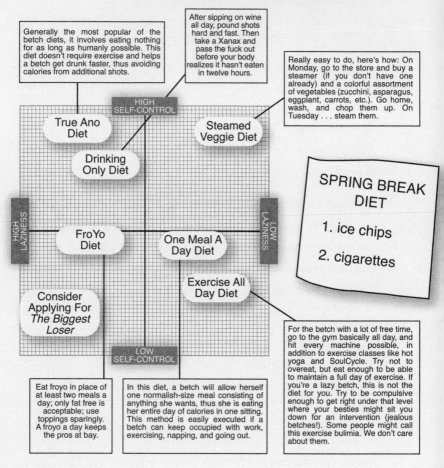

Generally the most popular of the betch diets, it involves eating nothing for as long as humanly possible. This diet doesn't require exercise and helps a betch get drunk faster, thus avoiding calories from additional shots.

After sipping on wine all day, pound shots hard and fast. Then take a Xanax and pass the fuck out before your body realizes it hasn't eaten in twelve hours.

Really easy to do, here's how: On Monday, go to the store and buy a steamer (if you don't have one already) and a colorful assortment of vegetables (zucchini, asparagus, eggplant, carrots, etc.). Go home, wash, and chop them up. On Tuesday . . . steam them.

True Ano Diet

Steamed Veggie Diet

Drinking Only Diet

HIGH SELF-CONTROL

HIGH LAZINESS

LOW LAZINESS

FroYo Diet

One Meal A Day Diet

Exercise All Day Diet

Consider Applying For *The Biggest Loser*

LOW SELF-CONTROL

SPRING BREAK DIET
1. ice chips
2. cigarettes

Eat froyo in place of at least two meals a day; only fat free is acceptable; use toppings sparingly. A froyo a day keeps the pros at bay.

In this diet, a betch will allow herself one normalish-size meal consisting of anything she wants, thus she is eating her entire day of calories in one sitting. This method is easily executed if a betch can keep occupied with work, exercising, napping, and going out.

For the betch with a lot of free time, go to the gym basically all day, and hit every machine possible, in addition to exercise classes like hot yoga and SoulCycle. Try not to overeat, but eat enough to be able to maintain a full day of exercise. If you're a lazy betch, this is not the diet for you. Try to be compulsive enough to get right under that level where your besties might sit you down for an intervention (jealous betches!). Some people might call this exercise bulimia. We don't care about them.

WORKING OUT: A NECESSARY MORAL DILEMMA

As much as we hate doing work and love going out, we're placed in an obvious moral predicament when it comes to working out. When ~~running~~ texting really hard on the elliptical, we often stop to wonder, am I doing too much work? But we immediately shake the thought away, because can you imagine what kind of heinous muploads you would have with a double chin?

Going to the gym is a fucking hassle, period. Sure we love showing off our sick new neon Nikes while casually staring at bros and dawdling on the stationary bike, but it requires serious effort. Things like popularity and free shots come easily to us, so having to combat the reality that one may not have the fastest metabolism is a fucking shock for some.

Sure there are some girls out there who don't go the gym and still have perfect bodies, but keep drunk-eating and wait a few years, and not only will you be hooking up with guys from the community college, but you'll also be that girl with the profile pic from three years ago. And you know how disappointing that girl is in real life. So unless you're gifted with a body of a twelve-year-old Ugandan, it's time to face facts. You have to either stop eating or exercise, but probably both. The key is to choose the right workout, while also not making yourself into some sort of obsessive gym rat. Let's take a look at some workout habits and some strategies for not turning into a marathon runner or something, because then you'd need to simmer the fuck down.

The overly fit psycho gym girl: She makes you feel like shit about the fact that while you're sitting on the couch hungover and about to order sushi, she's already en route to body bootcamp in her fucking Lululemon leggings. Sorry bitch, we commend you on your collarbones, but you're one triceps extension away from having veiny man hands. Chill out, Rocky Balboa.

SPORTS: THERE'S NO "I" IN TEAM

You'd think for writing a book about winning, we'd devote a little more time to sports. Think again. If you're one of those girls who considers herself an athlete, first of all, we probably beg to differ, and second of all, we hope you don't play anything bizarre like basketball or softball. Your interest in sports should be limited to things that highlight your personal superiority and winning qualities, so that pretty much only allows for nonteam sports with pricey accessories.

Tennis: If you're a female athlete trying to be on the cover of *Sports Illustrated,* you better play fucking tennis. It's the only sport that any standard betch would play on a competitive level. What's not to love about a sport that encourages dressing like a slut in tight outfits, lets you serve people without a law degree, and even if you never win a point your score is "love"? Talk about delusional dating.

Squash: Another country-club sport similar to tennis, but just like don't play this professionally.

Golf: It generally impresses bros when a girl is decent at golf because it means she's played often enough to know what she's doing, therefore she must have a rich dad. Just don't be *too* good because it's unattractive to outperform men in areas they're supposed to dominate, like golf. Also, we don't know many girls who are insanely good at golf for the same reason we don't know many butch lesbians.

Skiing: We love skiing because even though it's a sport, it's actually just a synonym for vacay. It even gets its own elitist happy hour, après-ski, plus it requires an entirely new wardrobe. Acceptable ski locations include: Swiss and

Austrian Alps, Aspen, Whistler, Vail, Jackson Hole, Beaver Creek, etc. (no East Coast!).

Equestrian: Riding horses is betchy because it involves the biggest and most expensive of accessories, plus you basically get to sit back and let the animal work while you look good and ponder what color your next pair of boots should be. However, competitive riding is generally a large time commitment, so if you're doing it past childhood you should like get some friends. Okay, Seabiscuit?

The marathon runner: To the rest of the world this girl might be called ambitious or an exercise bulimic, but to us she's simply the girl who used to be fat. Marathon girl is super type A, has a workout complex, and severe OCD that will probably manifest in other areas like trying extremely hard in school or taking on too many projects at work. This girl gets high off of telling people she's training for a marathon and she'd rather skip her mom's funeral than skip a day at the gym. Also note, she'll probably hit you up for money because she's "running for the children!" Don't give her any. When you're actively trying to prevent children, giving money to them is just silly.

> "The first time I see a jogger smiling, I'll consider it."
> —Joan Rivers

SoulCycle/Flywheel/general exercise-class fiends: This is the slightly more laid-back version of the marathon runner because this category involves annoyingly intensive workouts and you can't just leave when you're bored because there are like people around to judge you. Avoid consuming enough calories to burn off in these classes to begin with.

Yoga: Aside from the fact that yoga involves no work at all, the best part about it is that it makes you seem deep, meditative, and chill. Even though most of us are not these things, chanting out a salutation to the sun allows you to manipulate yourself into thinking you've reached Zen or like a state beyond hunger. But yoga is honestly the perfect activity because it allows us to be girly while active. Who would pay a monthly gym membership fee to get man muscles when you can pay thirty dollars an hour to stretch in a room and become super flexible?

Namaste, motherfuckers

Note: The distinction between the yoga betch and the hot-yoga betch is vast. Hot yoga makes you sweat and, therefore, is an actual workout. That makes it totally disgusting, plus your hair looks like shit afterward. We advise against having anyone see you leave class this way, so if you must hot yoga, hot yoga in a different country.

Be you the SoulCycle, yoga, or gym-rat betch, working out is about looking and feeling your best. Unlike schoolwork and bitchwork at your internships, working out is the only type of work that actually solely benefits you and that you can't get anyone to do for you. Nothing perturbs a betch more than having to be photographed with the fatty bestie, so if you're not working out you should definitely be partying in.

GETTING FUCKED UP: YAY!

Speaking of partying, you might think the reason that we "work" so hard to eat less and work out more is to live a longer, healthy life. Well, it depends on your definition of healthy. We eat less so we can get drunk at night on fewer shots and therefore fewer calories. While we may do this so often our liver has been assigned its own proof, at least we don't require a biannual angioplasty.

As a general rule, a betch's preferred method of ingestion is drinking. This is because being drunk is fun and gives you an excuse to do whatever you want without consequences. Have you ever heard a good story that started with "So I was having a mug of hot tea . . ."?

Blacking Out: A History

Betches have been getting drunk since the dawn of time. I mean, how else would we be so good at it? Knowing how to have an amazing time while simultaneously not being able to remember it is one of the hallmarks of a truly betchy evening (or day). With the exception of the drinking age being twenty-one, a problem made irrelevant by the invention of the fake ID, blacking out is one of the few activities that comes easily to us.

But as with all fun things we do, there are always haters and narcs trying to rain on our pregame. Take the 1920s, for example. Imagine if the American Temperance Society had spent their nights blacking out to the beats of Duke Ellington instead of going to church meetings and talking shit about our drinking habits in *Us Fortnightly*? Ugh, Prohibition. The worst.

But if *Boardwalk Empire* taught us anything, it's that Prohibition and the Volstead Act were a total fucking j. Even Volstead realized he was too socially awkward to go to Congress without a few shots of bootleg Jameson, so all Prohibition really achieved was making alcohol stronger and parties more exclusive. For us, Prohibition was kind of like having a table at Provocateur for a whole decade, a way to keep the fuglies out. Everyone knows temperance was for fatties who couldn't get bros to buy them moonshine.

Finally, after a few years, even the Senate started to crave vodka sodas, so Prohibz was totally dunzo. This didn't make that big of a difference, except to crowd the clubs and add people to the lines outside. Because of that, to this day, betches are forced to pretend like they're going to fuck club promoters and bouncers everywhere to avoid waiting among plebes.

How to Drink Like a Betch: Often

One word: shots. Betches love taking shots, because they're the fastest and easiest way to get drunk. Beware, though, shots are dangerous and impossible to turn down. You don't want to be the girl who passes out on the couch or like in the hallway, so the best way to take shots is to go by halfsies. If someone tries to tell you that halfsies are a bitch way to drink, ignore them. They're the ones who will find themselves face-to-asphalt in the next hour.

What We Drink

Before the pregame: Wine, while getting ready and often with dinner . . . and lunch.

At the pregame: Vodka or tequila are the only ways to go. Like if you wake up in the morning and don't see at least one empty handle of Svedka lying around the living room, then you're probably not waking up in your apartment. Postcollege readers will without a doubt have observed that midtwenties betches lean toward Grey Goose or Belvedere. For those who swear by Goose and say it tastes the best, you are stupid. It's just colder.

At the bar: Vodka soda, optional splash of cran or pineapple, paid for by a bro or the bartender who thinks that if he gives you enough free drinks you'll stick around later and fuck him. You won't, because you're not Miranda Hobbes.

Exceptions: Beer. Betches will drink beer on rare occasions. For example, a guy buys you one, during beer pong (tip: have a guy partner, smile coyly, and let him drink your cups), and at Super Bowl parties.

How We Get Drunk

A betch doesn't get "shitfaced," "hammered," or "slammed." We get "blackout." As in, *I was soooo blackout on Wednesday.* This might imply that we advocate being out of control. No, it's not about that, it's about having a good time but also not being an embarrassment to yourself or, more important, your friends. Therefore, the key to blacking out is to make sure you're with people who are slightly more drunk than you are. This way it seems like you have your shit together. If you wake up the next morning with a minor panic attack because you don't know where your phone is, congrats, you blacked out.

> **INSPIRATIONAL QUOTE FROM THAT OLD-ASS MOVIE *GONE WITH THE WIND***
>
> *"I'm very drunk and I intend on getting still drunker before this evening's over."*

So when your parents give you a speech about how you have to stop getting ridiculously drunk and that they're concerned you're becoming an alcoholic, just tell them not to worry and that everyone's doing it. Remind them that you're only as betchy as the extent to which your Facebook pictures look like a wedding montage of you and vodka, traveling the world together . . . one shot at a time.

What Your Drink Says About You

Spring break enthusiast.

You love clubbing, have high standards, and hate poor people.

You like the color blue and will name your kid something trendy like Skylar or Gandalf.

You're Chelsea Handler . . . seriously, she's the only one who ~~prefers~~ promotes it.

You're in college.

You're a tool.

You're a douchebag who orders this to let ~~everyone~~ the girl you're trying to fuck know you're not poor.

Russian parents.

For when you're hosting a pregame for people you don't like.

You're old.

Store was out of Svedka.

Wine: Because You're Chic

While betches will always be down to drink pretty much anything that will get us inebriated, there is one category of alcohol that will always hold a special place in our hearts: wine. In recent years, fine wine has enjoyed a resurgence in popularity among the middle class, taking its rightful place alongside voting and incest, on the list of activities that were once the exclusive privileges of the very rich. While it takes a lifetime to truly understand the complexities of fine wine, here's a crash course.

First, let's exclude Franzia or anything that comes in a box or plastic bag, because that kind of shit will get you roofied at a frat party. Nor are we about to go anywhere near a screw cap. Limit yourself to wines with names you can't pronounce that are made from grapes harvested during or before *Full House* season one.

If you don't love wine, you better keep that shit to yourself. Along with loving it for the sake of getting fucked up, loving wine (or pretending to) allows you to appear classy and sophisticated. So even though you smoke pot every day and wear clothes so tight that your dad would shoot himself in the head if he saw, you better fucking know a good pinot noir when you see one.

Doing Drugs: A Love Story

When a betch talks about her relationship with drugs, no matter the type, the word she'll always use is "love." Ridiculous, inconvenient, consuming, *can't-live-without-each-other love*. Even if the most she'll do is fuck with a joint or dabble in some brownie mix once in a while, she can appreciate drugs for the good times they are, and she knows it's not cool to judge others who buy bud by the ounce or do molly twice a week. Drugs bring people together and every hit you take brings the betch community that much closer.

While you should never actively judge a fellow betch for her drug use, the last thing you want is your bestie to end up on the next season of *Intervention*. Therefore, when it comes to drug intake, it's important to understand the line between recreational and fiendish. We personally draw the limit at consuming any drug other than weed or a mild daytime sedative when you're by yourself. If you ever find yourself blowing lines off your iPad solo at night, congratulations (?), you've got yourself a habit.

Let's break down *las various drogas*.

Marijuana: Put it this way, I just put down my bowl to type this sentence. Weed is all around you. Of course it's a gateway drug, a gateway to greatness. You think we were sober when we wrote this book? You think our founding fathers were sober when they wrote the Declaration of Independence *from scratch*? "Life, liberty, and the pursuit of happiness" is literally the highest thought ever, and there's no way that concepts so abstract could come without having hit something serious. Besides, they first had to *create* a government before they could go around banning shit, and call us crazy, but antidrug laws don't seem like the number one to-do item for the trendiest new country in the world. Now that we think about it, you know what probably happened? John Hancock was definitely soooo high he didn't even know there were people in line behind him.

> "Some of my finest hours have been spent on my back veranda, smoking hemp and observing as far as my eye can see."
> —Thomas Jefferson

Luckily for the world, weed is becoming more accepted. It's now openly displayed on TV, and it'll probably be completely legal soon, so to the weed-haters, STFU and deal with it, pun intended. I mean, have you ever heard of someone smoking so much weed that they died? If you're now allowed to talk about being openly gay in the army, I should be able to openly talk about smoking weed in my backyard . . . every day. Not only does blazing nourish creativity and promote peace, but its sale, once legal, is a surefire way to stimulate the economy. Betches 2016.

Prescription pills: Obviously the intensity of these pharmaceuticals ranges, but generally, popping a casual Klonopin here and there is a nonissue. Lots of people are prescribed drugs, and lots of people sell them to their friends. We don't really have strong feelings on the extent of acceptable pill use because everybody's different. Think of pill problems along a spectrum. All we know is that there are people who are totally okay if they take a bar with a few shots, and there are people who deem it absolutely crucial to take six roxies before going skiing. Barface or not, just don't get in my way.

Cocaine: For some reason, there is a very negative stigma

attached to cocaine. Why so serious? Why can't two people go into a bathroom stall at the same time? For this reason, coke has to be done privately, meaning it's an exclusive activity, not to mention expensive. The main thing that concerns us when it comes to coke is the number of people we've personally gotten to know on TV who've died blowing a casual eight ball in one sitting. (See: *Gossip Girl, Californication, Eastbound & Down,* the bus driver from *Billy Madison.*)

Molly/ecstasy: In the same way house music is moving from underground clubs to the mainstream, its sister drugs are as well. Like the way your parents did coke at Studio 54, times have evolved and now the thing to do is roll, wear neon, and watch a man on an elevated stage press buttons and raise his arms.

'Shrooms/LSD/acid: Experimental drugs to be done in exotic places like Amsterdam or your rich friend's aquarium room.

Meth/crack/heroin: Have you no respect for your inner elbow skin?

Responsibly Irresponsible: How to Avoid Getting Sent to Rehab

A betch must understand what it means to have self-control. This may sound counterintuitive, probably due to the fact that we preach drinking till you can't remember anything, but even with blacking out, there is a technique involved. That technique is called "don't fucking die."

The (general) motto we live by is always be responsibly irresponsible. For example, it's totally okay to go out and drink like an asshole, but don't drink like an asshole alone. Don't go out without your phone fully charged. Bring money. We even bring our health insurance cards with us when we know the night has real potential. The reason why we take such precautions is because we don't want to end up getting arrested or sent to rehab, and because we want to go out the next night. Remember, heaven is for fuckups and Promises is for celebs.

Handling a Hangover: The Aftermath

Everyone knows that being hungover sucks. Actually, we imagine being hungover is how nicegirls feel all the time: fucking awful. Maybe you just woke up on Lil Wayne's tour bus. Maybe your body feels like it got hit by a truck. Maybe you actually did get hit by a truck. Maybe you just decided to follow Rosie O'Donnell on Twitter. Whatever it is, your drinking has caught up with you, and now you're dealing with the consequences. You think apartheid sucks? Try being hungover on Father's Day.

LIST OF HANGOVER ESSENTIALS

1. Weed

Fortunately, betches know how to cover all their blackout bases ASAP so they can get right back to being pissed off and hungover. If you don't know how to get a new iPhone rush delivered, get the family lawyer on a call, or get out a couple of preemptive "Sorry I was so drunk!" texts in less than ten minutes, then you should probably just stay in.

Not only do hangovers provide valid justification to do nothing all day, but they offer a great excuse to talk about yourself. It gives your friends an opportunity to ask about what you did last night, and gives you the chance to let them know how ano your ankles look in your muploads, while simultaneously bitching about how awful you feel today. Also, you get to tell them all about your vomiting habits without them believing you're bulimic, as you take very secretive pride that you threw up last night's dinner.

In the end, no matter how bad a hangover is, a true betch knows how to rally. Drinking with a hangover is about as backward as fucking a bro while breaking up with him. But given the make-up sex you're bound to have with alcohol anyway, you're willing to look past the contradictions.

HOW TO PARTY LIKE A BETCH

Between the onerous task of getting fucked up enough that your drinking/drug tolerance is actually affected and recovering from the prior night's hangover by nine P.M., life can be a rough road. Truthfully, when we say we "don't do work," what we really mean is that we just do a different type of work than your average person. That's why it's important to conserve the energy that nicegirls use for productive tasks and channel it toward showing everyone how gifted you are at celebrating any occasion. We are big fans of specialization and believe that people should pursue the things they are naturally best at. For us, that means going out and having an amazing fucking time whenever possible.

One of the fastest ways to show the world that you're a boring nicegirl is to be lame and not party. So let's break down the myriad ways that fun people rage, while losers are busy sitting at home sprouting gray hair over the stress of their career ambitions. No fucking thank you.

Birthdays: How to Celebrate Yours without People Talking Shit about It

As someone who loves herself, it's natural that your favorite day of the year will be the celebration of the day you changed the course of history by being born. Birthdays are a chance to dress way nicer than everyone else, celebrate the fact that you're still young and hot, and host a big party for all your friends.

But remember that while this is your favorite day of the year, everyone else's favorite day is *their* birthday, and they give zero fucks about whose birthday they're celebrating specifically, as long as they're getting drunk. So we're going to tell you how to have the best birthday possible: get everyone wasted and don't piss anyone off.

Type of celebration: This varies by your age and location. If you're in college, a pregame, party, or bar tab is appropriate for most years, in addition to a dinner with close friends and perhaps a lunch or drinking activity on the actual day. For your twenty-first birthday, you should probably ask your parents to arrange some sort of open-bar sitch and, trust us, everyone will be really happy to come.

If you're out of college and live in a city, the same basic rules apply, but instead you should get a table or private room at a club.

However, after the age of thirty, you should move on to daytime celebrations with your husband and besties, otherwise people will think you're a fugly old cougar who can't find anyone who will marry you.

Birthday vacations: These are great for milestone birthdays (like twenty-one or twenty-five) to go party in places like Vegas or Europe with your besties. It's generally proper etiquette to pay for at least part of the trip for your friends. If you don't have a private jet to fly them there on, it's common that the birthday girl will pay for the hotel expenses and her friends who want to come will pay for their own plane tickets.

> "My birthday was yesterday, and everybody forgot. I got really dressed up and excited, and no one said a word. There wasn't even a party. I think sometimes people are really mean to the hot, popular girl."
> —Kelly Kapoor

Invitation: This obviously depends on the type of celebration you're having, but if you're going with the simple Facebook invitation, there's a particular technique involved. It has to be somewhat clever so people know you're funny, but not so clever that it appears you actually put any effort in. Always appoint two or more besties to be admins so they can invite the bros you like (so they don't think you actually invited them yourself). Make sure your close friends come early so you don't have to make awkward convo with any weirdo early arrivers. Only freaks show up anywhere on time, unless by special invitation.

Gifts: Birthdays are a great time to ask your parents for random shit, not that this is unusual. However, friends typically don't exchange serious birthday gifts, mostly because you should have too many friends to make this practical. Plus we prefer to spend our money on ourselves. Gifts are meant to come from your family, but your friends will typically chip in and buy alcohol or dinner at celebratory events. And if you refuse to pay for the birthday girl's drinks, you're either a really bad friend or like really poor.

BETCHES ON HOLIDAYS

Halloween: ~~People~~ Fat girls are always bitching that this holiday is just an excuse for girls to dress like sluts. We say, yeah, no shit. When it comes to choosing a costume, it is necessary to plan weeks ahead and it will probably be the most work you'll do all month. A true betch puts more thought into her Halloween costumes than Lindsay Lohan puts into her life. The key is to accentuate your best qualities while being both ironic and whorish.

In general, if your costume isn't extremely funny or clever (aka original) while also being slutty, then you should just dress as slutty as you can and do whatever the fuck is the easiest. *Oh, you know I look great in red . . . I'm gonna be, um . . . fuck it, I'm gonna wear my red bra and be the color red.*

New Year's Eve: We love NYE because it's like the world's biggest party. Some people say this night is usually a letdown. We say they were just too sober. This is a night to dress up like you're on the fucking *Titanic* and party hard with all of your friends. The reason this night is different than others is that people drink more champagne than usual. And balls drop, just like an episode of *Teen Mom 2.*

Valentine's Day: In celebration of Hallmark's ability to get people to buy you presents for essentially no reason,

NICE IS JUST A PLACE IN FRANCE ✦ 49

milk this shit for all it's worth and enjoy. Also remember that even if you're single, Valentine's Day is the perfect opportunity to take shots in honor of the fact that you've avoided becoming that fat girl next door who's busy downing semen and chocolates from her fugly boyfriend.

St. Patrick's Day: A time to be thankful for the 1840s Irish potato famine, which not only eliminated carbs and resulted in lots of skinny Irish betches but also brought millions of Irish to America so that we could all partake in this magical day of destructive, belligerent drinking.

4/20: 4/20 may not hold the same place in your heart it did when you were sixteen, but the holidays are important for remembering where we come from and the struggles that our people endured. So break out your old bowl from high school, visit your old dealer in jail, and tell your parents to fuck off. Spark up a j for us, it's not every day we light up for a cause.

Group Dinners: The Anxiety-Free Approach

The group dinner is simultaneously one of the most loved and hated activities. GDs are bittersweet. We love the activity and the ambience of eating out with our besties, but when the group gets too big or the guest list isn't right, shit can be fucking annoying. The general goal is to limit your group dinner to six people tops, all of whom you actually like and don't have to avoid speaking to.

But regardless of how successful (or disastrous) your dinner is, the process is universal.

The proposal: Since GDs sound like a great idea in theory, but in actuality can be a serious hassle, they would never happen if not for the initiator who plans it. The initiator of the group dinner is usually either the most bored or the most anal betch in the group. Or the fattest.

The planning: Not only does planning a large dinner involve taking into account other people's plans apart from your own but also the art of selecting guests is complex and risky. Invite too many of your besties' frenemies and the next plans you'll be making will be with your therapist.

Venue selection: Venue selection is a major deal. Inevitably, one of the besties will have a serious bone to pick with the planner over the restaurant choice because of the new diet she's on. Nothing is more annoying than the high-maintenance friend who insists on changing the plans.

The dinner: When you arrive, and with whom, are essential factors in the group dining experience. This determines the seating arrangements and therefore how much Xanax you'll need to tolerate those around you.

Eating is the least important part of the meal. Salad, drizzled with air. Vodka soda or wine. Maybe some form of chicken if you feel like you're about to faint, so everyone can know that you're not ano, just naturally skinny. Acceptable dinner conversation includes: talking shit about people or talking about yourself.

The check: Everyone hates the check. To avoid being the person who has to figure out the bill, it's a wise strategy to seem like one of the drunker characters at the table to avoid any expectation that you'll be helping with this nicegirl task. You throw your credit card into the pile and start working on postdinner plans. You say fuck you to the bitch who either (A) refuses to split the check equally (*But my salad cost twenty-one dollars and yours was twenty-three dollars!*) or (B) insists on using cash. If you're too poor to split twelve salads among eleven people, then just fucking stay home and have your housekeeper cook you dinner.

> ### BIRTHDAY DINNER ETIQUETTE
>
> If you're invited to someone's birthday dinner, you obviously shouldn't let her pay. Birthday dinners are the only time it's okay to attend a large event with people you don't like, simply because it lowers the portion of the birthday girl's meal that you have to pay for.

And don't even think about ordering dessert. Remember, this is a group dinner, not an excuse to fucking eat.

The Pregame: Getting Blackout in Peace

Being an alcoholic of Chelsea Handler proportions, you'll be able to find an excuse to pregame pretty much anything. Besides major events like birthdays, tailgates, dates, and clubbing, short of taking the LSATs and going to our first day of work, it's basically mandatory that we get fucked up before any and all activities. For all the drinking we write about, the pregame is the only part we can be sure we're describing accurately, and even that doesn't include the end. *OMG, I can't even remember leaving the PG!* is a common phrase to leave a betch's mouth.

The pregame is the thing of our generation. It's because we don't often drink for pure enjoyment. Instead, we drink to guarantee that we'll be drunk enough for whatever activity follows the pregame. If we didn't, we would need to rely on men to buy *all* our drinks, and I mean, we already need them to get a house and a baby, why do we need them to get us drunk, too? That's why all independent women pregame. So, no, Mom, I can't just fucking drink when I get there. If I wanted to be sober around strangers, I would take a bus.

If the morning after you still have vivid memories of your time at the bars/clubs/graduation/your grandma's ninetieth birthday party, you know you didn't pregame hard enough. *Wait, did I really ask my grandpa for a drag of his cigar last night?* That's more like it.

But more important, we enjoy the exclusivity of pregames. Who will we invite? Who will be snubbed? Facebook invite or word of mouth? This can make or break how much fun you have. Everyone knows that the best bonding occurs not over baking cakes and cookies but over the three-too-many mimosas consumed during the drunk brunch before a bestie's birthday drunk lunch.

The best way to avoid unwanted guests at any small pregame is to say that you don't have either enough alcohol, chasers, or room for more people in the apartment. While this is obviously not true, because you like have money, the annoying people who end up attending will probably feel bad and bring you a bottle of alcohol. This is obviously worth having them over for ten minutes before you go out. This brings us to our second strategy, which is to pretend that you are about to leave your apartment when you want them out. If it's too early to say you're heading to the bars, you can say you're about to leave for dinner or go to someone else's pregame, to which you can't invite people, sorry, because you "barely know the host yourself."

Remember, always bring your A game to the pregame. It's your responsibility to set an example for others, prove how hard you can rage, and fuck up anyone who tries to get in your way.

Clubbing: How to Not Do It like the *Jersey Shore* Cast

Thanksgiving Eve, New Year's Eve, Memorial Day weekend, Tuesday. What do these have in common, besides being the days your grandma calls you? These days are important because anyone who's important knows that her presence at a nightclub is mandatory.

So what do we love so much about these raging temples of house music, drugs, and debauchery? Simple answer: exclusivity. Honestly, what's NOT to love about an establishment that screens its entrants so the ugly girls can't come in and guys are only welcome if they buy bottle service that you get to drink?

The key to making an easy entrance and never having to pay for a drink yourself is to get to know at least two club promoters who will constantly text you, pleading with you to come to the latest openings. Often these promoters are just bros from high school who are trying to avoid getting a real job. But who's keeping track anyway? He's promising you a night of free alcohol, possibly even dinner, along with the chance to meet hot guys and minor celebrities. Let these bros feel cool for being able to pay $2,000 for this table just to have an excuse to talk to you.

THE HOUSE AND ELECTRO DANCE MUSIC REVOLUTION

'Tis the season to take molly

House music has always been a shady underground genre of music associated with partying until dawn and a lot of ecstasy, mostly in Europe. But since that's pretty much the funnest shit ever, a bunch of abroad betches came home and were like, *OMG, I miss abroad; that needs to go down here.* And just like that, the house music revolution began. Next thing we knew, SHM was casually playing MSG. And if you don't know what that means, this section is for you.

Put simply, going to a house concert or music festival gives you a widely acceptable opportunity to roll face while dressing like a slut in neon. Your parents had Woodstock, and obviously they were hungover for like a really long time because they haven't been to another concert worth bragging about since. Music festivals are like Woodstock, only better, and they happen twenty times a year and give you an excuse to travel to lots of different exotic cities instead of bumblefuck upstate New York.

Trendy Festivals (not all EDM): Ultra (Miami), Electric Daisy Carnival (travels), Electric Zoo (NYC), Coachella (LA, not only house music but still cool), Sensation (travels), Lollapalooza (Chicago), Bonnaroo (Bumblefuck, Tennessee—hippie festival), Burning Man (the desert).

More importantly, you'll need an entirely separate wardrobe for these events as well. Here's the dress code:

"Effortless" neon: The essence of the house music wardrobe is obviously some variation of a neon crop top coupled with jean shorts or leggings and cool neon Dunks. Bandeaus encouraged. But the key is to make it seem like you aren't trying to look cool, you just loooove neon.

Big trendy sunglasses: How else will people know you're rolling?

Hairpiece: A hairpiece can go either way. The more shit people are talking about your hairpiece, the betchier you are. Or you could look like a fucking tool. Hard to say without stalking your outfit on Facebook.

Handbag with secret compartments: No one wants to bother with a handbag while they're raging to Angello. This is the only time a fanny pack might be acceptable to carry, but only if it has your sorority's letters on it (or is neon) so it's clear that you didn't buy it on your own and you didn't find it in your grandma's closet. Anyway, our main point is that whatever bag you bring should have secret compartments to hide your drugs because security is usually strict at these events.

So, make sure to dress appropriately for the next concert or music festival that you attend. And by appropriate we mean look like a chic drug addict from the '80s.

Party Fouls: What You Can Get Away With

It should be obvious that having an amazing life often comes with unwritten consequences. We're not referring to dealing with a hangover or buying Plan B, we're talking about the shit that happens to you while you're out, and the material you use to build your repertoire of examples of why your life is "a complete joke," but also like really fun and enviable.

Have you ever been at a party where people were looking at you when they start chanting, "*Who brought the asshole?*" and suddenly you realize that you've knocked over an entire bottle of red wine on your friend's animal-skin rug? *Whatevs, it was begging to be destroyed.* Well, if the answer to that question is yes, we're right there with you. Although most of the time we try to maintain the essence of class and poise when navigating the social world, if you don't have at least one minor party foul a month, you probably take yourself too seriously. While you might ordinarily regret it, the hilarious story cancels out the humiliation.

PARTY FOULS: WHERE IS THE LINE?

Whatever the party foul may be, we're sure that there are a hundred betches in the world who are doing the same exact thing at the exact same moment. Sure they're not the classiest of moves, but they're okay sometimes. If you're doing them on a nightly basis, you should stop fucking drinking so much. No one wants to chill with Amy Winehouse (RIP).

✦ Losing shoes, cell phones, wallets, anything that's not literally attached to you.

✦ Falling down stairs or a table and ripping your clothes.

✦ Walking into a glass door.

✦ Eating five slices of pizza and a quart of mac and cheese.

✦ Eating your friend's food when she's not looking.

✦ Eating a stranger's food when he's not looking.

✦ Spilling your drink on people (purposeful or not).

✦ Accusing the bouncer of discriminating against you because you're white.

✦ Buying shots.

✦ Buying shots for people who didn't ask for them.

✦ Taking too many Xanax and passing out in public.

✦ Telling your friend exactly what you think of her annoying friend . . . in front of her annoying friend.

✦ Sending twenty-five emoticons to a guy you're hooking up with when a simple "hey" would've sufficed.

✦ Crying because it's Saturday and you can't go out for an entire two days.

✦ Snorting salt . . . accident or not.

If you don't have at least five stories of a time your friend had a hysterical fuckup that you can deliver on command, then you probably hate each other. Having a best friend who does stupid shit when she's drunk is so much better than bringing it upon yourself to take on the responsibility of being the idiot of the night. I mean, who needs to watch a Kardashian marathon when your Saturday morning entertainment can consist of watching your bestie and her boyfriend duke it out over which of them is the urinator who peed in their bed the night before.

[Side note: Seriously, we don't understand the whole peeing in your bed because you're so drunk situation, but we're happy we know people who do it, because it has to be one of the more entertaining phenomena to hit the first world.]

The moral of the story is: Keep your party fouls in moderation. Commit too few, and you're a boring floser; too many, and you're probably in a coma.

Damage Control: Sunday Morning Regrets

Sunday morning regrets (which if you treat every day as a weekend, you can use to describe any morning after), although traumatizing, leave a far funnier legacy than the sting of the embarrassment. Always remember, it's better to have drunk and fucked up than not to have drunk at all. But now that you've had your fun, here's how to cover your blackout bases so you can go right back to sleep.

Blackout texts or calls: Delete them immediately at the hazard that you might throw up at the sight of them again, and delete this person's number from your phone to ensure you will never do it again.

COMMON TEXTUAL REGRETS

One really embarrassing text: *I'm DTF.*

Sending the wrong text to the wrong person:
YOU: *I couldn't even feel John's penis when we were having sex.*
JOHN: *What?*
YOU: *Shit. Sorry, wrong text. Different John.*

Consistently texting the same person:
YOU: *Hey, what's up?*
YOU: *Come over.*
YOU: *Where are you? I'm at my apartment.*
YOU: *Are you not coming?*
YOU: *Fine, don't come over.*
YOU: *I'm naked.*
YOU: *You're either coming over or you're not.*
YOU: *Fine, I'm over it.*
YOU: *Over it dot com.*
YOU: *Seriously, where are you?*

Walk of shame: On those occasions when you've fucked a bro and it's not in the comfort of your own bed (likely a result of deciding to go where the free drugs are), you will have to endure the walk of shame.

When Lionel Richie wrote the verse "Easy like Sunday morning," it's hard to imagine that he was thinking of anything other than watching a betch take her morning walk of shame.

While making a mental list of everyone this bro knows and is likely to tell that you fucked him, you head out the door. Your level of embarrassment should depend on where you are. If you're in a city, just get in the first cab you can and pray you don't see your boss or anyone you would have to stop and chat with awkwardly. But if you're in college and you see that nicegirl from your biology class with her backpack clearly headed to the library, walk tall, betch . . . after all, your pumps make you look almost six feet. You'd rather walk through your college town with enough eyeliner down your face that you look like a member of KISS than let this betchhater think you have something to hide. She is clearly a fucking loser since she's on the way to the library, and hey, you got laid last night while she was reading Jodi Picoult!

Sex without a condom: Shit, have to get Plan B.

Losing shit: Losing shit when you're drunk is not the same as when you're sober . . . obviously. Most of the time when you lose something soberly, it's like *Oops I left my credit card at the restaurant,* or *Shit, where did I just put my phone!? Oh, it's in my hand.* Losing shit doesn't really get serious unless you're blackout and make decisions like *Ugh, I gotta take my jacket off, this shit is seriously obstructing guys' views of my skinny arms.*

We've all been there, and when we say *there,* we mean the morning after when you can't find your camera or your underwear. I mean, being a betch is hard enough, why does everyone expect us to keep track of all our belongings? *You're mad I "misplaced" your leather jacket? You're like sooo materialistic; I mean it's not like I lost, like, a person!*

Anyway, there are always haters like parents and poor people who are like *Ohhh, you're so irresponsible. You don't know the value of a dollar . . . blah, blah, blah.* But I mean, any Wharton graduate can tell you that fiscal responsibility is for those without any fucking money. So while normal people might waste time trying to hunt down the things they lost, a betch just orders new shit. We don't even tell our parents, we just embezzle money from our own bank accounts in order to buy the item again without our parents' noticing. *Mom, I told you I was getting a new phone. You must've been barred out, again. You're so irresponsible.*

You should never feel too bad about losing something really nice, because if it's nice and trendy, it's probably going out of style soon anyway. Think of losing shit like the casualties of any great war. In the war on sobriety, there are certain sacrifices we must make. As famous pro Abraham Lincoln once said, "We highly resolve that the shit you lost last night has not been lost in vain."

VACATIONS AND SUMMERS: IT'S A HARD-KNOCK LIFE

When she's accumulated too many hungover regrets to cope, a betch may find herself overwhelmed. Vacations are the perfect expensive excuse to relax, clear our heads, and show everyone how much tanner than them we can get.

When it comes to flying, we imagine any type of strife and starvation those skinny people feel in Africa is exactly how betches feel when we're not seated next to our besties on the plane. So if you're not flying private, it is completely necessary to make a huge scene on the plane in order to secure a block of seats near one another. Once you've thoroughly pissed everyone off, feel free to move around, shout profane things and proclaim how excited you are to get extremely wasted the minute you land. And if anyone objects or asks you to settle down, tell them to take a chill pill and politely offer them a Xanax.

Vacay with friends: Spring break or not, a vacation with your besties for a weekend, be it to the Hamptons, South Beach, or just to your liquor cabinet, never fails to entertain. As always, drink to oblivion at night and spend the day curing your hangover with iced coffee and Advil, any form of narcotic, and a vodka soda, in no particular order.

When betches are in the pool, we don't really move around. We just stand in a circle, laughing very loudly, and making sure our bikinis don't fall off. If Phelps doesn't swim on his fucking vacations, why should we? Saying you're "going in the ocean," because you're really hot from lying out in the ninety-five-degree sun for the past three hours, usually means a two-to-three-second toe dip in the water.

A NOTE ON PACKING

Let's talk about the unspoken "hassle" of packing. Packing for a vacation with your friends is almost as hard as paying someone to take your SATs for you—as in, not at all. It's as simple as this: You have a closet full of clothes, fucking pack them. Much to your disbelief, betches and George Costanza have one thing in common. We dress based on mood. Scared you'll pack too much? Stop! Everyone knows the fifty-pound limit is for poor people and pussies. And hey, the upside of traveling with your besties is that they already know that you'll be wearing three quarters of their shit and just about nothing of your own. Well, maybe your underwear.

Also, you wouldn't want your housekeeper packing your shit because like what if she packs as if she's packing for herself? *No thanks, Rosita, but I'm not going to need a giant, fruit-patterned head wrap.*

Vacay with family: You never want to turn down a vacation with the parents, as lame as it may be. Depending on the type of parents you have, they may not want to take shots, but they'll definitely keep the wine and martinis coming. Granted, either way, you're going to a hot place, you'll come out of the week glowing with a tan and the feeling that you just had a free vacay, which you did.

On the other hand, as our ugly-hot AP econ teacher once said, as his Trump-like hair flapped to the other side of his head, there's no such thing as a free lunch. Despite your luxurious vacation, you still have to listen to their incessant shit. *Why don't you go talk to those guys over there, they seem nice. . . . We might meet up with our friends for dinner, be a doll and please explain to their son in explicit detail the college admissions process.* It's like . . . fuck no?

Vacay with your boyfriend: Or should we say your bag caddy? Going on vacations with your boyfriend is great because he pays for everything, and the two of you can focus on important things like getting drunk and having sex instead of finding people to have sex with.

There are certain deal breakers to look for when island-hopping with your pro. Remember our motto that "rolls are for trolls." That is to say, if your boyfriend considers it "helpful" to take your rolling bag while you're stuck lugging around your Louis Vuitton tote, you should ditch this lazy loser. Make him suffer a little with your heavy shit; it's good for the soul.

No matter what type of vacation you're going on, remember to relax, kick back, and take a well-deserved break from the everyday stresses that life throws at you. Also remember to moisturize excessively upon return. No one likes a peeling betch.

How to Summer like a Betch

Unless it's raining, you better haul your ass outside, because the days are not only longer, but the toxic UV rays are also stronger than ever. With that, we present to you our guide to having the least productive and most fun summer ever.

WHERE YOU SUMMER AND WHAT IT SAYS ABOUT YOU

The Hamptons: Take a small percentage of betches and bros from the NYC scene out to the east end of Long Island for the weekend and you have a whole new level of exclusivity. If you're a tristate-area betch and you don't have a house here or a friend who does, you better fucking play sick every weekend. I mean, we've all seen *Revenge*.

Cape Cod/Martha's Vineyard: These places are much like the Hamptons in the elitist sense, but less Jewish, less flashy, and less located in New York. With more old money and Vineyard Vines.

Aspen: For those who dwell in warm-weather locales like Miami or LA, Aspen is a summer getaway—a place where you'll find lots of shopping, marijuana dispensaries, and less hot temperatures that still allow for tanning.

Nantucket: A combination of prep school/lax bros, WASPy girls wearing pearls, Jack Rogers, and Lilly Pulitzer, and tan surfers who just like to drink a lot. If you drive a Range Rover, pimped-out Land Cruiser, or an old-school Defender, then you fit right in. Knowing the bouncer and the bartenders at the Chicken Box is key so you can drink as many "life is good"s as possible. People who go to Nantucket would probably never set foot on Martha's Vineyard—it has too many chain stores and stoplights to be charming.

Not having a job: For the funemployed college betch, summer is really about avoiding boredom. Not an issue. Summer is great because you don't have to see irritating people in class and at college bars. If you're annoying, you'll probably have no friends, but if you're a betch, your schedule is merely a balancing act of choosing at which friend's pool to tan. Not having anything to do can suck on a rainy day when you realize that your summer life revolves around the sun's schedule. Still, bad weather is never a good excuse to get a job.

If you're doing the internship thing, tell your employer you'll be on vacation until July and get your start date pushed back. Also remember to make up a school start date that's three weeks to a month earlier than the actual one, so your employer knows you're outie by August fifth. This is especially true if your internship is unpaid. I'm sure I'm trying to "maximize my experience" by updating contact lists and getting supplies from Staples, under the guise of a fashion internship. If we enjoyed slave labor, we'd just get ourselves a real job in PR. Better yet, tell your parents you're studying for the GRE at Barnes & Noble, and when they ask why you returned so tan, just say you got a fucking window seat.

And if you are a betch with a job that doesn't stop for summer, the only suggestion we have for you is to consider planning elective surgery sometime in June, with a minimum two-month recovery period.

Wardrobe change: Summer means it's time to swap out your chunky leather boots and plunging V-neck sweaters for sandals, bikinis, and crop tops. Summer is the season when it becomes completely acceptable to dress like a slut disguised as being "stylish for summer." Every true betch knows to take this as a green light to break out your most revealing items, in a classy way, obvs. Add a massive pair of sunglasses to up the "get the fuck away from me" factor.

Outdoor dining: When given the choice to eat outdoors or indoors, betches always choose to eat outside. Too hot out for you? Fine, go eat your lunch indoors, and eat some carbs while you're in there.

Summer music festivals: Make sure your group photog comes along so she can take artsy pictures of you and your besties in a field wearing hippie clothing. If you prefer 1985 to 1960, break out your neon and follow Calvin Harris and your ecstasy dealer down the East Coast.

Summer flings: Summer by nature brings out a betch's wild side. There's something about being barely clothed around hot, tan bros that makes summer hookups really interesting. Show off how much skinnier and hotter you got this winter, while you judge the bitches who missed the memo that anorexia isn't a seasonal disorder.

Summary

From what you're putting in your mouth to where you vacation during the summer, everything you do sends a message about who you are as a person. It's about mastering all aspects of your life so you look like one complete, enviable package. I mean, Queen Elizabetch may live in Buckingham Palace, but if she were summering with Snooki at the Jersey Shore, do you think she would still be admired in the same way? Exactly. Fuck up any lifestyle element, and you'll just be another fat girl at the country club or the sober girl waiting on a long line at the bar. It's about having it *all*. To expect to be treated like a betch, you have to look and live like one. Keep this in mind, and remember that the type of life you deserve is nothing more than the type of life you exude.

Image

How to Appear Unapproachable and Hot

Face it, everyone cares how they are perceived by other people. Caring about your appearance dates back to like, forever. You think Eve wasn't concerned about what Adam thought about the size of her nipples or the couture leaf she used to cover her vag? Of course she was, just as you would be if that were all you had in your lingerie drawer.

In today's society, we have a lot more to worry about. Not only do women these days have to be self-conscious about what a guy thinks of our natural appearance, but we also have to think about contemporary concerns, like will a guy assume we're slutty based on what type of sepia filter we used for our profile pictures?

But like a fascist leader or any of the Kardashians will tell you, perception is like way more important than reality. Just as Hitler tried to make people forget that he wasn't Aryan, the Kardashians try to make everyone forget that they might be O. J. Simpson's children. How do they do this? By buying out cable networks and preaching about world domination and hair removal,

> "How you first meet the public is how the industry sees you. You can't argue with them. That's their perception."
> —Meryl Streep, best actress ever

of course. The lesson is clear. If you can fool people into buying the image you project, they will believe it and follow you on Twitter/to world war.

Since most people with eyesight judge others first and foremost on their appearance, half the task of making people think you're the shit is to look that way. In this chapter, we'll explain how to mold yourself into the outward representation of the put-together intimidating betch who goes by her own rules, or at least appears to. That's why it's called "image," not "reality."

> "Men seldom make passes at girls who wear glasses."
> —Dorothy Parker

Why You Should Care

You may be wondering: Why can't I just be myself? Invalid question. We're not saying you shouldn't be yourself, we're just saying you should be the hottest possible version of yourself. You may think it's necessary to spend time on profound self-improvement and reflection, but you actually need to spend that time at the gym. Many more people are blessed with traits like intelligence and virtuosity than with supermodel genes. But the ugly truth is that you're not doing yourself any favors by putting more effort into your career, character, or intellect than into your appearance.

This is because of something that people of science call the "halo effect." Wikipedia writes at length about it, but all it means is that if you're hot, people will automatically assume that you are happier, have a better job, have more friends, and get fucked more often than they do. While

> "I believe in manicures. I believe in overdressing. I believe in primping at leisure and wearing lipstick. I believe in pink. I believe happy girls are the prettiest girls."
> —Audrey Hepburn

these are correct descriptions of any betch, anyone can use the halo effect to her advantage. Simply by making yourself well-groomed and attractive, you can fool people into assuming you're great just because they're superficial idiots. I mean, whose fault is it that your decision to don a Theory blazer this afternoon led them to believe you're successfully employed? In all seriousness, if you want people to be prejudiced against you, go ahead and be ugly. It's your choice.

APPEARANCE:
HOW TO PRESENT YOURSELF
IN PUBLIC WITHOUT BEING MISTAKEN
FOR A HOMELESS WOMAN OR KE$HA

So let's say you're a nicegirl who's looking for improvement. Where do you start? Anyone who's ever had the good fortune to stare at Michelangelo's *David* while on vacay in Florence can appreciate the time and thought that goes into creating a masterpiece. No one is born with an ass that firm. Likewise, since betches consider themselves masterpieces, you should put yourself together every morning with the focus of an artist.

To be clear, we're not justifying taking an hour to put on your makeup. That is busted. Everyone knows that the first layer of foundation is for blemishes and the second is for insecurities, and no one wants to fuck a birthday cake. We're simply saying that a girl who doesn't carefully craft her look will be laughed at and given the nickname "Miss Frizzle" until she buys herself a flatiron. Nothing in life is free and if you don't take good care of yourself, no one will have any desire to buy you a drink, let alone a weekend getaway to Lake Como.

But like most things in life, you should tend to yourself in rea-sonable moderation. Caring too much is for social workers and

Jewish mothers. Your look should seem effortless, like you woke up this pretty, not like your stroll to Starbucks is the Miss America pageant and your whole life's happiness depends on looking stunning this Monday morning. A girl who wears too much makeup makes any rational guy wonder what the fuck she's hiding. Is she a Makeup Transformer? Guys will pass on hooking up with the hottest girl around if the rumor mill suggests they'll be waking up to Shrek the next morning.

Be conscious of the message you're sending. The way you treat your body and face directly correlates to the way you will be treated. Put out too much cleave? A bro will think that the same applies to your vagina. Whoever said beauty is in the eye of the beholder was like definitely blind or stupid. Everyone knows that beauty is only skin deep. If the love in your heart runs deeper than your pores, you are not a fucking betch.

Your Overall Look

Any artist who's ever achieved their piece de resistance knows that there are many different things to consider in crafting this great work. *Should I use watercolors, or will this charcoal better capture my intentions to chop my ear off?* In a similar way, you should think carefully about how you put yourself together. You are your own *Starry Night.* So what are the different aspects that will go into the re-creation of your fugly physique?

Be skinny: If you're not born with a naturally beautiful face, then being thin is your only recourse. If you're skinny, you will not only optimize your attractiveness given your unfortunate facial genes, but also guys will be less likely to realize you're ugly when they're drunk. On the other hand, if you're fat, this

"Sorry, we only carry sizes 1, 3, and 5. You could try Sears." — *Mean Girls*

will always be clear, even to the extremely intoxicated. I mean, people thinking you're hot when they're wasted is better than them *always* thinking you're ugly, right, Butterface?

Be tan: Everybody looks better when they're tan, even those "fair" people who won't let a single beam of sunshine touch their precious porcelain skin because they live in fear of sun damage and cancer.

TENETS OF TANNING

For three seasons of the year, betches march to the beat of their own drums. But when summer arrives, our routines are determined by only one thing: solar fucking noon. You may not know the date of the only lunar eclipse in the last two hundred years, but you definitely know the sun's angle at 1:35 P.M. and therefore which direction to rotate your chair. Be ignorant of solar noon and mourn the loss of a tan left pinky toe forever.

✦ Prime tanning hours are ten to two; an eleven-thirty wakeup is a no.

✦ Every day is a race for who can appear darkest, but everyone has their own tanning style. Some girls go for the bandeau top, while others welcome their tan lines as a message that *"yes I'm white, I'm just like, really, really tan."*

✦ Learn to ignore the JPB (aka the one who gets burned faster than she can get through an *Us Weekly* article), who will bitch about how toxic the sun's rays are while simultaneously smoking a cigarette.

✦ Tan-Your-Back Sunday: Having anxiety about an even tan? TYBS is a day to unwind from a long week of lounging and raiding the alcohol in your bestie's pool house. You're probably hungover, so feel free to sleep on your stomach, ignore your phone, and hopefully wake up dark enough that your race is ambiguous.

Yeah, we get it, being pale is your "look." You would look a lot more attractive if you were three shades none the whiter. Having color not only makes you look hotter and skinnier, but it also implies you are exotic and well-traveled, especially if you are bronzed off-season. If you're not going on vacay, we still don't suggest you go fake tanning or get a spray tan in the winter, because people will call you orange and poor . . . in other words, a Cheeto.

Hair: How Big Is Too Big?

Straight: When you're young, you learn that all boys love straight hair. We understand that blow-drying and ironing take awhile, but listen, the same applies to losing weight: If it only takes 5 seconds, you're doing it wrong.

But even straight hair can go terribly wrong if you make some crucial mistakes. Unless you've just recently escaped from a psych ward, if it's pin-straight, your part better not be in the middle of your fucking head. Straight hair, when done properly, should be somewhat angled and parted in an interesting way. And the zigzag part is great, as long as you want people to think you have a weave.

Wavy: When it comes to wavy hair, the more natural-looking the better. Barrel curls fell out of style sometime circa Shirley Temple, and sculpted waves say "I'm Molly Ringwald in *Sixteen Candles*."

Curly: The bigger your hair is, the skinnier you should be. Ask nine out of ten guys on the street, and they will tell you that the curly look just doesn't do it for them. It broadens the face. It simply must be tamed, unless you want people to ask about your new condo at Pride Rock.

Colored: Hair color is extremely important. The amount of money girls spend on their highlights is fucking absurd, yet completely necessary. If the color of your natural hair looks like the rust on a two-month-old razor, it's time to accept that Mother Nature needs to be helped. Bore a man with your mane and he'll be bored while entering you.

Short: Don't even get us started on short hair; just because you're a celebrity doesn't mean you get to go out looking like a lesbian grandmother. Unless you have a gorgeous face—think Natalie Portman or *maybe* Michelle Williams on an especially good day—eh, nah, not even then. Just to be safe, keep it below the shoulder. No straight man wants to fuck Justin Bieber or the kid from *Liar Liar*.

Eyebrows: There Should Be Two

A dead giveaway of a betch is the kemptness of her brows. If you go on vacation with your bestie, and she doesn't immediately have a panic attack at the realization that she forgot her tweezers, we're sorry but you've been spending time with a poser. By the same token, if it looks like one of your besties hasn't been to Rahima the threader in a while, you are well within your rights to mention that if you wanted to hang out with Frida Kahlo, you'd go to a museum.

"Oh that's bullshit," you may say. *"If my dad doesn't recognize my new haircut, why should a guy even pay any attention to the two-inch strip of hair above my eyes?"* Because your dad isn't trying to fuck you . . . we hope?

Guys are always thinking about sex. Think about the conclusions they'll be making about the bottom half of your body if they see that the upper half of your face is a hairy mess. If bros wanted to go on a safari, they'd book a fucking trip to the Amazon.

Nails: Unmanicured Is Worse than against a Chalkboard

Your nails should *always* be done. Ever notice that the most confident betch in the room is usually the one with a flawless, chip-free manicure? We, of all people, understand the hardships of fast-paced texting, but the moment you spot an abnormality in the texture of your mani, to Ruby Cho you must go.

Keep it simple, keep it square. Unless it's trendy, putting a bedazzled design on the nail of your ring finger will directly delay that finger getting a real diamond. Nicegirls and my five-year-old cousin, neither of whom is getting laid, get leaves and flowers painted on their nails.

> **NOTE:** When it comes to manicures, always go Asian. Not to sound racist, but we recognize that those from the Far East hold a monopoly on nimble and artistic crafty fingers.

Makeup: To Make Up for the Fact that You're Ugly

When it comes to makeup, there are very few girls in this world who know what the fuck they're doing. But even for the naturally gorgeous, makeup is a necessary tool for enhancing God-given beauty and exuding a certain air of competence. Correctly applying makeup involves both manipulation and skill, so it's no surprise we love it.

You don't need to be Bob Ross to make yourself look good, but there are definitely some guidelines to follow for applying makeup for every occasion. Let's look at the appropriate ways to leave your house without looking like Taylor Momsen or that bro from Green Day.

To class or work: To perfect this look, it should appear that you're not wearing any makeup at all. But, of course, this just means you have to be particularly good at doing it. You want this look to say, *I don't care how I look when I leave the house, but, yes, I'm naturally this fucking beautiful.*

Do: Apply some basic eyeliner, one coat of mascara, and a small amount of bronzer to avoid looking deathly pale from doing drugs and drinking all weekend.

Don't: Wear bright unnatural shades of eye shadow in the day, unless you work at the Spearmint Rhino.

When going out: We all know that girl who thinks she's hot enough to go out with no makeup on. What we're all dying to tell her is, *You're not even close to pretty enough to pull that off.* Instead of saying it, we cringe at her face, which is a horrifying shade of ass.

Do: The smoky eye is the key to appearing hot and intimidating. However, if you don't know how to do this right, please consult someone who does. No matter how see-through your lace crop top is, do it wrong and you'll still look like a chimneysweep. This isn't *The Little Princess.*

Don't: Wear your concealer as your lipstick (who would do this? Guidos) or match your eye shadow to your dress or lipstick. Clowns chill at the circus for a reason.

The Mascara Rule: For nighttime, use multiple coats. Everyone knows that the thickness of your lashes is directly correlated to the fuck-off vibe you exude. In some cases, like if you're going to Ultra, you can skip intense eye shadow and do colored lashes. But do this only if you can pull this off, and don't go out looking like a Bratz doll. If you look stupid, it's not our fault. Look in a fucking mirror before you leave your house.

CLOTHES: HOW TO DRESS
LIKE A SLUT (THE CLASSY WAY)

We're not about to explain to you the ins and outs of modern fashion trends. Suffice it to say that the fundamental intention of your everyday dress code is to look somewhat slutty but not like a whore. If you find it bizarre that we encourage looking slutty, we'll admit that unlike most great ideas, this one wasn't ours. The fashion industry has been lowering necklines, raising hemlines, and making clothes progressively more transparent ever since colonial garb fell out of style. Just watch the *Victoria's Secret Fashion Show* and tell us that America doesn't love dressing slutty.

Dressing promiscuously begins as early as middle school. Remember buying your first thong at age twelve to avoid VPL[3] in your first pair of Hard Tails? That was just the beginning. As time went by, our efforts to dress like sluts (while still appearing classy, of course) got more serious with each passing year. Soon wedges turned into six-inch stilettos and we were buying Juicy tops that were two sizes too small so the 00 stretched all the way across our chests.

In terms of brands, (straight) guys usually don't care what brands you're wearing, as long as you look hot in them. Sure they want you to be fashionable because they want to make sure they're not dating a social outcast, but their knowledge is pretty limited. Guys just want you to look skinny and feminine in whatever you're wearing—be that a sweater and jeans or a tube dress and pumps. So if you think wearing man shoes or Birkenstocks makes you "chill," you should go the fuck home to ponder why you're going to die childless and alone.

---

3   Visible Panty Line. But the word panty . . . just ew.

Trashy or Classy: Where Is the Line?

Why spend so much time thinking about what to wear when you could be doing other things? Because getting dressed involves walking the hazy but crucial line between looking classy and looking trashy. The ultimate goal is to attract bros with your slutty attire (as opposed to your slutty actions) while avoiding being labeled as such. The question to ask yourself is: *Exactly how much of my perfect body can I expose to the world without being mistaken for someone Eliot Spitzer would date?*

You should think of every day as a new opportunity to try out ways to look hot without appearing literally naked. From when we were merely young ~~brats~~ girls watching Cher Horowitz rock her endless array of midriff-baring shirts, we anticipated the day when we could sport our own crop tops. That day is today. And if you feel too timid to wear a shirt made for a fifth grader, remember: Hiding your stomach is for lesbian gym teachers and fat people.

> "Sometimes you have to show a little skin. This reminds boys of being naked, and then they think of sex."
> —Cher Horowitz

The art of dressing provocatively is kind of like driving ninety-five miles per hour on an interstate highway while avoiding a speeding ticket. Just as your goal should be to go as fast as possible without getting three traffic violations, a true betch knows how to optimize her skin exposure without looking like the easiest bitch in the bar.

There is a very big difference between dressing like a slut and dressing like a *slut*. Cue the distinction between the overt and the covert whore. The idea is to maintain a decent level of dignity while simultaneously making your father rue the day he ever decided to reproduce.

The overt slut's boobs are more out than Perez Hilton. She's just one casual drop of her iPhone away from a "bend and snap" that

THE OVERT VS. THE COVERT WHORE

Overt = pairing fishnet stockings with a dress you've cut so the hemline lies half an inch below your ass.

Covert = wearing jeans so tight that you have to do a gymnastics routine to get them on.

the whole bar will remember. But the covert betch knows how to play it cool. She rocks her one-shoulder cutout dress with just the right amount of side abs exposed to drive bros crazy.

Remember, dressing like a slut does not mean you can go around fucking guys whenever you want. You have to make men work for that shit. The slutty outfit should be just enough to preview so this bro can fall in love and become your bitch for a few weeks before you (maybe) decide to put out. As Beyoncé says, "If you've got it, flaunt it." And if you don't got it, then you can always raid your fat friend's closet for Spanx and a bubble dress.

> *"Sexiness should not be overt. Something shapeless that drapes across your hip, hangs off the shoulder; something that cowls in the front, drapes low in the back, that's sexy."* —Rachel Zoe

Accessorizing Your Wardrobe

Sunglasses: The bigger they are, the more likely you'll be mistaken for a celebrity. How do you know when your shades are of adequate size? When they're the size of Anna Wintour's or they weigh more than your head. Seriously, nothing says "fuck off" like a massive pair of Tom Ford or Chanel sunglasses. Not only do they scream *I'm fucking important, bitch. Move out of my way* *or I'll spill my gigantic iced coffee on your head,* but they also tell the world, *I'm really wealthy and therefore better than you.*

But sunglasses aren't just an attitude thing. They also shield your eyes from the bright sun when you're hungover and, even better, save you from having to make eye contact with anyone. They're like the invisibility cloak of stop-and-chats. And on the off chance you actually find yourself speaking to someone, don't forget: the darker your shades the more openly you can judge other people.

High heels: These are a staple of intimidation. The taller you are, the less shit you take. We're not talking about that three-inch nonsense; it's four or higher. And to state the obvious, heels make your legs look five pounds lighter and your ass five years younger. Flats are what you wear if you have a leg deformity or a disease that left you toeless. Howevs,

> "*Flats, to me, is like a disease.*"
> —*Lisa Vanderpump*

if that's your sitch we have a feeling you have bigger concerns than looking hot, like finding the cheapest stem cells on the black market. Remember, even Ryan Seacrest wears lifts.

WHAT YOUR HEELS SAY ABOUT YOU

Kitten heels give off an extreme nicegirl vibe. They're not called lion heels for a fucking reason.

Wedges are tricky but good for a casual or daytime event.

Espadrilles are hard to pull off and most people can't. If you think you can, get a second and third and fourth opinion.

Ankle shoes or boots are great if you don't have cankles or big calves. No one likes a stubby betch.

Handbags: The guide to choosing handbags is fairly simple. If you're carrying it during the day, it should be as massive and trendy as possible without breaking your frail skinny arms. But when it comes to nighttime bags, less is always more. Your daytime bag is about making a statement, but your nighttime bag is about efficiency. Think about it, when was the last time you got a compliment on your purse while you were in the middle of falling off a club table? Exactly, fucking never. For the evening it's best to go with a classic clutch or a purse that's big enough to fit all your shit but small enough to show everyone that you're not still carrying your work bag.

HOW TO ASK FOR SHIT FROM YOUR PARENTS

This will work for most things.

Summary: Introduce the idea, tell them why you deserve it without actually saying you deserve it, then let them know you're thinking of a way to save money on it. Works like a charm. If all else fails, beg but don't whine. The last thing you want, and the best way to get shut down, is having them accuse you of being an irresponsible spoiled brat who's under the impression you're entitled to everything.

The Spiel: *Hiiiii, Dad, so I've been really researching a lot of things online lately, and I really don't want to ask you to buy me anything I don't severely need. I understand that money is, like . . . a big deal. But I saw this amazing* [insert item that you want] *online and I just don't want anything else! It's like really, really nice and no one else has it.* [Unless your dad is Bruce Jenner, he won't have a fucking clue if this is true, nor will he give a shit.] *I just don't want you to be nervous about how much it actually costs. . . .* [This is where your acting skills are vital. You want the idea of buying you something around the $10K line to cross his mind.]

Then he will give you *the* look and ask you how much it costs, and if you're lucky, he'll shell out a number. *What is it, ten thousand??*

OMG no way! You think I would ever ask you to spend that? Of course not, only five!

Okay, fine, you can get that. Love you.

Congrats, betch, you've just mastered the delicate art of manipulating your dad. Don't feel bad about it. There are worse things happening in the world, like genocide or new episodes of *Mike and Molly*.

Pick your strategies wisely and never give up. Whoever wrote, "You can't always get what you want" clearly has never gone shopping with a betch.

Scarves: Scarves are the ultimate wardrobe-maker. Ever seen *Confessions of a Shopaholic*? You might remember that the entire movie was based on a girl trying to get her hands on a stupid fucking scarf. And who can blame her? You could be hungover and wearing a pair of Juicy sweatpants and an American Apparel shirt, but put on a scarf and suddenly you may be confused for Nicole Richie. And if you think scarves are to be worn only in cold weather, that's like saying you'll only eat froyo in the summer. Betches need their scarves like they need their Adderall: all year long.

Expensive skin shit: If you don't have at least forty or so bottles and tubes of moisturizers, creams, and oils in your bathroom for your besties to envy and test out, then you might as well move to South Side. Since there are so many products available to choose from, it's always best to just buy the most expensive shit available. More expensive is more exclusive, and since it's probably not an effective treatment anyway, this is the most effective method of choice. Remember, you're never too young to start using stem cell regenerative antiwrinkle creams made from the golden apples of Switzerland and bottled in the finest huts of Indonesia. Our motto is, if it's good enough for Gwyneth, it's good enough for us. What better way to show you're better than everyone if not with your elite skin-product regimen that no one can see.

STATUS SYMBOLS:
WHAT THEY SAY ABOUT YOU

Being shallow and judging people solely by their appearance is absolutely nothing to be ashamed of. On the contrary, it is the wisest way to live, if only for the sake of efficiency. Who doesn't *actually* judge a book by its cover? Would you buy a magazine if it had a bunch of fat people dressed in clothes from the Gap on the cover? We sincerely hope not.

Similar to stereotypes (which is how everyone thinks, regardless of what they want to believe about themselves), status symbols convey a lot about a person in very little time. The distinction between a status symbol and a random expensive item is that a status symbol is not always about anything in particular like price, style, or quality. Certain objects have obtained a degree of prestige that is completely arbitrary—but powerful—*just because*. Like why do you and everyone you know buy Burberry rain-

> "With the greater part of rich people, the chief enjoyment of riches consists in the parade of riches."
> —Adam Smith, CFO, America
> ^high thought

A NOTE ON COUNTRY CLUBS

Ever since slavery was abolished, there have been few institutionalized ways for rich white people to show how much better they are than everyone. But while most people rejoiced in the land of liberty and justice for all, white Republicans stayed one step ahead of the game. They needed a way to preserve the timeless tradition of old white people who only interact with other old white people and occasionally their ethnic servants. And that's why they invented country clubs.

For a betch, the country club mainly serves as a dating resource. Everyone there is already preapproved by the family and a large board of directors, with the added bonus of looking hot in a polo. It's like an adult Greek system, where the only hazing you'll have to endure is wheeling your grandma to the breakfast buffet.

Belonging to an elite country club is our parents' way of saying: *We're better than everyone who isn't a member and most who are,* and gives them a place to show off their accomplished, financially dependent children, Dad's golf skills, and Mom's Botox. If you have a certain amount of wealth, it's almost weirder if you don't belong to one. Like, if your dad was never approached to invest money during a round of golf with Bernie Madoff, you're probably poor. And if he was, we guess you're poor now. With that we urge you to go clubbing at the one place where it's socially acceptable to wear a skort. Be classy. Be elite. Join a fucking country club.

coats? Because two inches of plaid around your wrists are absolutely essential for people to know that you shield rain in style.

People's desires to own certain status items aren't the least bit economically or practically rational. You want them for the conclusions others draw from your ownership. Do you want people to think that you're lucky enough to have money but too dumb to know how to spend it? No. You want people to think that you have plenty of money and plenty of cultural awareness to own the right things. Reflect on this for a minute, and then go ask your dad to borrow his credit card.

Materialism: A Defense

In life there are many symbols that alert us to the culture of those around us. The French have Hermès, our gay BFFs have black V-necks, and nicegirls have no plans this weekend.

Status symbols, like morals, are relative.

Take this scenario. A betch asks for something entirely reasonable, like a Chanel bag, and her parents respond, "I don't care what everyone else has, go tell a starving African child how badly you need another purse." But here's the thing: this response is easily refuted with evidence that is completely grounded in verifiable psychology (therefore proving that nicegirl college researchers were put on this earth to find ways for betches to outsmart people using "science").

INSPIRATIONAL BETCH FROM HISTORY: MARIE ANTOINETTE

It totally sucks that she got beheaded, because her house was awesome and Kirsten Dunst showed us that all she did was party and live lavishly. Our only issue with her is her promotion of carbs.

Any smart betch is well aware of the African starvation sitch; we've all attended numerous charity events, and some of us might even envy their success at dieting. *Kony 2012!* But the reason we don't compare ourselves to these tragic populations is because they're not psychologically relevant when it comes to purses. People—no matter their socioeconomic class—only mentally compare themselves to their immediate peers, not people outside their reference group. In other words, having a Chanel bag is as important to you as empty beer cans are to the hobo who lives outside your apartment—without that purse, we might as well be starving. The fact that we have a lot of money in comparison to a tsunami victim is just about as important to us as the existence of dollar stores.

> "Oh Lord, won't you buy me a Mercedes-Benz?"
> —Janis Joplin

As a betch, you can be sure the only status symbols you're interested in are the highest ones, naturally. That's why when you see some bitch prancing around with a 1996-style Coach bag with powder blue C's all over it, you're certainly not envious, but Jenny from the block most definitely is.

Caveat: Trying Too Hard and Caring Too Much

As with everything, there are a few caveats to keep in mind when judging others based on material things. We all know it's off-putting when people are flashy with brand names, confusing this with status. But on the other hand, even if you're the picture of an upscale fashionista, the manner in which you judge people can betray your own insecurities.

We're talking about the girl who makes a mental note when her bestie wears non-winter white in the winter, gets her own private hotel room on spring break, or refuses to attend a birthday dinner because the venue has zero Michelin stars. While we might joke about these things and talk shit for fun, we don't seriously give a fuck. It's not normal when your elitism impacts your social life negatively, no matter how many private jets ~~you have~~ your dad has. It indicates that you are personally defined by money and status on such a profound level that it renders you unable to relate to people. If you can't relate to others, then it's virtually impossible to manipulate them, and you will likely fail at most areas of life that you can't outright pay for—especially relationships, both romantic and not. The one thing money can't buy is genuine affection from other people. You'll know you're this person when you have more Birkins than birthday wall posts.

Always remember that the goal is to be put together but in an *effortless* way. Appearing to try too hard or care too much detracts, no matter how cool or trendy you can claim to be. Cultivating an aura of ease is equally important as what you own and how you show it. Just because your bronzer is expensive doesn't mean we need to see more of it.

SOCIAL MEDIA IMAGE: HOW TO LOOK LIKE THE SHIT ON THE INTERNET

Now that we're well into the digital era, your online persona is now equally as—if not more—important than your real-life identity. How you act and appear on social media platforms is pivotal to your image. Just like you wear cover-up to fool others into thinking you are not a walking advertisement for Proactiv, the virtual version of that is detagging any and all close-up HD pictures of yourself.

But just because you've mastered the art of looking unrealistically hot to the casual Facebook stalker doesn't mean you can still parade around cyberspace like a freak. The key, as in all aspects of life, is to act like you don't care. A few years ago people who didn't have a Facebook account were deemed mysterious and above all this shit. Now if you don't have one, you're probably just really fat.

So how do you remain an enigma to the online world? That's what you're about to learn.

How to Use Facebook to Show Everyone You're Better than Them

While Facebook is a double-edged sword, we really can't deny the potential for mass manipulation that comes with an account. It wouldn't be an understatement to claim that this website is both the greatest and worst invention to ever hit planet Earth. If you could clock the hours spent on this miserable site, you probably could've successfully figured out a cure for cancer in that amount of time, yet you barely passed high school biology.

When it comes to Facebook, more is always less. While FB started off as something elite and cool, now the people who use it the most are the biggest freaks on the planet, which we're chill with, because it's now easier to spot them and then ignore them in the real world.

Statuses: Ugh, what to say about the fucking stupid shit that pervades your news feed; the nicegirl word vomit that invades your life in the form of Facebook statuses. The occasional location change is okay, like if you'll be in Vegas or the Hamptons for the weekend, or the two times a year you're permitted to post a link or a comment that's ironically funny. Overloading your Facebook wall with your own personal thoughts is the same as telling everyone you think you're fucking hysterical. There are only a handful of people *that* funny in this world, and guess where they are? Not updating their statuses with quotes by Anon. Seriously, if you do it more than the amount permitted, you can't sit with us. Not just you, like, any of us.

"Likes": That tiny thumbs-up sign says so little yet so much. But call it what it is, this is a betch's subtle form of attention-seeking, like making a positive statement and affirmation of friendship without having to put in the effort of forming a full thought to make a comment.

Would you ever like something someone did on Facebook if you didn't like the person? Exactly. It's your way of saying, *See, everyone, I have friends who care about my opinion and we have inside jokes and I'm on the inside, and even though this comment was neither written by me nor addressed to me, I totes get it.*

But remember, be sparing with your "likes" and *never* like something you have written, unless it's clearly ironic.

Wall posts: Wall posts say, *We are real friends who keep in contact often and have things to talk about. Here is one of our inside jokes you won't understand. I could have just as easily texted this comment, but I need the world to know how close we are.*

Use wall space to share funny videos, inside jokes, and old pictures through which you can reminisce on ~~old times~~ the week after spring break when you were really tan.

Finally, consider this: If your birthday isn't on Facebook, were you ever even born?

Image and privacy settings: There's always a tension between maintaining exclusivity and showing how cool you are, while making it hard for employers and your grandpa to stalk you. Try to err on the side of privacy.

As we said before, the coolest people either don't or "appear not to" use Facebook very often. It lets them remain mysterious and elusive, like a virtual labyrinth.

Hiding your pics or your wall is chill, but hide both? You're up to something shady.

You also shouldn't "like" too many pages or join too many groups. Generally avoid the use of Facebook apps, and if you do use them, don't tell anyone. There is nothing worse than the receptionist at your dad's office friending you and then constantly sending you notifications of how many cows she's just unlocked on Farmville.

Tags and profile pictures: It's indisputable that extreme anxiety accompanies the difficult task of choosing profile pictures, as well as the decision to tag or untag your pictures.

Things to consider when making this decision: (A) How hot/skinny do I look? (B) Who am I pictured with? (C) If I didn't know me, what would this picture say about me? It's always important to judge yourself from the point of view of the public, not just your closest thirteen hundred friends.

Your profile picture should highlight your best features while simultaneously showing the world that you have your shit together. The wrong profile picture is one in which you look completely wasted or like a whore. A picture of you in your bathing suit from a vacation is permissible, but your profile picture album can only have one bikini shot. More than that, and you're officially trying too hard. Also, the minimum number of pictures you need to have tagged to ensure you're not a social leper? Let's say two hundred for guys and like seven hundred for girls.

It's enough stress to make you want to pop a Xanax.

Sharing photos: Let's face it, going out and taking pictures with an actual digital camera is so 2009. Do you know how much money we've spent replacing lost and/or broken Canon PowerShots? However much one costs, times fucking seventeen. Thank God that phase of life is over, because we were ready for bigger, better, and chicer things, most commonly known as muploads and Instagram.

Camera phones are amazing in that they allow you to capture a funny or especially cute moment as soon as it happens. People will know exactly where you are and how much fun you're currently having, while they are at home stalking you. A mupload screams, *I'm too cool for Facebook albums, but my life is just too fabulous to not share this pic of my best betch vomming in her own bag!*

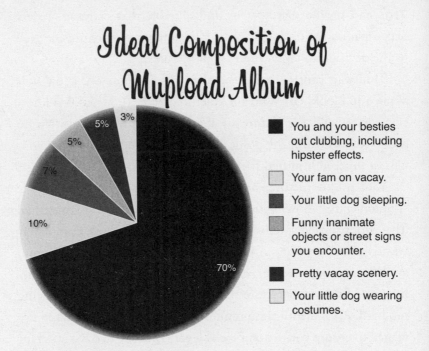

Ideal Composition of Mupload Album

3%
5%
5%
7%
10%
70%

- ■ You and your besties out clubbing, including hipster effects.
- ☐ Your fam on vacay.
- ■ Your little dog sleeping.
- ■ Funny inanimate objects or street signs you encounter.
- ■ Pretty vacay scenery.
- ☐ Your little dog wearing costumes.

Friends' privacy settings: It's undeniably irritating when your friends' albums are set to only their friends. *What the fuck is the point of looking like I'm having fun in these pictures if John can't even see them?* It is okay to ~~ask her to~~ hack into her Facebook and change her settings, but only if she is your bestie.

Stalking: Remember last Monday when you had literally nothing better to do than look through your third cousin Julie's vacay pics from her Bahamas album? Halfway through, you probably caught yourself and thought, *Why the fuck do I care about this?*

Facebook stalking is dangerous. Choosing the right time and place is crucial. Every betch knows not to do this during class or work, where there's always potential that the guy in the desk or cubicle behind you could know your boyfriend's ex-girlfriend and would find it strange that you're carefully stalking each of your mutual friends. Oh, and whoops there he sees his own profile on your computer . . . 'kward.

Another reason not to fall down the Facebook stalking rabbit hole is that there are few more awkward moments than when someone you barely know drunkenly reveals some personal information they clearly found out about you from stalking your Facebook. As betches, the rest of the world is obviously extremely curious about our whereabouts and outfits, but it's super creepy when you tell me you loved the dress I wore to my uncle's wedding in Minnesota back in June.

Back-stalking: The only thing better than regular stalking is back-stalking. It's looking at someone's pics backward to see how fat they've gotten since high school. Or even more fun, back-stalking yourself. There's obviously no better reason to be up until three in the morning than being Adderalled out and looking back on June 2007's spring break pics. *Oh my God, I look so young here. I can tell because I'm missing that one little drugs-and-alcohol-induced forehead wrinkle.*

How good is your Facebook game?: Facebook has made it a million times harder to get over an ex because you now have to be constantly reminded of what he's doing and with whom. But you can also do the same. Should you call a guy out for something he's done on Facebook? It shows that you've seen it, which you know they know you have. But do you really want them to know?

On the other hand, Facebook is the best possible tool to piss off an ex-boyfriend or a guy who isn't "ready" to date. If a guy breaks up with you, have your besties mupload pictures of you with other guys. But remember, don't be the muploader because your act will be transparent. As with all things, the key is subtlety. Oh, and make sure to check that your bestie is FB friends with your ex.

Example of someone with no FB game: Eduardo Saverin's psycho Asian GF.

Relationship statuses: Should you be in a Facebook relationship? It's really up to you and how you think your relationship is perceived by others. If you're an annoying couple, we recommend putting "In a relationship" (without each other's names) or nothing at all. The only reason people put specifically who they're in a relationship with is because they want other people to know.

And, of course, with a relationship there's usually a breakup. To maintain the classy, gradual Facebook split is one of the hardest parts of breaking up. First you change your profile picture, then you discreetly hide your relationship status. It's only a matter of time before people are asking each other if you broke up. Remember to not be too antagonistic on Facebook, like obviously deleting shit. That's fucked up.

Chat/messages: Chat is actually the wildest form of communication in that bros no longer have to ask for your number. They can find you on Facebook after you meet and nonchalantly chat you. You merely need to have met them in a bar once three years ago or sat behind them in French in sixth grade for them to have an opportunity to flirt with you. Although chat kind of sucks because of the nature of how open it is; a lot of annoying people will inevitably chat you because you're popular, so they would. Two thousand people are available to chat? *Sry ct.*

Pokes: Just . . . no. Poking is for fifth-grade boys who tease girls they like for having cooties, and the nerdy kids who never leave their dorm except to go to class. Different ages, same amount of sexual experience.

Twitter—How to Show Everyone You're Better in Fewer than 140 Characters

When Twitter first came out, everyone was like *What the fuck is this, why would I ever use a website solely devoted to Facebook status updates?* Nothing sounded lamer than a site that restricts your thoughts to 140 characters. Our musings are way too complex to be subjected to limits like that. Limits are for poor people's credit and road signs.

But then something happened. One day we realized that Twitter was cool and we just had to make an account so we too could give our followers detailed play-by-plays of our lives via hashtags. *Just checked into Fontainebleau, Miami! Sitting next to @chelseahandler at #dinner! #NowEveryoneKnowsHowRichIAm #ImBetterThanYou.*

Twitter is like a more selective Facebook, so your really creative and hysterical ideas are distilled down to their absolute funniest. And the more popular you are, the more people will want to follow you. Like Spider-Man's uncle once said, "With great power, comes great tweets."

First and foremost, Twitter provides us with yet another outlet to remind everyone that we're hot shit. If you don't tweet something funny about you and your besties being at "the groolest new restaurant!!" then you might as well have not even been there. Unless you're muploading, of course.

But before you go and tweet whatever's on your mind, you should know that everything you tweet can and will invite criticism, from your choice of topics to your Follow Fridays. Just like with Facebook, the key is to never overdo it. Tweet too much, or retweet too often, and consider yourself unfollowed.

Tweeting at friends: This is the safest way to tweet. If you think what you are about to say is funny enough for Twitter but not funny enough for the Internet (as they say), then your best bet will be to tweet it at a friend. This way, if what you just said makes little sense, everyone will just assume it is an inside joke and continue with their day. However, if you forget to mention your friend or make the ballsy move of purposely omitting their name, you risk disapproval and judgment from your followers. *Did you see what Liz just tweeted? She was definitely sitting there planning that tweet for about thirty minutes. Like, stop trying so hard.*

Retweeting: Retweeting a celebrity and retweeting your friends are two different situations that can say two very different things about you. When you retweet a celebrity you are saying that you are smart enough to understand what he/she is tweeting about. Say Bill Maher tweeted back in February 2012 calling Rick Santorum "Christy McSweatervest." Retweeting this will suggest to your followers that you not only understand why this is funny, but also have a keen sense of political humor, even though you actually thought this was a "Jesus dines at McDonald's" kind of joke.

Retweeting your friends is similar to liking something they

say on Facebook. It proves that you are not only in on the joke but that your relationship is also, in fact, much closer than the loose yet mutually respectful bond of your average follower/fol-lowee.

Flirting: Unless you are having a private conversation, flirting should never happen online. Like your alcoholic uncle, it's inap-propriate, aggressive, and makes everyone uncomfortable. If a guy happens to initiate a flirtatious conversation via Twitter, you may answer back. But be sure that your response is witty and not obvi-ous. And remember, the first time you tweet an emoticon is the last time anyone will think you are normal.

Instagram: How to Look Hot Through a Filter

As many of our longtime fans might remember, we got Instagram way before anyone else. Don't get us wrong, it was a total fluke, simply because we thought it was a speedy drug delivery app. Instant grams . . . could you blame us? Imagine our confusion when the app didn't even ask for our zip code, instead prompted us to take a picture!

What's this, a chic and pretentious new way to mupload? That'll do, iPhone, that'll do.

So what makes Instagram different? The appeal lies mostly in two things, the geo-tagging feature and the filter effects. With photo maps and geo-tagging, we can ensure that everyone we know is clear on exactly how many vacations we've taken this year. Meanwhile, the color effects help us understand what life would be like in *The Wackness* or the "We Found Love" video, but with less violence and diversity.

You see, with Instagram, everyone's an artiste, but not one who bothers with complexities like aperture or shutterspeed. Instead you'll say things like: *Commendable efforts on the Amaro, betch, but when my picture has a bluish hue, Walden is best for accentuating contrast.* Sure, you have no clue what you just said but on the bright side, the drop effect is perfect for obscuring the dud.

Suddenly your besties who you thought never ate are all foodies. Why? Because if you mupload food onto Facebook, people will assume you're going to eat it, whereas on Insta, you're simply showcasing your appreciation for plating technique. *How did you get your tuna tartare to look so lively?*

By the time this book comes out there will probably be more rules of conduct when using Instagram but since it's only been around for such a small amount of time, here's a short guideline.

❶ Upload pictures within an hour of taking them. It's calledInstagram,notwait-a-few-days-and-bombard-your-followers-with-twelve-pictures-of-a-wedding-you-attended-last-weekend-agram.

❷ Following people on Instagram is way more casual than Twitter so it's like, whatever.

❸ Twitter hashtagging rules apply: Don't be a literal loser. If you take a picture of an empty plate, #plate is not cool, #dinner is.

❹ Drunk-liking Instagram pictures is dangerous but sometimes fun. Drunk uploading Instagram pictures is dangerously fun.

❺ And finally, unless you think life looks better with one giant spray tan, be sparing with Kelvin. You'll thank us later.

So betches, next time you encounter a really beautiful tulip or an especially long blade of grass, carpe diem. Fuck Kodak, it's called an Insta moment.

Looking back on all of this, can anyone remember what the world was like without Facebook, Twitter, or Instagram? Can you imagine what kind of people we would be if Zuckerberg weren't such a social-climbing loser? Or if whoever the fuck created Twitter didn't care they were losing millions of dollars in the first five years of starting a business? Probably less narcissistic and just generally better people. But hey, that would be really boring. Let's raise this next shot to the nerds who created the social media sites we call home, because talking shit just wouldn't be the same without being able to showcase it on a network of six billion people.

THE ART OF BEING LATE: HOW TO SHOW PEOPLE THAT YOUR TIME IS MORE VALUABLE THAN THEIRS

If people are always telling you to hurry up or they remark that you're consistently late to everything, these are some of the telltale signs that you are cool and important. While the ordinary are encouraged to show up on time or even early, you have your own internal clock and everyone else should probably follow it. Or wait.

We simply don't have time to be on time. Some say this is rude, but think about it, why would we ever be early? Being early means that we would have to wait for people, and we don't do that. People wait for us. Who's the first person at a party? Not you. Not even if it's your own birthday. Being late is one of the most quintessential ways to show people that you're better than them and, therefore, your time is more valuable.

If you think our being late is obnoxious, think about the corporate world. Is the boss ever first to show up to a meeting? No, the minions are. Take a lesson from the corporate bitches. As the queen of your bestie realm, it's your responsibility to show up late.

Being late or inattentive is especially important when dealing with guys. Keeping a guy waiting for your text, your call, or your arrival is one of the best ways to build his anticipation. Being early demonstrates earnestness and, frankly, being excited to talk to a boy is a little bit pathetic. You may have just spent

> "I am invariably late for appointments—sometimes as much as two hours. I've tried to change my ways, but the things that make me late are too strong and too pleasing."
> —Marilyn Monroe

the entire day experiencing minor heart spasms from fear that you have nothing to wear on your date and you may have sent an unhealthy number of pictures to your friends for outfit feedback, but this is the last thing you want the guy to know. Showing up several minutes late will convey to him that you not only just happened upon this Alice and Olivia blouse in the back of your closet, but also that the date was the last thing on

DISCLAIMER

It is *never* okay for someone else to be late if, by chance, you make it somewhere on time. Does Kelly Cutrone wait for Stephanie Pratt to figure out what a computer does before she asks her to print some labels? No fucking way. In return for her tardiness, your bestie will forever be told that things start at least half an hour earlier than they do, to ensure that this travesty never takes place again.

your mind. If you're on time, or worse, show up before him, it's still planted in his mind (even if it's subconscious) that you didn't have anything else to do but think about him, therefore making spending time with you less prized.

Some nonbetches say they are "fashionably late." People who use this phrase invariably sound like tools. This has nothing to do with couture. Betches are just late by nature, because we're super busy with important ventures like getting manicures or waiting for the barista to remake our iced coffees. *Whoever said Skim Plus was the same as Skim was seriously disturbed.* If you get called out for being late, just remind this petty peasant that anything worthwhile is worth waiting for.

Always remember, the early bird catches the worm. Worms, ew.

APPEARING DOWN-TO-EARTH: HOW TO FOOL PEOPLE INTO THINKING YOU'RE NOT SUPERFICIAL

Now that we've basically given you a road map to crafting your surface-level image, it's important to understand that it's not socially acceptable to acknowledge how superficial you are. If you appear to have some hidden depth to your personality, it gives those who know you a chance to uncover it. This adds to your mysterious, complex image and further attracts people to you.

A NOTE ON CHARITIES

It's no secret that we are all inherently selfish and care very little about the well-being and success of those around us. However, in today's society it's quite unacceptable to say that shit out loud. As a person of means, it is expected that you give back to the community around you, if for nothing else than some good old-fashioned PR. Everyone remembers that show *The Fabulous Life of . . .* [insert celebrity name here]. The show always ended with a bit on charities because, well, it's hard for people to not want to kill you if your life is too fabulous and they don't have the delusion that you're doing something good for mankind. Even if it's a bullshit charity, like Hugh Hefner's restoration of the Hollywood sign (which is the biggest way of saying, *I literally don't give a shit about anything but getting my dick wet and making sure I'm not the single oldest thing in California*). This quiets the haters.

Charity events also provide you fancy occasions to dress up and pay thousands of dollars for a ticket that you can use as a tax write-off. Charities help you meet important people who are rich enough to attend the event, and who are in a position to help impoverished aspiring socialites who can't afford beautiful footwear.

As with anything in life, you'll often find yourself faced with the option of doing something the legitimate hard-working way or taking a shortcut. Obviously you should always choose the road less difficult. In other words, why actually *be* down-to-earth when you can just pretend?

The importance of seeming down-to-earth often goes overlooked, likely because very few people actually are, and those who have this quality generally tend to congregate far, far away from true betches. However, being considered down-to-earth, much like being hot, has its perks. People will probably make other positive generalizations about you: you possess a lot of world knowledge, you're not materialistic, you talk less shit than others, and you like to stay above petty drama.

The more generalized assumptions they make about you, the less work you'll have to do to project your image of nonchalant perfection. In other words, you can take time to actually learn about the news, or you can just project a persona that makes people assume you know about it. Let's look at some techniques for seeming down-to-earth:

Say something is expensive: You may occasionally get yourself into a situation in which you are with a friend who is not as rich as you. The aim is to avoid offending her, while subtly letting her know that you are superior.

For example: "Gas is really expensive these days. A gallon is like the price of my iced coffee."

Make random comments about how sad it is for poor people to be poor: As a down-to-earth betch, you must realize that things aren't so peachy for most people. To relate to the masses, it's important to sporadically express your awareness and sympathy for the plight of povos.

For example: "Oh, I've *seen Hotel Rwanda.* Seriously ground-breaking film."

"I felt really bad for that homeless woman, so I gave her twenty-five dollars. That should get her at least a bus ticket and some soap."

BOOKS YOU SHOULD SPARKNOTE
(OR JUST WATCH THE MOVIES)

Because everyone who attended like eighth grade has read these and will know if you get the plot wrong.

✦ *To Kill a Mockingbird*

✦ *The Great Gatsby*

✦ At least one Shakespeare play

Pretend to like artsy movies: But not too many, that makes you a freak from like a small liberal arts school. It's okay to say you like some old movies or movies out of the mainstream, like *Vertigo* or *Pulp Fiction.*

For example: "The cinematography in *Kill Bill: Vol. 2* was like so visually captivating. Can't wait for Aronofsky's next one. Wait, I meant *Requiem for a Dream.* . . ."

"*Mulholland Dr.* was like, so surreal, but whatevs, *Silencio* is chic."

Pretend to know about the environment: Much like being a vegan hipster, caring about the environment is really useful for pretending to take our focus off ourselves. Plus news about the environment is really easy to keep up with. All you ever have to know about the environment is that it's going to shit. Remember, even

Cher Horowitz gave her water skis to the Pismo Beach disaster relief.

For example: "My kids are gonna be really attractive, so there better be a world for them to fucking live in!"

"I love SunChips! They're made with the power of the sun!"

Having a token hated body part: Whoever said "nobody's perfect" had clearly never met a betch. However, going around telling the world what is obvious might make them think you're a huge narcissistic bitch and want to sabotage your amazing existence. For this reason, every betch has a token hated body part that she can plug into conversation when the need presents itself. (See: *Mean Girls*: "My pores are huge." "My nail beds suck." "I get really bad breath in the morning.")

When you name something that you hate about yourself, it should always be easily fixable. Like, "I hate my eyebrows when they're unthreaded" or "I hate my hair when I get out of the shower." But you love your eyebrows when they are threaded, which is always. And you adore your hair five minutes after you get out of the shower. So, really, you're perfect aside from those five minutes.

For example: "My ankles look so fat after flying, you know like to Europe. It's so embarrassing to land at De Gaulle with chubby ankles."

So you see, the key is to make sure you appear down-to-earth enough so people don't think you're a completely dull soulless bitch, but not so down-to-earth that people feel like they can approach you whenever the fuck they want. It's an art, really.

NOT KEEPING UP WITH THE NEWS: HOW TO PRETEND TO KNOW WHAT'S GOING ON WHEN YOU HAVE NO FUCKING IDEA

As a betch who merely pretends to be down to earth, you can excuse yourself from dealing with any of life's unpleasantries, no matter how big or small. That being said, we've heard that, besides the parties we attend, there are actually some pretty big events going on in the world.

Luckily our dads warned us that it's poor etiquette to ever talk about politics or religion in public. So for the most part, social norms will save you from ever having to express your worldview and then back it up with, you know, logic or evidence. Therefore the best way to address politics is to do so only when it's an absolute necessity and to keep your answers light and neutral. And since many people seem to think it's important to know what's going on, you want them to think you have at least a vague idea. Here's how . . .

> "I don't read books, but I do love fashion magazines."
> —Victoria Beckham

How to Fool People into Thinking You Know about the News

Just as expectations of women have evolved so that ignorance is now frowned upon, so has technology adapted to help us cope with this new world order. And just when you thought ten minutes of CNN was all it took to drive you to suicide, Twitter came along and changed everything. Even the most oblivious betches can be in the know. Twitter provides us with a quick and handy tool for us to find out what's going on, in case our parents call and want to talk about something other than how much money we need this week. Let's be honest, though, if Kourtney Kardashian's tweet *Wow!! Ding dong the witch is dead! #osama* hadn't prompted us to turn on the TV to some really tan guy giving a speech about Osama bin Laden's death, we probably would've just assumed she was overjoyed about her bitchy Middle Eastern manicurist finally quitting.

> *"I get the news I need on the weather report."*
> —Simon and Garfunkel

HOW TO ANSWER NEUTRALLY ON POLITICAL ISSUES

On immigration: "I'm pro immigration because my housekeeper, Josephina, was like the sweetest, we even got her Rosetta Stone English for her bday!"

On gay marriage: "Obvi love it, my hairstylist Tony is the best!"

On the election: "I never decide until I get to the voting booth, that way my vote is less partisan."

On the 1 percent: "Let them eat cake."

On abortion: Depends who's being born.

In addition to having a vague sense of what topics are being discussed in the news, you should also have an arsenal of answers, in case you ever want to prove to people that you're not only hot but also capable of forming an opinion. Even if it's incorrect, it's cute that you tried. Remember, you're a girl, no one's expecting you to run for president or anything.

The key is to have a general awareness of the most important things that are going on. We'll admit that sometimes being clueless is more embarrassing than it is cool or aloof. There's a fine line. But generally, follow this table of what you should know to be considered normal, and when you'll be considered a Washington, DC–touring, *West Wing*–watching, news-junkie floser.

It's Okay To	It's Not Okay To
Care about the environment.	Care enough to use a Thermos.
Know we're in a "financial crisis."	Actually be in one.
Know who the president is.	Know who the secretary of defense is.
Have followed the 2012 election.	Root for the fat candidate.
Enjoy movies exploring political issues.	Enjoy movies exploring political issues that don't feature George Clooney.
Be prolife.	Keep your bastard baby at sixteen.
Follow CNN on Twitter.	Actually read their tweets.
Vote.	Vote based on a thoughtful exploration of the issues or a basis of anything other than what your dad says.

HOW TO MANIPULATE YOUR PARENTS INTO THINKING THEY RAISED A NORMAL CHILD

Regardless of where you are in life, your parents will always want to know that you're not fucking up the person they spent so much of their time, money, and energy raising. Unless you want them constantly calling and checking up on you, the key is to reassure them that you're being a responsible adult and not wasting your life away. They know when you're at work or in class, so they've pinpointed your open window of time you can speak to them. You want to make this window as small as fucking possible. No one wants to be interrupted during lunch with her besties or a pregame, to have her parents asking annoying questions like, "How are you? What have you been up to? When are you coming home?" *Mom I'm in the middle of a shot. Can I call you back later!?* It's unlikely you will be able to answer this way, which is where we come in.

Some might call it lying, we call it putting your parents' worries aside. When you do speak to your parents, make sure to give them a vague idea of all the things that

> **INSPIRATIONAL SCENE FROM** *10 THINGS I HATE ABOUT YOU*
>
> WALTER STRATFORD: [*Bianca and Chastity are sneaking past Bianca's father.*] Should've used the window!
>
> BIANCA: Hi, Daddy!
>
> WALTER STRATFORD: Hi . . . where're we going?
>
> BIANCA: Well, if you must know . . . a small study group of friends.
>
> WALTER STRATFORD: Otherwise known as an orgy?
>
> CHASTITY: Mr. Stratford, it's just a party!
>
> WALTER STRATFORD: And hell is just a sauna.

they want to hear. *Oh no, I haven't really gotten a chance to go out this week, I have a lot of work to do. I've got a big project coming up.* Yeah, you didn't have a chance to go out on Wednesday, but you're planning on making an appearance on Thursday, Friday, and Saturday, and they don't really need to know that this project is due in a month.

We're not saying you should actually be fucking up your life, getting drunk every night, and potentially getting fired and/or failing out of school. That's information you might want to let them in on so they can solve your problems for you. But as long as you have your life together, they don't need to know your process for getting your shit done.

Your parents grew up in a different time; they never had Facebook, Twitter, or Blackout Wednesday. Things have changed, and they'll never really understand that. You should approach answering their questions in a way that will placate their worries about you and let them go on with their lives. Let's face it, most of us are hooking up with bros we meet at bars, going on sporadic dates, and not really settling down, but that's the last thing your parents want to hear. So here is the surefire way to appease your parents' concerns about your dying alone or being a giant lesbian. *There are definitely guys in my life, just no one that I've found worth my time. I just don't really like anyone at the moment, you understand.* They will understand, and change the topic.

When it comes down to it, your parents just want to know that you're happy, so give them that, but don't make it too obvious. For girls, there's a significantly greater pressure on us to find the perfect boyfriend to eventually marry, and if you're single, it's especially irritating to get the question, "So is there anyone special in your life?" *Yeah, Dad, his name is vodka and we've gotten to know each other over the years pretty fucking well.*

Summary

In a world where we're constantly being reassured that it's what's on the inside that counts, it's essential to understand that's bullshit. Sure, having the right Chanel sunglasses, the ideal summer home, or the perfect breed of Maltese to stick in your Louis Vuitton won't make you any more interesting, but it will make you more envied, more appreciated, and more respected. A wise betch once said, "Everyone becomes boring, but people with money become boring slower." And even if you don't have material possessions, pretending like you have your shit together is the best way to have your shit together until you actually do. No one wants to hang around a mopey, crying, poor loser. So hold your head up high, reserve your smiles for those who really deserve them, and let the world know it's your bitch. Elle Macpherson wasn't fucking joking when she said out loud what everyone else was thinking. Image is everything.

Dear Betch,

I started thinking about the etiquette of the text message sign-off. I am unsure about the policy on finishing a message with X's and O's. Because betches have so many people texting them, what is the best way to approach the X/XX/XOXO sign-off to the betches, bros, pros, and family in our lives? How do you maintain control, and therefore win, but still appear to have a soul? Please clear this up for me!

Love ya,
Nervous Betch

Dear Nervous Betch,

If you're actually *that* nervous about how to sign off on a text, we suggest you ask your doctor to up your Xanax dosage. With that said, no one signs off a text, except maybe your mother. But even with moms, it gets so fucking annoying when they write *Love, Mom* in every single message.

Important: the more sign-off abbreviations you send to a guy, the less attractive you become. As in, MWAH TTYL LYL XOXO. You might as well say, "I'm fugly; don't text me again." When it comes to a guy, if you want to stop texting, just stop—they aren't looking for an elaborate good-bye.

However, in e-mails the sign-off can say a lot. Use "Sincerely" if you're trying to be more formal and "Thanks" or "Talk soon" for the friendlier good-bye. Use "Best" when you want to be passive-aggressive, like in an e-mail to your sorority's e-mail chain.

Best,
The Betches

Social Life

People Who ~~You Like~~ Are Worthy
of Your Friendship

THE BESTIE GROUP CIRCLE

When you think about what has molded you into the person you are today, besides your family and your perfect genes, the most obvious answer should be your friends. People always say that once you graduate college, it's very difficult to make new friends, but it's like, why the fuck would you want to make new ones when you already have so many? Honestly, being a friendless loser is much less work than being a betch with way too many friends. At least losers don't have to deal with the pressure and anxiety that planning a birthday dinner involves. *Ugh, I might have to have two diff dinners, one for my school friends, and one for my home friends.* But wait, *which one do I invite my camp friends to? No one ever told me growing up would be* this hard.

> "*I get high with a little help from my besties.*"
> —The Betches

Despite these stressful elements of being popular, having droves of besties has many more benefits than it does drawbacks. When you only have a few BFFs, it's difficult to specialize. What do we mean by specialize?

Whether it's to constantly entertain you, to be your personal photographer, or to always be down when you want to go out, every single one of your friends serves a distinct and probably singular purpose in your life.

THE BETCH CODE: AN INTRODUCTION

Because Girl Code is for nicegirls.

While betches aren't always the most moral people, there are certain lines we shouldn't cross when fucking over our fellow females, especially those we call our friends.

We understand that when it comes to relationships, the lines of betchdom become a little blurry.

For example, everyone is familiar with that girl who hooks up with a guy one time and forever claims him as "hers," even though he wouldn't ever (soberly) touch her again with a ten-foot pole. This girl is annoying and will often say you're a "bad friend" if you even think about hooking up with this bro.

But this is why the Betch Code exists. So to all of you delusional daters out there who figuratively, and hopefully not literally, pee circles around guys whose family stories you memorize yet who can barely pronounce your first name, chill the fuck out. Do yourself a favor, spend less time googling guys' family trees on ancestry.com and commit the Betch Code to memory. Then maybe your friends will spend less time daydreaming about what it will feel like to slap you across the face.

We've devised a points system for those of you who are clueless as fuck and/or have no soul. The system could otherwise be called the "Are You a Bad Person?" list.

You will see the points system dispersed throughout this chapter. Disregarding it can and should get you black-listed, leaving you to hang out with the sexually active band geeks and the girls who eat their feelings.

Here's how it works: Add points for every item on the checklist that rings true for something you've done. If you have more than three points, don't do it. If you have less, go get yourself laid. If you have three exactly and act on it, you're either someone who can manipulate your way out of looking like a horrible person (aka someone we would hang out with), or you're going to get yourself punched in the face.

The Bestie

It is perfectly natural to have a problem with trusting too many people. This is what your bestie is for. She is your motherfucking BFF. She's there for you thick and thin, knows you inside and out, would literally ~~die for you~~ help you get your tampon out if you accidentally had sex while on your period. She helps you bear the burden of all your deepest secrets and holds your true "number" in her vault of confidential information. She's the girl you've known forever, she's the person who's in on 95 percent of your inside jokes, and she's the wind beneath your ~~wings~~ private jet.

Your bestie is your most trusted shit-talking partner, because you two are so in sync that your brains operate on the same frequency. Scientists can't truly explain the silent conversation you just had over lunch about the girl with tree-trunk arms who walked by. Before you had time to do as much as raise an eyebrow, your bestie said, "Holy fuck, that bitch's arms are the size of West

BESTIE TWIN SYNDROME

To further prove that two heterosexual girls pairing off is a widespread epidemic, there's even a condition out there to describe this phenomenon: the Bestie Twin Syndrome. Sure, people might occasionally mix up your names, but when you have BTS, people will start mixing up your faces into one fucking betch, even when you don't look alike. And if you do happen to look alike, well then get ready to have your names fused into one. If you ever hear the name Meslie used to describe a person, don't be naive, this is clearly a duo with BTS named Mel and Leslie. What dipshit would actually name their kid Meslie?

Afghanistan." Being able to tune into what your friend is thinking not only makes your life easier, but it also gives you so much more free time to figure out what you're going to wear tomorrow or why your period is a week late. Just because science can't explain bestie telepathy doesn't mean you can't rely on it.

As long as you're not one of those floater girls who basically uses the friends she's acquired over the years as intermittent friends (aka the people she uses to go out with while she's in between boyfriends—see: the Limbo Bitch), then you will always have one bestie by your side, both figuratively and literally. And by "literally," we mean "in pictures." Then who's the one taking the pictures? The group photog, of course.

The Group Photog

Now we don't mean to imply that the group photographer is not worthy of your friendship or of being in your tagged photos. No, everybody likes the photog, because she controls your virtual life. Besides muploads, this girl has sole authority over your FB profile. If you're a bitch to the photog, she might "accidentally" forget to crop your arm out of the picture in which the rest of your

THE LIMBO BITCH

We're not talking about that nicegirl game played while sipping virgin piña coladas at Hawaiian luaus. Nor are we referring to the place betches probably chill in right before they enter hell. No, LB's the girl who has a lot of friends when she's single, but when she gets a boyfriend, she disappears off the fucking planet. Then when her relationship ends, she tries to make like she never even left and starts partying even harder than the rest of us.

Sometimes it's hard to decipher if she is only hanging out with you to pass the time while she looks for her next one true love. Shit gets confusing when your friendship with someone is dependent upon the frequency with which they're getting fucked.

Now if you don't really give a shit about this friend it's usually like whatever. You feel no obligation to give a shit that she leaves because you were never that tight to begin with. Therefore you often welcome her as another bitch to party with when she's single. Her return will often be preempted by an outreach to *grab dinner and catch up!* It's kind of like if your mother got remarried and abandoned your family, only to return after many years bearing alcohol and breakup stories. If you're a more astute bitch, her fake presence is usually irritating, and you resent her using you for your popularity and inner circle. Like, if I wanted to babysit a pathetic single girl obsessed with finding a boyfriend, I'd watch a fucking Katherine Heigl movie.

body happens to look really skinny. Piss her off and next thing you know, she's setting her albums to "friends only" and directly throwing your Internet reputation in the garbage.

THE BETCH CODE

Is it okay to hook up with a guy your friend has hooked up with once?

- **+1:** If your bestie has hooked up with him once (+ only .5 if she's not a friend you would ever hang out with alone)
- **—1:** If your bestie can't remember hooking up with him
- **—2:** If your bestie was so fucked up she doesn't remember that she threw up on him
- **+1:** If he threw up on her

But the reason why the photog is a very important job is the very same reason why you would never want to be her. She has the upper hand in your online image, but she's cursed with some seriously taxing social responsibilities. While you enjoy your Sunday afternoons sleeping, brunching, and watching movies you've already seen ten times on TBS, the photog is sitting at home, uploading and editing the 320 pictures she took of everyone over the weekend. This would be one of the only times we would advocate thinking about others, so go ahead and offer to bring her an iced coffee. I mean, it would really be in your best interest to make her happy while she's captioning and tagging (and selectively deleting) photos of you.

So why would anyone want to assume this stressful position in the group? Probably because she's the betch who craves the control that comes with the job and wants to show everyone how amazing her life is. She has the Godlike power to upload a pic in which a girl you all hate looks like Martin Lawrence in *Big Momma's House*. Also, some people just like photography. We may not understand it, but we're down. There's no doubt that some pictures actually look really cool in black-and-white, but if you upload a picture of yourself in B & W, then you're clearly a weirdo who's trying too hard. But if people see that you're not the one who uploaded the awesome black-and-white photo, it's totally a win-win. The picture of you looks sick, and your photog got to exhibit her skill at "art" (read: filters).

The Anal Betch

No, this isn't the girl who won't stop talking about the one time she let it slip in. This is the girl who is the biggest overachiever of the group, or just should be clinically treated for OCD. Probably based on some psychological issues, the anal betch is like the group photog but more intense. When you and your besties want to do something that's slightly less casual than meeting at a bar, such as going out for dinner, the anal betch will call dibs on planning the evening. And seeing as putting in effort is not really your forte, go ahead and refrain from weighing in unless she's really fucking it up. If you don't have this girl in your group of friends, then the one who initiates the group din is either the dud (see below) or just the fattest.

The Dud

Remember how all of your friends have a special task and bring something to the metaphorical table? Well there's always an outlier, and we've dubbed her "the dud."

Ask anyone in your bestie group what they think of the dud, and they'll obviously say that she fucking sucks. Even though no

TALKING SHIT 2.0: ABOUT YOUR BESTIES

Talking Shit 2.0, which is distinguished from regular shit-talking by its complexity and nuance, is all about your friends and their secrets. Every bestie group knows that you're allowed to talk shit about your besties but *only* if it's to your mutual besties. Otherwise you're like a really bad friend or something.

Talking about your friends behind their backs usually happens when one has noticed that a bestie is changing for the worse. Like when one of your formerly awesome besties is turning into a psychopath and has been try-ing way too hard to make the ongoing inside joke "who's going to be the first to fuck the dealer?" a reality.

And let's not forget about the bestie who's been MIA lately because she's with her boyfriend at all times or try-ing extra hard at work. Her absence makes it even easier to talk shit about her because she's not around. She might as well just send a mass text that says, *Since I have some-thing "better" to do than hang out with you, you're all allowed to talk shit about me.*

Some people say you should keep your friends close and your enemies closer. We say that's for paranoid weir-dos and the mafia. Every betch knows you're only as pow-erful as the amount of bestie secrets you have stored in your gossip arsenal. So the saying should really go: Keep your friends closer so you have more to say when you talk shit about them later.

girl in the group would truly consider the dud their personal bes-tie, she's somehow been able to play her cards well enough that no one has a good enough reason to just kick her the fuck out . . . though we all secretly wish she'd find some nicegirls to sit at home with and knit mittens. Let's face it, bros are just not that into the dud . . . ever. To guys, she's more of the hit-it and quit-it type, if they even hit it at all.

She's the friend who's always on the end in group pics. She's cute enough, but she's not prettier than you, so you always look hotter standing next to her. She's great for the times when no one else wants to listen to you complain about your problems, but when she starts to talk about her issues, you sort of zone out. Even though her presence is irritating during the sober portion of the evening, she's great as a wingwoman because you never have to feel bad about ditching her. Also, she'll fuck anything in her line of sight, so she's a reliable match for the wingman of the bro who you're trying to get with.

Every once in a while, it'll come down to a crucial decision: watching *Dancing with the Stars* with Great-Aunt Sally or going barhopping with the dud. Depending on your great-aunt's dialysis schedule, it's perfectly acceptable to choose the former.

The lesson here, betches, is that everyone has their niche in society. But duds, beware. Make sure you stay generous and inof-

---

THE BETCH CODE

Is it okay to hook up with a guy your friend has hooked up with multiple times?

+2: If your bestie has hooked up with him more than three times (+1.5 if she's not a friend you would ever hang out with alone)

+5: If your bestie is currently hooking up with him but they're not exclusive

+3: If your bestie has hooked up with him but he's made her cry

fensive. We might be willing to take in a stray dog, but we sure as fuck won't be picking up its shit.

And if you're not sure who in your group is the dud? You're it.

The Bat-Shit-Crazy Betch

The token crazy friend has superior abilities to talk shit, tell really funny stories, and make everyone around her appear sane to guys, so she often goes by the name bat-shit-crazy betch. Because the BSCB may come in several different forms, there's a flavor for every bestie group. Let's take a look at the various qualities the BSCB may possess.

Compulsive need to rage: While we're almost always down to rage, the BSCB gives this an entirely new meaning. She's usually the girl that lost her virginity in seventh grade, regularly pounds shots at ten A.M. while everyone else is taking turns vomming from their hangovers (or breakfast, whatever), and was doing lines behind her laptop screen in freshman year econ. This girl is your favorite person to party with, has fucked upward of forty bros, and generally serves to make your insane habits feel comparatively normal.

Psycho breakdowns/tantrums: Some BSCBs have some sort of real and diagnosable (but untreated) psychiatric disorder, be this OCD/ADD/manic depression/generalized anxiety disorder/is just fucking nuts. She may appear normal most of the time . . . until she starts spontaneously crying in the middle of the library, or when the Bachelor eliminates the girl the BSCB most identifies with. If her breakdowns are minimal (read: not too inconvenient), then this BSCB can have you laughing for hours. However, if her psychosis is extremely intense, we suggest you be careful about getting too close, because you might be spending those hours in the hospital waiting room.

Sociopathic tendencies: One of the most dangerous BSCBs is the type that is a sociopath/borderline personality/pure fucking evil. This girl is stealthy. She may initially come off as completely sane, but she has some seriously evil plans for destruction. While most betches are harmless and generally awesome, the sociopath BSCB allows her boredom and/or insane ambitions to get in the way of living life like the rest of us. Watch out for this bitch or she'll steal your boyfriend, your dignity, and your self-esteem. The only options are to make sure you're cool enough to bawl her out, or you better get your ass on her good side.

The Token Asian Betch

The problem with befriending the girls we've described up till now is that you can't decide what kind of friend they are until they do

---

THE BETCH CODE

Is it okay to hook up with a guy your bestie has had sex with?

- **+2:** If she had sex with him once (-2 if it was after she was roofied, +10 if he was the one who roofied her)
- **+5:** If your bestie has had sex with him more than three times (+3 if she's not a friend you would ever hang out with alone)
- **—1:** If the girl who's TGF has had sex with him
- **+2:** If your bestie had to Plan B his baby
- **+3:** If you went with her to CVS

something indicative of their personalities, like whip out a camera or send death threats to some guy. However, the one girl we haven't mentioned in our bestie circle is pretty easy to discern. It's the Token Asian Betch.

Now, you may not be BFF with the TAB, but you definitely have a school friend whose home friend has one, or vice versa. Regardless, they exist, and they're great because they add diversity to the group, the possibility of homemade sushi for dinner, and an occasional free manicure. The TAB stands out from the group because of her Asian flush at pregames, tiny bone structure, and high SAT scores.

The TAB's parents are often either FOB business moguls who she's embarrassed of or Jewish lesbians from the Upper East Side. And, unfortunately, she'll be plagued for life by her parents' urging her to stop dressing like a slut and become a doctor or attend MIT. But despite her parents' strict rules and high expectations, the TAB is usually either a complete BSCB who parties really hard while fucking any bro she can or the kind who never puts out and dates Wall Street pros.

Honestly, we love the Token Asian Betch because, when she's not sleeping in the library, she's usually tearing shit up at a club. Asian betches bring that special flavor to the bestie group, they're like the sweet-and-sour sauce to our steamed chicken and broccoli. And to any Asian betch who's offended by this, maybe you can teach us how to play the world's smallest violin?

The Gay BFF

Since we're on the subject of diversification, can you think of anything that would expand the boundaries of an all-female group of friends more than a penis? No, you can't! This is exactly why our last, yet very important, addition to our bestie circle is the gay BFF.

If betches had a religion (no, we don't count going to synagogue or church once a year for thirty minutes before sneaking off to Starbucks as "religion"), then our gay best friends would be the high priests. Thankfully, like all spiritual guides, gay best friends are both total fucking experts in how to behave, and completely emotionally removed from whatever questionable behavior we confess to them. This role used to be filled by our housekeepers, until we realized that anyone who walks around the house in a PAPA GINO'S PIZZERIA XL T-shirt and homemade jorts is probably not someone we should be looking to for advice, no matter how nonjudgmental they are.

Gay best friends are both brutally honest and also weirdly unemotional about whatever you do, so you don't feel like they're judging you in a mean way. Like the kid with Asperger's who gave the group a D when the professor asked what the team's grade should be, they're the referees of the betch life, objective bystanders who you can trust because they have no (fore)skin in the game.

THE BETCH CODE

Is it okay to hook up with a guy your friend has ever dated?

Rule of Thumb: If your bestie ever dated a guy, always ask if she's okay before you do anything even if she's been over him for "years."

+1: If your bestie went on a date with him

+5: If he made her pay

+2: If your bestie went on more than two dates with him

+7: If he's your bestie's ex-boyfriend (+4 if their relationship ended more than two years ago, +2 if it was more than five)

+100: They're currently dating, *you whore*

The most amazing trait of the gay bestie is that they *love* drama and always have way more scandalous stories than you, which makes you feel like less of a slut. You're guaranteed to feel better about having sex with three different guys last weekend when your gay bestie says he just had a foursome in the Equinox bathroom that morning.

The entertainment value and emotional guidance that the gay bestie brings to a betch's life make them the only real form of guy friend. You know you can count on your gay bestie to be your sidekick at all times, constantly telling you how hot and fabulous you are. Since they want to turn you into the ideal feminine embodiment of themselves, they always have your back when you feel like talking shit, or when you're having an anxiety attack about a fashion emergency. Since being surrounded by girls all the time is fucking annoying, a gay BFF provides the perfect dose of testosterone without your having to feel self-conscious about anything you're doing. And you get to be their beard for their grandma!

The gay BFF is the ultimate addition to the bestie group. You get your biggest fan, your psychologist, and a friend who will never look better than you in a miniskirt all rolled up into one. Since girls are inevitably all competing with one other, having a gay bestie is like a breath of fresh air. It's like rooting for your immigrant housekeeper to get her green card. You can selflessly support this person, because your goals are so mutually exclusive.

When in Doubt, Don't Branch Out

Now that you've gotten to know the cast of bestie characters in your life movie, what does it all mean? Why is your bestie circle so close? It's important to have good friends who "get you." These friends will always be there to validate your lifestyle of needing to always be tan and complaining about your overflowing closet.

In your lifetime you're going to come across a lot of haters who might think the number of iPhones you've had to replace this month is a tad excessive. Your besties, on the other hand, have already accepted you for who you are: an innocent girl with butterfingers and alcohol-induced short-term memory loss.

Every betch knows there's no greater pain than meeting a new person who doesn't understand your jokes or get why you have your dad's credit card number memorized. (No, it's not in case of emergencies. What am I, poor?) Getting to know people outside of your bestie circle is like writing an essay and having to start it over again, for no fucking reason.

We're not saying that making new friends is a bad thing. Go ahead, go out for drinks with people from work. But more often than not, these people who you call your "work friends" are almost exactly like the people you've known your entire life. Plus or minus a summer home or two.

So why don't we spend time trying to meet new people? That's like asking when was the last time you saw Mary-Kate hang out with anyone other than Ashley. It's essential for girls to have a support system of close female friends. In fact, it's unhealthy and weird not to. When it comes to branching out, you should branch like a palm tree: not at fucking all. We don't know shit about gardening, but would you want your social life to imitate the trees of Beverly Hills or some bushy thing in a forest? Fucking thought so.

But None of This Applies to Me!!!

Sorry, but you're clearly a floser or a nicegirl. You obviously aren't friends with a BSCB because no girl who recreationally skips her meds would spend time with someone who plays Jenga on Thursday nights. But cheer up, now that you've studied the delicate art of being a betch, you can put this book down and befriend a hot Asian and a homo, while still maintaining a core group of besties. You'll thank us later.

GUY FRIENDS: A FAIRY TALE

Some of our favorite friends are the ones who possess the one thing a betch doesn't: a penis. We'll say straight-up that guy friends are a joke. Saying you have guy friends is kind of like pretending you have a true appreciation for movies like *Citizen Kane*. *It's such a cinematic masterpiece, you know, with innovative lighting and shit.* There may be a small amount of truth to it, and you like the way it makes you seem in theory.

However, there is another movie that is much more on our level and happens to shed light on the honest truth of the real relationship between men and women. It's called *When Harry Inevitably Fucked Sally*. It says everything that needs to be said on the topic of guy friends, namely that they all want to fuck you. But we're going to go beyond that and show you the real benefits of having them and, specifically, what they can be used for. But first, we must address why you don't—and will never—have a male friend who isn't a flaming homosexual.

If you're a true betch, no guy would actually want to hear any of your shit-talking about other girls and other shallow nonsense. Men and women don't realistically have that much in common, especially not when it comes to nonflirtatious small talk. Do you really think bros want to sit and listen to you talk shit and reiterate the benefits of Diet Coke all day? Fuck no, that's why you're not really yourself around your guy friends, which is why they're not *really* your friends.

Here's simple evidence: When you are going for iced coffee

with your female friend, you might not put on eyeliner, but if you were to go with your guy friend, you'll definitely apply eyeliner, and maybe even straighten your hair. If you're not nodding in agreement, you're probs a lesbian or you're too fat for it to even make a difference.

Being a highly confident and attractive girl makes it difficult to encounter a straight male who doesn't want to get us in bed. If you have a boyfriend who claims to be friends with this really hot girl who, in his words, "is really great," there's no way he's not thinking about having sex with her (if he hasn't already).

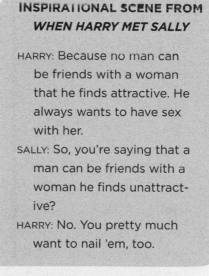

INSPIRATIONAL SCENE FROM
WHEN HARRY MET SALLY

HARRY: Because no man can be friends with a woman that he finds attractive. He always wants to have sex with her.

SALLY: So, you're saying that a man can be friends with a woman he finds unattractive?

HARRY: No. You pretty much want to nail 'em, too.

You may think, *I have a guy friend who I haven't hooked up with,* but please don't take that as a sign that you're safe from a drunken make-out session in the future. There's a reason why you are friends. He obviously likes you as like a person, so why wouldn't he want to hook up with you? It's probably not that you're unattractive because consider this: Are you friends with any really ugly girls? No. No one wants to be around unattractive people, so the same applies to female-male relationships. If he hangs out with you in public, he thinks you're good-looking, therefore he's attracted to you, therefore he wants to fuck you. It's in the math. Guy friends are for lesbians and funny fat girls.

Classic examples include Monica and Chandler and Ross and Rachel and every other straight and single (or not) television and movie couple to ever exist who claimed to be "friends." Bull. Shit. There are no exceptions to this rule. We dare you to come up with one, real or fictional. There's a reason why on a show called *Friends,* four out of the six main characters ended up coupled off.

But don't let this earth-shattering myth of guy friends get you down. It should be nothing new, so nothing has to change. Best of all, having guy "friends" can have tons of benefits for you. Let's take a look:

❶ They make you appear chill, like you can actively engage in nonbetchy conversation that isn't gossip, even though you don't know what that is.

❷ You can find out the latest scoop on guy drama. Who beat the shit out of whom? Who's been fucking whose ex-girlfriend? Who secretly likes *The Notebook*?

❸ Guys who you are interested in dating will see that you are able to sustain a friendship with another male, which is kind of a stamp of approval that you're not extremely annoying and therefore potentially dateable. It also might make other guys jealous of the relationship you claim is "super platonic. Jason and I are just besties since we were in that class together in Florence!"

❹ Since all bros are also aware of the fact that there's no such thing as being friends with a girl, others will assume that he likes you, making you appear more desirable to guys who you're like actually trying to hook up with.

❺ Going out for meals with guy friends will get you to eat less, because who eats actual meals in front of males? Hilary Doof professing to Chad Michael Murray in *A Cinderella Story* that she would rather eat a cheeseburger over a salad is a joke because (A) that's not true and (B) it's a retarded movie.

 They will hopefully feed you with superficial sports knowledge you can use when talking to bros you actually give a shit about.

All in all, the illusion of having guy friends is kind of like believing in Santa Claus, or that plus-size models are the look of the future. But having this realization about guy friends doesn't mean that we're ready to get rid of them anytime soon. So keep these imaginary guy friends around, but be prepared for that inevitable moment when you'll either have to make him cry or blow your rape whistle. Or even worse, succumb to the pity fuck.

HOW TO TEXT LIKE YOU'RE KIND OF A BIG DEAL

In this day and age, texting is by far the main form of communication among social circles. Knowing what to say and when to say it is pivotal in the image that you give off. It's time to take a look at the ways you can use texting to manipulate others and show that you care less about them than just about anything else.

What you're allowed to text about: It's weird to initiate texting over mundane things. Save that for iChat or gchat during work hours, when the other person is clearly bored. If you're texting someone with a *Hey, what's up,* you better be following that up with details about a pregame tonight or something at least as exciting as that you finally set the date for your chin job.

It's poor etiquette to text things that could waste someone's time, such as, *I'm getting a manicure,* or *So I've decided that head-*

bands are now my thing. What you say should have high entertainment value.

When a casual conversation is over: Ends with *Thanks* or any variation of *Okay.*

How to strategically avoid people: With texting as opposed to BBM, this has become a lot easier. Now you can find out that Rachel wants you to pick her up from the airport without her knowing whether or not you've seen it, and you can ignore her because you were "napping."

How to strategically avoid agreeing to plans: When someone texts you to see what you're doing, and you just *know* the follow-up is

---

THE DRESS CODE OF AGREEMENT:
THE VARIOUS VERSIONS OF "OKAY"

When a word comes in several forms, it's often difficult to discern its meaning. The most commonly used example of this is the various formats of the word "okay." You may use this word every day, but the way you say it usually holds a deeper meaning about your seriousness.

OKAY = Black tie

OK = Business casual

'KAY = Casual Friday, but you're still at work

KK = Casual

KKKKKK = Superhyped up on Adderall

K = A jeans and a tank-type casual or could be passive-aggressive (meaning "fuck you")

OKAYYYY = Casual but reluctant like *Honestly you need to stop texting him when he knows you're supposed to be in a work meeting.* Response: *Okayyyy.*

going to be *Wanna chill?*, the iPhone gives you the ability to buy some time while you conveniently go "run errands with your mom."

Caveat: Be wary of your use of other forms of social media while ignoring people. Like, if you're ignoring your friend but you answer the group chat that she's also in . . . congrats, you just blew up your own spot. The same goes with tweeting from your phone. *I know you're not dead! At least pretend like you're doing something else!*

The Text Psychopath

The main thing to remember when considering a text is that you don't send texts, you just get them. And none for Gretchen Wieners.

Avoid the following like you would a wedding without an open bar, lest you be labeled a text psycho.

Texting the same person more than three times: It used to be that only one text was acceptable and then BBM came around, which was like instant messaging, so it was kind of okay to send multiple messages. Because of that, we'll allow three now. Any more and you're annoying/harassing. Especially if, after your three texts, the person responds with the *Kk*. The Kk is not your excuse to initiate a new topic.

Calling people when texting will suffice: You're allowed to use the "phone" function on your cell when you're talking to your parents, just so that the conversation ends quicker. And you're allowed to call your bestie, but only if you're waiting for her because she's fucking late or if you're walking to work and just *that* bored.

Never leave a voice mail unless it's going to be: "I'm fucking leaving without you, bitch."

Assuming you don't have a boyfriend, you should never *ever* call a guy. Unless it's to tell him you're pregnant and it's his. Calling a guy means you've secured yourself a quiet space and taken time out of your day to entirely devote to speaking to him. Meanwhile, texting allows you to be in contact while not giving anyone your full attention.

Initiating texts with guys (daytime): Do this seldom, and never twice before the guy has initiated at least once. And only if you have a reason to text him a specific thing that he would consider relevant, interesting, and not weird or random. You never text *Hey, what's up* without an extremely worthwhile follow-up or an invitation to something that you're hosting later that night. Ever. You don't want this guy to think that you're casually thinking about him throughout the day for no apparent reason.

> "Men don't respond to words. What they respond to is no contact."
> —Sherry Argov, *Why Men Love Bitches*

Also, never text a guy who has given you his number and not asked for yours. If he wanted to speak to you badly enough, he would have made sure he had your number. There's a special spot reserved in hell for guys who are so lame that they have to offer girls their number. The treasure does not do the hunting. This guy should know that you have more important things to do than casually "check in" with him. You're not his parole officer or his fucking camp counselor.

Also, always be sure to wait anywhere from ten minutes to two hours before answering any texts from guys, even if you saw it immediately. The bigger an asshole he is, the longer you should wait. I mean, sure you could be a complete loser with no life who has nothing to do all day but constantly check your phone, but he doesn't have to know that. . . . .

One last thing: If a guy does not text you back after you have initiated texting, he is *not* into you.

Initiating and ending conversations (daytime, boys and girls): You should generally try to avoid sending the last text of a conversation, as letting someone else have the last word means that you are choosing not to let the dialogue continue.

Unless of course you're fighting with your good friend, in which case you should continue to confront her until you have the last word on why Lady Gaga is really annoying and not creative and original like she tries to seem.

But with a guy, you definitely don't want to have the last word. If you do, it means he stopped caring first. Who starts and ends the conversation is a big deal and says a lot about how annoying you are and how badly you want to continue talking to this person.

Late-night texting: Is defined as an initiated conversation after ten thirty P.M. and before five A.M., usually on the weekends.

In other words, at two P.M. you cannot text a guy *Hey, what's up?* with nothing to back it up, but after ten thirty at night, this same phrase has a new meaning, mainly: *Are you interested in having sex with me tonight?*

You get fewer points if you initiate the drunk late-night meet-up, but at least it means you're not the one being booty called, rather you are the booty caller. It's generally best to avoid, though, because down the road it may lead to rejection. Very risky. This is unless, of course, he's your back-burner bro and you don't really care what he thinks, because you have no desire to increase his affections for you.

You should never initiate late-night sexting. Sex should be inferred, and never blatantly said. It's all about suggesting to "hang out." There are lots of things you can do at three A.M.

Deleting texts you regret sending: Frankly we would rather look at photos of dismembered natural disaster victims than an unanswered *I miss you* from Saturday night. You can't be looking at that shit every time you look in your inbox. Therefore, deleting is necessary sometimes. Just do it and move on.

Saving texts where an SAB said something nice to you: Now, the iPhone allows you to pick and choose which texts to delete, not just entire conversations. If you find yourself in a place of constantly deleting bad shit and saving only nice shit, you're feeding into your own delusions. Texting isn't fucking PhotoShop. While you can accentuate the background in a picture to make your arm look skinnier, you cannot crop out the part of the convo where you told Ben you shaved for him.

The solo question mark: You've all gotten and sent the question mark before. The question mark is an extremely passive-aggressive move because it usually comes from a place of latent anger and growing tension with someone. It's says, *?*, but it means, *This is my last fucking warning before I start talking shit about you to anyone who will listen. Don't make me pull out the call.* You know you're in deep shit when you're getting a call.

The question mark with a guy: No.

In general: There is no greater way to make a guy go crazy over you than to ignore his texts. To wait is acceptable, but to ignore is simply divine. This is especially difficult if you really like a guy, but often doing the opposite of your instincts is what gets you the biggest prize. Unless a guy truly has been amazing to you and you're sure it's reciprocal, the occasional ignoring of texts is a surefire way to have a guy constantly thinking about what you're doing, who you're with, and why you're not answering his texts. If a guy is sending you a question mark because you haven't answered his texts, you can answer and exclaim in a cheerful way that you're sorry you've been so busy and you forgot to answer. Bam. Even if you were insanely deep in the hole before, you're now officially winning.

Bottom line: As in all aspects of life, maintaining the upper hand in any situation is always of the essence. Texts are hard evidence, so make sure you think through the texting vibe you give off and what your texts say to others. It only takes a few faulty, annoying texts to turn one into the guy who only gets texted for a ride home from the train station or the girl who only gets messaged for a copy of her take-home final.

PEOPLE YOU DISLIKE: HOW TO DEAL WITH THEM WHILE NOT APPEARING PSYCHOTIC

While your natural charm and manipulative wit will draw many allies and admirers throughout your life, it's inevitable that you'll encounter conflict with a number of people who cross your path: guys, family members, other betches, enemies, acquaintances, bosses, feminists, fuglies. And though little girls are taught from a young age that "getting along nicely with one another" is paramount, the truth is that whatever kindergarten teacher gave you this idea was absolutely fucking you over. Sheltering children from reality is not beneficial to their survival, *thank you very much, Miss Lippy.* This is because the very idea of "getting along" is in direct conflict with looking out for number one.

Staying on top means not being weak. Since you are enviable and people hate those they envy, be ready for people to start shit with you. Abandon the delusion that being nice is necessary. As long as you're not like two hearings away from court-ordered anger-management class, disagreement isn't a bad thing; it's a way of setting the social pecking order.

Imagine that a longstanding frenemy of yours told a group of mutual male friends that you have the herp. If the mere thought of this doesn't enrage you, it means you're either timid and lame, too barred out to care, or you actually *do* have herpes. Even if that's the case, though, you should still want to cut the bitch who outed you.

We're not saying you should be combative or constantly trying to prove yourself. Having beef with a lot of people is a sign of low self-esteem and a defensive nature, probably because you had no friends as a child. The goal is to always be—or at least appear to be—a chill person.

Much like any aspect of being a betch, the key to fighting like a betch is to hardly fight at all. You can win any argument simply by keeping your cool and letting your enemies defeat themselves. This is accomplished by not doing anything obvious, while using tactful suggestion and empirical evidence of how fucking superior you are. You can think of this as acting like an aloof bitch, but the more common term is passive aggression. After all, physical aggression is beneath you (unless you're from Staten Island).

Handling Altercations: How to Remain on Top

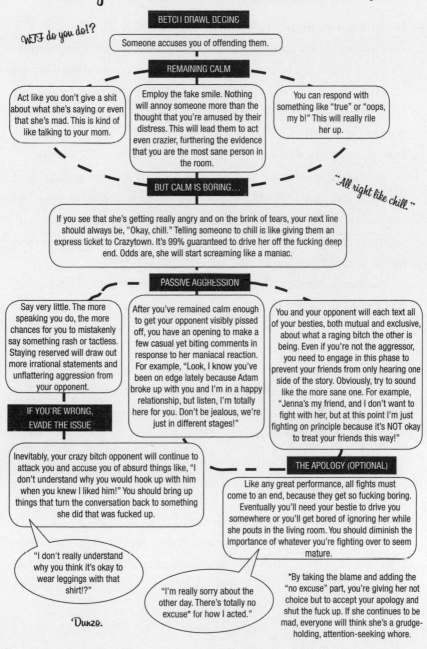

BETCH BRAWL BEGINS

Someone accuses you of offending them.

WTF do you do!?

REMAINING CALM

Act like you don't give a shit about what she's saying or even that she's mad. This is kind of like talking to your mom.

Employ the fake smile. Nothing will annoy someone more than the thought that you're amused by their distress. This will lead them to act even crazier, furthering the evidence that you are the most sane person in the room.

You can respond with something like "true" or "oops, my b!" This will really rile her up.

BUT CALM IS BORING…

"All right like chill."

If you see that she's getting really angry and on the brink of tears, your next line should always be, "Okay, chill." Telling someone to chill is like giving them an express ticket to Crazytown. It's 99% guaranteed to drive her off the fucking deep end. Odds are, she will start screaming like a maniac.

PASSIVE AGGRESSION

Say very little. The more speaking you do, the more chances for you to mistakenly say something rash or tactless. Staying reserved will draw out more irrational statements and unflattering aggression from your opponent.

After you've remained calm enough to get your opponent visibly pissed off, you have an opening to make a few casual yet biting comments in response to her maniacal reaction. For example, "Look, I know you've been on edge lately because Adam broke up with you and I'm in a happy relationship, but listen, I'm totally here for you. Don't be jealous, we're just in different stages!"

You and your opponent will each text all of your besties, both mutual and exclusive, about what a raging bitch the other is being. Even if you're not the aggressor, you need to engage in this phase to prevent your friends from only hearing one side of the story. Obviously, try to sound like the more sane one. For example, "Jenna's my friend, and I don't want to fight with her, but at this point I'm just fighting on principle because it's NOT okay to treat your friends this way!"

IF YOU'RE WRONG, EVADE THE ISSUE

Inevitably, your crazy bitch opponent will continue to attack you and accuse you of absurd things like, "I don't understand why you would hook up with him when you knew I liked him!" You should bring up things that turn the conversation back to something she did that was fucked up.

THE APOLOGY (OPTIONAL)

Like any great performance, all fights must come to an end, because they get so fucking boring. Eventually you'll need your bestie to drive you somewhere or you'll get bored of ignoring her while she pouts in the living room. You should diminish the importance of whatever you're fighting over to seem mature.

"I don't really understand why you think it's okay to wear leggings with that shirt!?"

Dunzo.

"I'm really sorry about the other day. There's totally no excuse* for how I acted."

*By taking the blame and adding the "no excuse" part, you're giving her not choice but to accept your apology and shut the fuck up. If she continues to be mad, everyone will think she's a grudge-holding, attention-seeking whore.

ENEMIES: THE OBJECTS
OF YOUR ANIMOSITY

Now that you know the fundamentals of how to behave in any confrontation, it's time to take a closer look at your opponents. Know your enemy. In general, the group of people we dislike can be divided into smaller subsections of types of people we hate for different reasons. You might know that you dislike a person, but unless you know which category of repulsive he/she is, you won't know how to most effectively destroy them. It's a very dynamic system.

A nicegirl might say that we could avoid all this negativity if we'd just be kind. Whatever. No one respects someone who lets others walk all over her. It's one thing to let people borrow your skirt; it's another to act like it's okay that they didn't dry-clean it before returning it.

Although betches usually have lots of besties around, we don't feel a need to extend that warmth to girls outside of the innermost circle. It's not that we necessarily dislike them for any real reason, it's just rare that we would have anything particularly nice to say about them. It's kind of an ambiguous disinterest, trending toward the negative. It's a universally accepted truth that girls don't like other girls, so it's really just a matter of degrees, and those degrees can make all the difference.

Social Climbers

Social climbers are not so much hated as pitied. But accidentally get too close to one and you'll soon realize just how painful these types can be. As a naturally all-around amazing person, it's basic logic that everybody else is less cool than you. Enter the people who wish they weren't: social climbers.

The thing with SCs is that although they may essentially suck, their desire to achieve higher status means they are easy to manipulate. SCs are easily identifiable by their constant need to demonstrate their social value. Don't worry about their bad intentions or conniving ways. Fuck ladders, a true betch knows it would take a fucking cherry picker to get higher than you. See below for how to categorize the social climbers in your life.

Types of Social Climbers

Manipulative Ability →

The Group Snake

a.k.a. Gretchen Weiners... A pro at using her besties' secrets against each other; motives are unclear and she flies under the radar; may be confused for a people pleaser but she's really just a professional shit-talker with pathological tendencies.

The Successful One

Her personality is less miserable than the rest of these; she's fun to go out with and offers her big apartment for pregames so you don't really care that she manipulated herself into your group of friends.

The Talker

Talks a huge game and doesn't do shit; namedrops people from intensive Facebook stalking; claims to know connected people; is "on the list for a table" everywhere, every weekend, except not.

The Giver

A rich girl who sucks so she has to use material possessions to climb the ladder to appear cool; pays for a lot of shit, offers lunch at her country club, and does unwarranted, unasked favors in exchange for social currency, a.k.a. being associated with you.

Usefulness to Your Life →

Frenemies: Second-Class Enemies

Unfortunately, everyone is all too familiar with the proverbial thorn in your side, muddy spot on your suede Tod's loafers, the ingrown nail your pedicurist failed to remove. We're talking about the frenemy.

The frenemy is often another betch in your circle. You've probably been "friends" with her for a while, and this history is what makes the dynamic interesting. Since a frenemy is someone you know well, she probably has some dirty secrets on you, like the fact that your boobs aren't real or that time you accidentally had anal sex.

It would just be awkward and potentially problematic if you officially cut each other out, though it's widely known that you fucking hate each other. It's also expected that she comprises a large piece of your shit-talking pie, but because your social lives are so intertwined, it's not worth starting World War IV over just anything. It takes more work to permanently turn your friends against the frenemy than it does to accept the status quo. Plus exiling someone from your friend group projects immaturity. She's there to stay.

So, how do you know when your relationship has reached frenemy status? Sometimes the feeling of frenemyship is subconscious, and you might not even express it aloud. But, typically, you just hit a fucking wall. You wake up one day and the thought of seeing her face makes your blood boil. You can be certain you have a frenemy when you find yourself experiencing pure feelings of happiness at her misfortune. *Becky's boyfriend cheated on her? And her dad cut her off? Fuck, yeah, best day of my life!*

You should model your strategy for handling the frenemy on the United States' position in the Cold War, silent and smart. Just like America's first vacay to the moon is highly debatable, so is the rumor you floated that your frenemy's ex-boyfriend wants hook up with you. What they can't prove won't hurt you. We're not saying you should start rumors, but far be it from a betch to do the work required to contradict a convenient one.

If you're not sly enough to execute the strategic ousting of this friend, you need to suck it up and live with the frenemy. Think of your friendship with this girl as you do flat-ironing your hair. It's annoying and kind of fake, but you realize there's no better way to deal with it. Best to make the most of your unfortunately unavoidable "friendship." It's better to listen to your whiny frenemy at her beach house than hang out with your actual friend at a public pool, right?

To someone outside the bestie circle, navigating these elusive friendship dynamics can be complex and dangerous. Just remember that everyone has their shit with each other, and it's hard to always know how people are feeling about you (though if you're an intuitive shit-talker, you can surely figure it out). And don't let yourself get discouraged, there are always going to be betches who are really jealous of you . . . just ask Julius Caesar how hard it is to be the most popular girl in Rome.

The Arch Nemesis: Members of the WYDEL

The girls on your Wish You Didn't Exist List, or WYDEL, are your top priority shit-listers. Any mention of a girl on your WYDEL most likely triggers an involuntary "UGH, I hate that bitch; I wish she didn't fucking exist," usually followed by exaggerated stories of your encounters with her (all of which demonstrate that she's a complete psycho). If you're a less vocal betch, you'll probably go with the understated but still effective, "Bitch is miz." Either way, the automatic response from your bestie group should be, "Yeah, she sucks." Your besties are required to hate your arch nemeses; if they don't show the appropriate amount of disdain, get rid of them. That's just, like, the rules of feminism.

So how does someone go from being your run-of-the-mill, ambiguously disliked fellow betch, to the girl you daydream about gaining eighty pounds and working at Dairy Queen? Ah, let us count the ways.

Types of Arch Nemeses

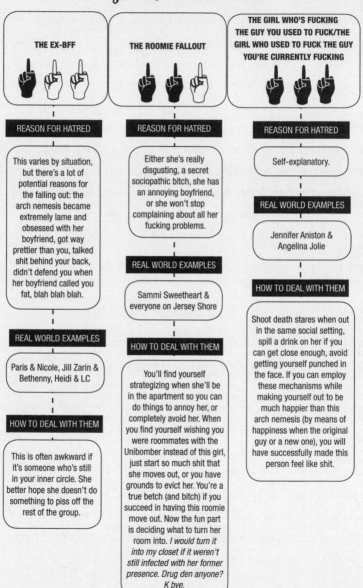

THE EX-BFF

REASON FOR HATRED

This varies by situation, but there's a lot of potential reasons for the falling out: the arch nemesis became extremely lame and obsessed with her boyfriend, got way prettier than you, talked shit behind your back, didn't defend you when her boyfriend called you fat, blah blah blah.

REAL WORLD EXAMPLES

Paris & Nicole, Jill Zarin & Bethenny, Heidi & LC

HOW TO DEAL WITH THEM

This is often awkward if it's someone who's still in your inner circle. She better hope she doesn't do something to piss off the rest of the group.

THE ROOMIE FALLOUT

REASON FOR HATRED

Either she's really disgusting, a secret sociopathic bitch, she has an annoying boyfriend, or she won't stop complaining about all her fucking problems.

REAL WORLD EXAMPLES

Sammi Sweetheart & everyone on Jersey Shore

HOW TO DEAL WITH THEM

You'll find yourself strategizing when she'll be in the apartment so you can do things to annoy her, or completely avoid her. When you find yourself wishing you were roommates with the Unibomber instead of this girl, just start so much shit that she moves out, or you have grounds to evict her. You're a true betch (and bitch) if you succeed in having this roomie move out. Now the fun part is deciding what to turn her room into. *I would turn it into my closet if it weren't still infected with her former presence. Drug den anyone? K bye.*

THE GIRL WHO'S FUCKING THE GUY YOU USED TO FUCK/THE GIRL WHO USED TO FUCK THE GUY YOU'RE CURRENTLY FUCKING

REASON FOR HATRED

Self-explanatory.

REAL WORLD EXAMPLES

Jennifer Aniston & Angelina Jolie

HOW TO DEAL WITH THEM

Shoot death stares when out in the same social setting, spill a drink on her if you can get close enough, avoid getting yourself punched in the face. If you can employ these mechanisms while making yourself out to be much happier than this arch nemesis (by means of happiness when the original guy or a new one), you will have successfully made this person feel like shit.

MANAGING THE OUTER CIRCLE:
FAKE IS BETTER THAN NOTHING

Seeing as these people in your outer circle are most certainly not your friends, you simply can't be mean directly to their faces. The term is "social butterfly" not "social barbarian" for a reason. The key to successfully remaining civil with them is to treat them with as much fake respect as you can muster up. Now, we are in no way suggesting brownnosing is appropriate in any circumstance; after all, only your ass should ever be kissed. The best form of communication with your less attractive pseudo-acquaintances is through flattery.

Compliments and Flattery

It's important to remember that everyone, even fat and poor people, have something decent about them to be complimented, even if it's just that they're a "really good friend." Always remember, flosers can have their moments, for instance: they've made it far enough in life to be within the reach of your flattery. The key is to find whatever strength got them there and exploit it to your benefit.

The idea is to compliment others in a sparing but meaningful way—when you want something from them. Some may deem taking advantage of people as manipulation, abuse, or being disingenuous, but those people are weak and stupid. Commenting on the relative strengths of others is commonly called flattery. For this method to work, your compliments have to be based on the truth. Even our bestie Helen Keller could smell a bullshitter right off the bat. Like, don't go around telling your friend who has obviously gross frizzy hair that you'd kill for her curls. She'll know you're full of shit and will assume the same applies to everything else you say.

However, if someone's hair looks really good one night, make sure that you praise it effusively. This will reward you because she'll permit you to borrow her hair product, blow-dryer, and iron for the next two weeks.

In some cases, however, the benefit you will reap from giving a compliment may simply be for your own personal entertainment. Examples:

"I didn't know you were going to make it out tonight!" (*I can't believe you're showing your face in public when everyone knows your boyfriend just cheated on and dumped you.*)

"I love your shirt, it's actually so much more flattering than I thought it would be!" (*Wow, Spanx must make that top. Where are your rolls hiding?*)

Sure you can offer backhanded compliments to your closest besties, but this tool really shines when striking up a conversation with someone in the outer circle. For instance, if you don't have anything to say, tell them their ugly shirt is really unique. *Is that Missoni for Target?* If anything, these are great conversation fillers and the perfect way to pass the obligatory two minutes of small talk. Since these situations often occur in passing—at class, at a party—complimenting someone, be it a backhanded one or simply a lie, is a surefire way to keep the conversation from turning mad awkward.

Stop-and-Chats

These specific circumstances in which you have to stop what you're doing to speak to someone you don't want to talk to are accurately described as "stop-and-chats." Obviously they're fucking annoying, but true betches like them because, when handled well, they are useful for gaining intel with which to talk shit later.

Hopefully you will come away from a stop-and-chat with some interesting gossip to pass along. Perhaps you just bumped into someone from high school. Now remember, you must have the conversation without looking too eager to text your besties what happened, *Bumped into Katie Smith at Starbucks, looks like shit.* It is important to make sure she has

> "*He wanted to stop and chat with me—and I don't know him well enough for a stop-and-chat.*"
> —Larry David, inventor of the stop-and-chat

taken at least two steps in the opposite direction before you start fervently tapping away at your iPhone.

On the other hand, if you're ever in a situation in which you'd rather shoot yourself in the head than speak to the person approaching, you should use your phone as a tool. Either pretend you've just gotten a call or text while hanging your head low, but always be sure to prepare your fake smile.

OPTIMIZING YOUR STOP-AND-CHAT

1. You don't want to be seen looking like shit, so be careful what you wear to certain places. You think you're just running out while hungover to quickly grab an iced coffee in your pajamas with eye makeup down your face, but you never know who you might see. There's no greater annoyance than running into an ex-boyfriend when you're looking like shit and being forced to partake in the boilerplate stop-and-chat convo: "Hi, how are you?" "Good, how are you?" "I'm good, how are you?" . . . "Good."

2. Beware that what you say in the stop-and-chat may be repeated to multiple people, so you shouldn't reveal too much personal information or information about anyone else. Oversharing is dangerous and takes a stop-and-chat from a friendly encounter to an impending contorted rumor. "I'm just here buying Plan B for Alex!"

can soon become "I heard that girl Alex gave herself an abortion!"

3. The hungover stop-and-chat can be avoided with big sunglasses, excessive use of your phone, and a fuck-off look on your face.

The Fake Smile

A betch's main weapon in life is not a gun, a knife, or even her car. Instead, it's her ability to turn up the corners of her lips into the shape of a perfect fake smile.

Nothing makes you appear weaker than showing real emotion. Only when everyone thinks that you like them will you gain total control. Remember, fake emotion is the path to real happiness. Plus, ignoring someone you don't like is just plain rude.

The fake smile may also come in handy when being introduced to a mutual friend. Of course you're not actually happy to meet someone new. You probably already know this person, having casually come across her Facebook pictures before. Seeing as you most likely store completely useless knowledge, you probably have a small file cabinet in your gossip arsenal about her. So when you say, "Heyyyy, nice to meet you," what you're really thinking is, *Hmm . . . I wonder if it's true that she fucked three guys in one night without a condom. Would it be a bad time to ask? Are we on that level yet?*

Just shine your best FS and she'll think you're like the nicest person ever.

But remember, don't smile too hard. There's nothing less appealing than speaking to someone whose face is stretched to the point where you question the last time they've moved a bowel.

How to Pretend to Care about a Conversation When It's Not about You

While we're on the topic of forced conversation . . . you think volunteering at a soup kitchen is bad? Try talking to people about their jobs or, worse, their family. It's literally the fucking worst. But have no fear, we've had enough practice with this that we've developed handy tips to have others fooled into thinking you give a shit about them.

Eye contact: We can't overemphasize the importance of eye contact when pretending to care what people are saying. Other than the entire discography of Huey Lewis and the News, *American Psycho* taught us one thing: You could be planning how you're going to systematically murder someone and their entire extended family, but as long as you're looking them in the eye, they have *no fucking idea.*

Nods of approval: Coupled with solid eye contact and a few well-placed "mhmmms" and "rights," every time you give a nod of agreement you're saving yourself from needing to construct an intelligent sentence or ask a thoughtful question. Gross.

Occasional smile: Knowing when to insert the fake smile only requires about five percent of your attention, but the rewards are massive. You'll know when to whip it out because the other person will be smiling. Take the hint. Not only will they think you're paying attention, but they'll also think you actually agree with them! Which you might, who knows? You weren't listening.

Pay attention to small cues: If, between daydreaming and admiring your manicure, you happen to catch onto the general topic of convo and realize that this person is talking shit about someone insignificant to you but very significant to them, throw in the casual "What a fucking bitch." It's a great way to reassure them that you're on the same team. Besides, you most likely hate that person too.

Adderall: Pop one of these and you're set. You no longer need to pretend, you *do* care. *A lot.*

Summary

As we navigate the tumultuous waters of betch life, shit can get hard. That's why it's important to have people you can be yourself around. But more than that, it's important to have a girl whose summer house you can tan at. Keeping that in mind, choose your friends wisely. Every bestie group gives off a vibe, and it's important to make sure yours shows people that you are hot, fun, and fabulous. So get rid of your frenemies, throw your duds a bone, and cherish and honor your BFF. Life is long, and without some valuable companions you'll become the skank who claims she only has guy friends or, worse, an entourage that includes Rumer Willis and like no one else.

College

Using Higher Education to Get Ahead

Ah, the paradise that is college. To outsiders (and our parents), spending four years at a collegiate institution is an expensive privilege that gives us the chance to fill our minds with knowledge and enables us to take on the world as educated, literate, and informed individuals. Luckily we already have those qualities when we arrive at college, at least according to our application essays. This means you'll have more time to spend doing things you enjoy, as opposed to making study guides and attending orchestra practice, which you may or may not have lied about to get into college. *National champion at the intramural glee competition? You bet I was!*

As much as we hate doing work, going to college (and graduating from it) is an absolute necessity. No one is interested in a girl who's so stupid that her high school diploma is her greatest achievement. College is a symbol of sophistication and class, though we doubt either of those words will describe your experience there.

You don't need to do extremely well in college; you just have to fucking go. For you, college won't be so much about

> *"The aim of a college education is to teach you to know a good man when you see one."*
> —William James

getting an education as being able to say you went. It doesn't *really* matter where you go, as long as the name sounds good. Why should you care about going to a good school? Simple. In addition to the boring qualities like intelligence (which you'll find few men rank highly when choosing a wife), good colleges are signals of wealth, power, and status. People will think more highly of you, and when you inevitably need to look for a job, your employer will make assumptions about your qualifications based on where you went. We know, because that's how we hired people to work for us. Ultimately it will require significantly less effort to find a job if you went somewhere prestigious.

When picking which college you'll attend, you should aim to go to the one with the best name that is also the most fun. These tend to be larger schools with strong Greek systems and a football team that could potentially make it to the Rose Bowl. Even if no one besides Charlotte York would say it out loud, attending SUNY Plattsburgh will just not give you the same street cred with employers or future mothers-in-law as attending Harvard. It's not a coincidence that there are no presidents who boast Springfield Technical Community College on their Wikipedia pages.

NOT DOING WORK IN COLLEGE: HOW TO REVOLVE FOUR YEARS OF YOUR LIFE AROUND DRINKING AND HANGOVERS

If you're smart enough to get into college, you should be smart enough to shape your life once you get there. If you can't manipulate your schedule to create as much free time as possible, you won't be able to do any of the other fun shit we talk about in this chapter. The goal is to spend as much time as possible blacked out, having sex, or getting high and very little time actually working toward a degree. If this contradicts your goal of going to college to become educated, we're going to educate you that the true "education" in college lies in your social life. After all, it's already paid for and your college GPA will prove irrelevant later in life, just ask anyone who got a ring before twenty-seven.

But please don't be confused by our academic ennui—failure is not an option. Ideally, you should approach the academic aspect of

> "If you want to get laid, go to college. If you want to get an education, go to the library."
> —Frank Zappa

college as you would other simple but necessary tasks, like ordering dinner: casually. Getting passing grades is important for many reasons, like keeping your parents happy enough to continue supporting you financially. It's absolutely not acceptable to be that girl who is on the verge of failing—that makes you a boring, unmotivated loser. We just mean that you should never find yourself in the library on the weekends or like after four P.M. Trying too hard in school is a waste of the effort and time you could be using for worthwhile causes, such as building your drug tolerance or perfecting your blow-drying technique.

Don't be ashamed if you started college doing more work than necessary. Often it takes time to learn the shortcuts and tricks that lead to college success without effort, but we can help you cut the learning curve in half.

Course Requirements

Your parents or an academic adviser might point out that the reason you're at college is to take classes, but we know the truth. It's kind of like the time you stopped by your frenemy's birthday pregame. You were trying to make yourself seem nice by going, when you were really just there for the alcohol. Classes/your frenemy are obvs the worst part of the pregame but they're also the reason it's happening.

Therefore it's necessary to enroll in some classes so you can continue using them as an excuse to not do anything else. *I'm like sooo busy with my one class on Tuesday!* The first step in any successful college experience is picking your schedule, leaving yourself with an overwhelming amount of free time to do all the getting fucked up that we mentioned before.

❶ Never enroll in any attendance-based classes. If you don't need to go, it might as well not exist.

❷ No night classes or Friday classes, or anything before noon or after four . . . so almost never.

❸ Never take a class without a friend, unless you plan on relying on yourself to do work, also known as educational suicide.

❹ Male professors > female professors (easier to manipulate, easier on the eyes).

❺ Never enroll in a class for which the description reads: "Will explore female roles in society." This is code for: "Taught by a femi-fascist lesbian professor who will fail you for being pretty." Not to mention you'll have more luck finding a boyfriend at a shelter for battered women than in any class listed under gender studies.

❻ Prioritize classes that are popular with athletes. With more athletes in a class, there's greater motivation to attend. Also they are probably dumb as fuck so you can copy off the homework that their tutor did for them.

❼ Small seminars are always a bad idea. You can't fuck around on your computer the whole time and, seeing as you will be the hot girl who's always late with the thirty-two-ounce iced coffee, they'll always notice when you're not there.

So betches, when you're miserable sitting in class because you failed to follow our guidelines, just remember the golden rule in scheduling: you can always fucking drop it. There's nothing worse than showing up to a class you thought sounded easy and then finding out it isn't. Trust us, if we managed to get an A plus in a class called Cell Reproduction, Senescence, and Death with no knowledge of biology, you can too. *Senescence . . . like senile!*

How to Avoid Assignments at All Costs

Once you've secured seats in the easiest classes your school has to offer, it's safe to say that you'll probably never sit in them, physically. If you do this right, the only time you'll ever find yourself inside a college classroom will be for your finals . . . and still, you can probably get away with skipping those. Regardless, it's clear that you'll have to devote at least a small amount of time to ensuring that you pass with the grades sufficient to keep your credit card. Here are some of our favorite work evasion techniques.

"Class friends": We can't overemphasize the importance of having class friends. They literally got us through college, and to this day are saved in our phones as *Taylor Econ, Jamie Bio, Amy S. Art History.* CFs are very easy to identify and befriend, and they are the key to getting your work done without doing any. These are the jovial types who will try to make extensive conversation with you on the first day of class, while you're resisting the urge to vom on them due to your hangover. You should be as friendly as possible, since the first day of class is probably the only time you'll attend, and it's best to leave a positive and lasting impression. As in, don't vom.

HOW TO WRITE AN ESSAY

If you ever find yourself writing your own essay, don't panic. After much life experience, we've devised an exhaustive list of ways to manipulate your assignments to minimize your workload. Let's say you have a paper that's supposed to be eight to ten pages. When you hand in said paper, the page number may say eight, but we say you can get away with only writing four. Here's how:

✦ Forget double-spaced, 2.5 lines is the only way to go.

✦ Fuck headers and footers, there are no such thing in your world. Your intro paragraph should start somewhere circa five inches down the first page. And you better milk your title for all it's worth—bold, underline, and size 16 that shit.

✦ Whatever the margin requirements, add .2 inches.

✦ Periods, commas, quotations, and all punctuation can and should be size 14. Always two, occasionally three, spaces between sentences.

✦ If your professor is a nicegirl, you can probs get away with making her believe that you thought a cover page was included in the page requirements. *I even included clip art!*

✦ If your professor requests that you turn in your paper electronically, you NEVER send it in a Word doc where they can see that your chosen font size is intended for someone with cataracts. Magicians never reveal their tricks. Three little letters: PDF.

Finally, for the in-class essay, if you know you've bombed, try throwing out your own paper and then accusing the teacher of losing it.

Class friends are always nicegirls, but not always the quiet, boring (vindictive) kind who think you deserve to fail as punishment for your lack of effort. The best CFs are the ones who are proud of their nerdy ways and want to be powerful corporate women one day. They probably think that your lax attitude toward life is hilarious but also a little pitiful (aka they'll feel sorry for your academic struggles and help you because you're not threatening). You should resist your urge to mock these people (to their faces), because they are your gateway to perfect grades. They have impeccable notes and because of their natural niceness, will be *thrilled* to give them to you. Finally, it should be obvious that you should never associate with these people outside of class, they're called "class friends" for a reason.

The double exchange: This is one of our favorite tactics, because it involves doing so little while getting so much in return. It's kind of like sex for a guy who's horrible in bed. What you do is you split an assignment in two, tell a class friend that if they do the first half you'll do the second, then tell another class friend that you'll give them the first half if they do the second. Voilà, you exchange both halves to the respective CFs, and you've successfully done nothing. To execute this, at least two distinct CFs are required per course. Some may call this cheating, we call it delegating.

Google: If you're ever in a tough spot where you don't know an answer during a test, the best thing to do is to look it up on your phone. Under your desk, obviously. Again, some might argue that this is cheating and defeats the purpose of school, which we've always found to be ridiculous, and here's why: If the goal of education is to prepare you for the real world, and if in the real world you can always look up the answer on your phone, what about this method is not educational? The only thing we learn from memorizing facts is how to be extremely inefficient. What do you think Wikipedia is for?

If it's the cheating aspect you have a problem with, you should realize that everyone does it, so technically it evens out, from a practical standpoint. If you don't cheat, you're at a disadvantage.

> *"Information is not knowledge."*
> —Albert Einstein

We once read in some notes from a class friend that it's okay to cheat if everyone else is cheating because of a theory called "moral relativity." That works for us, so if you can't do the phone thing, you've gotta go old school and copy off of the paper of the smartest Asian within eyeshot. While we won't give you detailed directions for cheating with friends, we'll say that the "one knock on the desk for A, two knocks for B" method has a 99 percent success rate since middle school . . . until you get the psycho teacher who gives two different test versions, then you're fucked.

THE ASIAN CHARM

Before you enter a test or a big presentation, touch three Asians. Not sexually, just give them a stealthy tap on the shoulder. If they ask you why you're touching them, just say, "For good luck, duh." We don't even feel bad that they do better than us on the SATs, since they've been enrolled in Kaplan since they were six years old.

How to Manipulate the University System

Remember when you were young and your mom would call up your teachers and bawl them out for giving you a "bad grade" on your spelling test because it was like totes unfair and you forgot to take your Adderall that day? Then suddenly the next day you were accepted into the gifted students program? Well, this is a rare instance when you should take a lesson from your mother. If your assignment avoidance tactics aren't working and you fuck something up, you'll inevitably need to convince someone important, be it the professor or the administration, that you're a conscientious textbook-loving loser who not only deserves to pass but also deserves to get like a really good grade.

Extra time on tests: If you're smart enough to obtain an endlessly refillable Adderall prescription from your shrink, you should also be sure to have him send over a letter to your university about your condition and how you need extra time on tests. While we obviously don't want to actually spend more time on our tests, the goal is to be able to take your test in the "extra time room." This is usually a haven of unsupervised betches and bros who are all extremely hopped up on Adderall and always willing to share their answers.

> **INSPIRATIONAL SCENE FROM**
> ***CLUELESS***
>
> MEL: You mean to tell me that you argued your way from a C plus to an A minus?
> CHER: Totally based on my powers of persuasion, you proud?
> MEL: Honey, I couldn't be happier if they were based on real grades.

Manipulating your professor: This technique is much like manipulating your dad in that it involves talking an old person into giving you what you want. Usually all it takes to convince a professor to raise your grade is a fifteen-minute stopover at office hours, where a combination of well-timed tears and a feigned interest in the course subject will do the trick.

Ignoring college requirements: Sometimes a school will decide that they want students to be what they call "well-rounded," which basically translates to the fact that communications and marketing majors might have to take things like science labs. These classes are heinous because they involve work and are typically filled with foreigners who can't speak English, yet who somehow still ruin the curve for the hot people. If you're ever forced into one of these classes, the best move is to find someone in student services who will be your four-year bestie, as in, willing to risk their career by helping you get out of requirements. Just mention something about high school AP scores and your parents' traumatic divorce.

If all this manipulation grows tiresome, we recommend taking a semester to recover. Under the guise of getting college credit and cultivating your worldly air, of course. Yes, we're talking about studying abroad.

STUDYING ABROAD: HOW TO CULTURALLY IMMERSE YOURSELF IN FOREIGN ALCOHOL

If you want to be able to say you maximized the number of fun and cool Facebook pictures you took in college, then you need to "study" abroad. Going abroad is the best way to have an extremely fun semester while pretending to become more globally aware. Taking pictures with your besties in front of the Louvre and some Roman ruins totally means that you're well versed in the cultural importance of these things, and that your tour guide was a hot historical genius.

But while nicegirls go abroad looking for a chance to fully immerse themselves in local cul-

> "The cool thing about being famous is traveling. I have always wanted to travel across seas, like to Canada and stuff."
> —Britney Spears

ture to expand their worldviews and language skills, the only thing a betch expands while abroad is her father's credit card bill. Studying abroad is essentially a four-month vacation funded by one's parents . . . also known as partying in the best clubs in every city across Europe.

The abroad itinerary consists of attending classes maybe three days a week, buying chic clothes in strange sizes, and testing out the weed in various cities while ~~sightseeing~~ being hungover in front of old shit.

But going abroad isn't just about the drinking and traveling. You'll also learn how Europe shows its love for disabled people by doing away with frivolous American things like handicapped ramps

> "The fact is, with every friendship you make, and every bond of trust you establish, you are shaping the image of America projected to the rest of the world. That is so important. So when you study abroad, you're actually helping to make America stronger."
> —Michelle Obama

and elevators. And don't worry about the language barrier. The big secret of all foreign countries is that *everyone* speaks English! Well, at least anyone you'll ever want to talk to. Upon going abroad to Italy, you thought you were going to become fluent in Italian? Think again! Experiencing cultural diversity goes as far as having a McGill student in your Wines of Tuscany class.

What Your Abroad Destination Says About You

London: You want to have a serious internship while abroad. That or you like the royal family, bad teeth, bad food, and have an aversion to foreign languages and sunlight.

Paris: You like fashion and art and took French in high school. You'll learn throughout your semester in Paris that French people really fucking hate Americans and will do whatever possible to ensure that you have a miserable time in their city and never want to come back. If you aren't busy fighting off pickpockets while your garçon refuses to serve you iced coffee ("I'm afraid zat is impossible. Le ice is out of season!"), you're probably sitting in a cab with a driver who's purposely running up the meter by giving you a scenic tour of twenty-five extra arrondissements.

Switzerland/Vienna/Budapest/Belgium/Berlin, etc.: You want to be different but still have your besties nearby to visit them, or perhaps you want to spend your semester skiing while looking for excuses to gorge yourself on melted cheese and chocolate.

Barcelona: You told your parents you would become fluent in Spanish there, even though people in Barcelona speak Catalan. But you're really going there to get fucked and fucked up, and to be in the general vicinity of a lot of drugs.

Madrid: IDK, do you like *jamón* in and around your mouth at all times?

Seville: You want to go to Spain but think you're "too chill" for the Barcelona scene.

Rome: When choosing between Italian cities, the general rule is that men go to Rome and women go to Florence. Why? Gladiators, obvi. So if you're abroad in Rome you're most likely a guy, or a girl who wants to go where the guys are. Or you have a Corinthian column fetish. Rome, so phallic right now, Rome.

Florence: You pretend to be into like art history and the Borgias but really you're more into YAB and wine. It's pretty much guaranteed that the only thing you'll have to show for your semester in Italy is a new leather jacket, for which you did not bargain sufficiently.

THE HARDSHIPS OF ABROAD

We know we've probably given the impression thus far that abroad life is easy, but we would be lying if we said that European living doesn't have its drawbacks. It's like you go there to get a sense of history, but it turns out half the cities are stuck in the century they were built. The key to your abroad apartment probably looks like they used it to spring prisoners from the Bastille. Let's talk about some challenges you'll face that you can bring up in future job interviews.

No one does work: While it's amazing that you get to spend the semester drunk, keep in mind that this behavior is the native custom. The only people more skilled than betches at doing nothing are the Europeans. It would be generous to say that the economies of Spain and Italy, when combined on a good day, move slower than erosion.

Gypsies: Oh man, they're everywhere. Whether they're interrupting your outdoor meal to sell you a fucking leaf, or they're hurling their baby at you so you'll drop your purse and they can steal it, there's only one way to stop these crazy nomads. And that is by demanding that they give you their tears.

Eviction: You laugh now, but eviction is a real problem that many abroad betches face. Literally everyone we know was at least threatened with eviction. Your crazy landlord will try to evict you for crazy reasons, like being drunk Americans who walk around in heels at four A.M. every day and wake the building. *Maybe if your walls weren't so skinny!* It's best to handle this situation by telling him your dad is the ambassador.

Restaurants that refuse to charge more than one credit card: It's like can your dainty little renaissance machine not endure more than one swipe per group of American girls who just spent their meal staring at shrimp that still had their heads attached?

Prague: You like to have fun and you don't mind if you do so in a place that's culturally still behind the Iron Curtain. You don't mind being assaulted by hairy men because the clubs are really fun. It's a little too bro-y (too much beer and prostitution for our taste) but whatevs, it's still like really pretty. Also, it's cheap as fuck. We're pretty sure you can buy a Czech baby for five hundred koruna.

Amsterdam: Okay, we get that Anne Frank studied abroad here, but nowadays, unless you want to spend your semester abroad in a comatose state, keep it to a weekend visit, okay? The only people who spend a semester here probably have a black light and a poster of Bob Marley hanging above their bed.

Copenhagen: You enjoy the igloo life or are trying to take real classes. Neither is okay.

Edinburgh: Pretty but also too fucking cold. How do those bros walk around in skirts all the time?!

Australia: You've been all over Europe a bunch of times and want to cultivate your outdoorsy side by doing things like skydiving, posing next to baby tigers, and wearing flippers. You also harbor a deep appreciation for semester-long tans and blond rugby players with hot accents.

Tel Aviv: You're Jewish and you love that about yourself. You will come home with a nameplate necklace of your Hebrew name (or what you think is your Hebrew name) and will forever pretend to completely understand Middle Eastern politics.

Buenos Aires: You want the Europeanness of Europe and the heat of Australia. If you're staying in the Americas, it's the most normal place to go. We hear the clubs are fun, and BA is no doubt the spot to hear the latest remixes of "Don't Cry For Me, Argentina."

Capetown/China/Egypt/India, etc.: We doubt the type of hemp-wearing, open-minded vegan who would go to these places has been able to make it this far into the book, we'll leave it at that.

SPRING BREAK: HOW TO GO HARD WITHOUT GOING ~~HOME~~ TO JAIL

As wild as abroad life can be, everyone knows that a semester is a marathon, not a sprint. Let's talk about another way to use your college years to kindle your alcoholism in a shorter, more intense and more debaucherous way. Nothing compares to the best week of college life, spring break.

Spring break marks a time in a girl's life when all preconceived notions of "appropriate" are thrown out of the window, when the words "sleep" and "tonight" are never used in the same sentence, and when the arrival of your period is a greater fear than dying alone. It's the craziest week you'll experience all year, and you'll be spending it with your best friends beneath the tropical sun and many hot bros. What more could a betch ask for?

Spring break is both the best and most ridiculous thing to hit modern society. Like, how is it *actually* possible that there's an entire week when it's socially acceptable for your parents to pay thousands of dollars so you can go to a tropical island and get obliterated day and night, while alternating between getting fucked on the swim-up bar and getting railed against your balcony's railing? It's like going abroad, but you don't even have to pretend to be having a cultural experience. Unless your parents are gullible enough to believe that you're going to learn something in Cabo.

HOW TO GET YOUR PARENTS TO
PAY FOR SPRING BREAK

The Spiel: *As you know, spring break is coming up and I think everyone in my class is going. I don't want you to think that I desperately need to go on this trip, but OMG did I tell you I got an A in Chemistry? Yeah, everyone else got C's and B's; it's shameful. Anyway, I don't think it will be that expensive, I have to check, but I'm fairly sure that if I sign up early we can get a serious discount.**

Do you see what we did there? You basically told them that spring break is coming up, that you're being very responsible and frugal about the trip, that you deserve to go on the trip, but without ever actually saying you want to go. Let the idea marinate, get another good grade on an exam (or tell them you did), find the price, round down, and call them back in a few days. We guarantee it'll be fully funded.

*This doesn't work if you're poor.

The most important thing you can do on spring break is party as hard as you possibly can. But since Natalee Holloway is not on the list of girls we emulate, you need to make sure you survive spring break. Watch out, because we're about to enlighten the shit out of you.

You see, the key to a successful spring break is to have the time of your fucking life but to embarrass yourself only a little. Read: Keep it right below the level of the most shitshow girl in your SB group. Sure you may think you look so cool being wheeled to the hospital but you won't think so when you're stuck in an infested Mexican hospital bed while everyone is at the beach taking shots.

Do's and Don'ts of Spring Break:

How to Avoid Arrest, Deportation, and Embarrassment

Do . . .	Don't . . .
Dance on tables.	Fall off tables and not notice that your tube top is at your waist. *Where are my boobs? Oh, there they are. All over the Internet.*
Take shots at 7 A.M.	Take seven shots in one minute.
Buy *mucho drugas* at *la farmacia.*	Get stopped at customs because you're so wasted you forgot which state you're from.
Come home from the club in the morning and smoke a blunt on the balcony.	Have sex on the balcony in full view of everyone else smoking on their own balconies.
Take a bar on the plane.	Get fingered on the plane. (Okay, fine, do. But be sneaky about it. It's not over till you land.)
Do drugs and have sex with people you normally wouldn't.	Have sex with those people in exchange for drugs.
Get thrown in the pool.	Get thrown into white slavery.

Unfortunately, there will come a point in life when the only vacations you'll go on will be with your family (*vom*) or boyfriend/husband/kids. In ten years, when your spring break consists of taking your two-year-old on Space Mountain fifteen times, you're going to need to think back to your glory days. Fuck roller coasters, remember there was once a time when the club was your amusement park, the only rolling you did was on E, and your favorite ride was the bro underneath you.

COLLEGE SOCIAL LIFE:
HOW TO KEEP FRIENDS
AND ALIENATE (THE RIGHT) PEOPLE

As with any time in your life, you are defined by those with whom you surround yourself, and this is never more clear than who you're friends with in college. College gives you a chance to start with a clean slate of new friends for you to manipulate and talk shit about. And every college freshman will tell you that your freshman social life starts with your roommate.

The Freshman Roommate: Avoiding *The Roommate*

The freshman-year living situation presents a rare occasion in which you'll be living with someone who isn't necessarily your friend. This poses a challenge, and making the wrong decision definitely has consequences.

First of all, betches don't live with randos because we already know everyone worth knowing, and no college ever fails to fill the year's quota of freaks. Guess what, these weirdos are all choosing random roomies, while all the betches are pairing off. Never go rando. Agree to live with a total stranger, and you run the risk of inhabiting a twenty-by-ten space with a nerd, a narc, or, worse, a girl who calls it "the Facebook."

Choosing your roommate is a delicate process. Betches will usually choose to live with their bestie's sister's bestie's younger sister, or their camp bestie's bestie from their teen tour. Moral of the story: always make sure your roommate is someone's bestie. They're the only ones we can trust.

When you're put in a situation where you're forced to meet several girls who are going to your school, like a weekend visit or meet-up before freshman year, you'll know when you've found your roommate. You will have similar interests, find the same things funny, and most important, talk shit about the same topics and people. This will inevitably be followed by that moment of: "OMG, should we just like live together!?"

However, if you're set up by a mutual friend with someone you've never met, checking the girl's Facebook is absolutely the most important factor in agreeing to live with her. Your potential roommate should be pretty so that you can go out together and she'll be a good wingman, but not so pretty that there's any debate over who the hotter roommate is. Checking her Facebook to make sure she's not a freak, had normal high school friends, and her list of favorite movies doesn't include *Free Willy 2* are among the most essential college prerequisites.

Once you've found the lucky girl who gets to inhabit the same room as you for an entire year, cut to the start of freshman year— 99 percent of the time your roomie situation ends up one of three ways.

Tweedledee and Tweedledum: These two are peas in a fucking pod. They are those stupid, annoying freshmen who can't help but let the entire fucking campus know that they're roommates. Half their tagged photos are the two of them doing the same pose at different frats with the caption LOVE YOU ROOMIE or BEST ROOM-MATES EVAAAA. *Thank you for easing our concerns that there might be trouble in freshman paradise.* Most of the time, Tweedledee and Tweedledum tune this down after freshman year even if they remain besties and/or roommates, which they usually do until one or both gets a boyfriend and they become jealous rivals in a race to the engagement ring.

Casual roomies: This is most common. You're friends, you get along, you have occasional roommate issues, but generally things are chill. Lots of people have no idea who your roommate is. You're friendly enough to ask to borrow her top, but not so friendly that you'd ever agree to be sexiled.

Mom and Dad (filing for divorce): You hate each other so much that you would consider murdering her, along with whoever else facilitated your living together and anyone who ever suggested it would be a good idea. You've more than once considered killing her in her sleep, and you've been looking forward to the day you move out of your dorm more than your own fucking wedding.

Remember, be careful who you choose as your college roommate, because it can either become the gift that keeps on giving or a self-induced sign-up to have the most frustrating year of your life. Remember, just like *The Roommate* taught us, go rando and you could wind up with a lesbian BSCB who's so obsessed with you that she tries to kill you and, like, hates kittens.

GREEK LIFE

For a girl who aspires to have a social life in college, joining a sorority is pretty much a necessity. There are a few colleges at which this is an exception, but the types of people who go to those places are usually sweet, down-to-earth, or enrolled at Brown. Either way, we're not interested.

On a "Greek" campus, being in a sorority not only puts you in the perfect position to meet frat bros who you will later claim you didn't have sex with, but it also provides you a house in which to live and engage in activities, such as organized judging of people, getting dressed up, and pretending to be nice to others for your own social advancement. Having trouble meeting actual friends? Just give this national university-sponsored organization upwards of one thousand dollars a semester and you've got "sisters" for a lifetime! Not only do you gain about a hundred automatic besties, but you also have a whole new slew of people to ruthlessly manipulate all day long. So how do we select the lovely ladies who, by contract, are obligated to be our sisters? Two words: sorority rush.

What Is Sorority Rush?

If we had to define it simply, rush is a completely superficial way of deciding who will join your sorority, based primarily on what they look like, where they're from, and your mutual Facebook friends. Your rush experience as a freshman will essentially determine your entire college social life. It will change who you're friends with and the guys you meet, which is basically all that matters. Sorry to blow up the spot of Panhel boards everywhere that spew bullshit like, "Everyone will end up happy, no matter what house she's in." They are lying to you—mostly because how can they possibly know if everyone ends up happy? News flash: Some people will end up happy, others won't. Honestly, it doesn't really make a difference, because the two things all sororities have in common is that (1) girls live in houses together, and (2) girls generally don't like each other. No matter how you feel about your prospective "sisters," it's undeniable that we need rush as an institutionalized way to judge others objectively, and therefore establish our own superiority by sorting freshmen into houses.

The Reason to Rush: It Is What It Is

When it comes to rush, there are two things you need to understand. One: In order to get into a sorority, you need to go through rush. Two: Rush is fucking stupid.

For instance, is it fair that fraternity rush involves blacking out and doing drugs while sorority rush involves sober conversations and pearls? Fucking no, and that's why as soon as this book is finished we're going Erin Brockovich on all universities with Greek life. JK, we're way too lazy.

At fraternity rush, you're judged if you can't drink enough alcohol. At sorority rush, you get the stink eye for taking a sip of hot chocolate from the girl who just offered it to you.

Anyway, despite our angry tangent and the fact that rush is sexist, outdated, and like really fucking boring, you should definitely still do it. This is the way it is. This is why it sucks. This is why you have to do it anyway. It's simple, if your school has a dominant Greek system and you want to spend your weekends at parties rather than at the recreational rock-climbing center, you have to be in the Greek system. Your goal is to get into the house with the hottest and most fun girls, because they are the ones who hang out with the hottest and most fun guys. Clearly you'd rather be the ugliest girl in the hottest sorority than the hottest girl in the fugliest sorority. Why? Because if you're a six hanging out with a bunch of tens, you could maybe pass for a seven, but if you're chilling with all fours, you'll probably seem more like a five. And, according to math, seven > five.

So if your aim is to be surrounded by douchebag frat bros, join a sorority. The only thing less attractive to a frat guy than a GDI is the herpes on his dick. However, if your aim is to make kind-hearted lifelong friends who will stick with you through thick and thin, best to go join a book club or like chill with your mom.

How to Judge a House by the Number of Blondes in It

In many cases, a particular college will have one sorority that's considered "the best house." If this is the case at your school, that sorority is the one you want to be in. However, at most schools, there are a number of top-tier houses that will all effectively earn you the right reputation.

If you find yourself choosing between two or more comparable houses, it's best to join the one that fits your demographic profile. In other words, if you're a Jew from New York, you probably won't feel comfortable in the house where everyone wears pastel sweater sets and has grandparents who refer to slavery as "the glory days."

Choose your house wisely. You become the people with whom you surround yourself. Being around ugly, nice, fat people might make you feel better on the inside, but you just gained a metaphorical fifty pounds on the outside.

How to Succeed in Rush without Really Trying

It's fairly easy to get into whatever house you want, assuming you're hot, skinny, and rich. During rush, the role of every betch is to act fake happy and look the hottest she can, while appearing classy. Think Bryce Dallas Howard in *The Help*.

You're not supposed to talk about boys or alcohol at rush, so you might as well say we need to pee standing up, for all the conversation topics left in our repertoire. Here's the truth: You should mention one or both of these topics nonchalantly so that you give the impression that you're a chill girl. The key is not to overshare. If you're blabbing about all the guys you date, you'll sound like a slut.

But a casual mention of your wild New Year's Eve in Miami establishes that you're far from enjoying poetry readings. It also helps to avoid hooking up with the boyfriends and/or fuck buddies of the sisters in the house (though, if she's not particularly influential or cool, this is less important).

The shadiest fact about rush is that the sorority sisters' opinions of you have already been determined sometime around orientation week thanks to Facebook and your reputation (or lack thereof) among the frat stars. If the older girls haven't already seen you at parties or heard a frat guy refer to you as "that hot freshman," then you're way more fucked than if you never rushed to begin with. There are a few exceptions to this, like if you somehow managed to be exceptionally hot and cool and still fly under the radar. However, the chances of being *that* hot and still unknown are on par with getting a bid to Hogwarts.

If you don't get into an "acceptable" sorority, it's best to just not be in one. We know we said that being a GDI is equivalent to euthanizing your social life, but being in a bottom-tier sorority is even worse. Finally, remember that you're more likely to get into a particular house if you fit the geographic/religious/hair-color profile. The only other trick is to have an alumni legacy, because then they're legally obligated to let you in. Talk about true friendship! It's like *The Sisterhood of the Traveling Pants* except they didn't let Carmen in because she's fat.

On the Other Side: Rushing Freshmen Sluts

So maybe you and your sorority sister haven't been speaking for months because you each hooked up with the other's boyfriend. Come sorority rush, this is as evident to the incoming freshmen as the fact that you're rating them on a scale of one to five and stalking their prom date on a giant projector screen during the nightly voting sessions.

As a sister in the house, rush is pretty much about wearing nice clothes and watching your tan fade from sitting inside talking to moronic freshmen all day. Essentially the only solution to this problem is to get as drunk as possible without being so wasted that you can't speak and/or walk; remember, you're "classy." Throw a few Xanax in your iced coffee and soon you'll find yourself thrilled to talk to anyone, or even better, you'll be so fucked up that you get sent upstairs to take a nap.

Sorority rush is crunch time. So put your ugly sisters in the kitchen, put aside the fact that you hate 80 percent of the girls in your house, and silence any qualms about deceiving others (*Hello, Hitler Youth!*). This is no time for truth, honesty, or virtue. This is sorority fucking rush.

COLLEGE BROS: ATHLETES AND FRAT DOUCHEBAGS

When it comes to college, a betch will find herself surrounded by a plethora of guys who bring something uniquely douchey to the table. Nowhere will you find a greater concentration of these shady assholes than in fraternities or on sports teams—or both, if you're really looking to get (mind) fucked.

Fraternities

Obviously frat bros are more common than athletes, as the only talents required to join a fraternity are the ability to chug a gallon of milk and like form sentences. These bros are also more available to do things like drink and have sex, because they don't have to wake up for six A.M. weight-lifting sessions.

When dealing with fraternities and the brothers within, you can pass judgment using standards similar to those you use for sororities: birds of a hot and shady feather flock together. It's important to realize that guys who are/were in frats are distinctly different from those who aren't/weren't. This is because pledging is torture and teaches them not to be a pussy. Character-building activities include spanking one another, drinking copious amounts of beer and not urinating, and being faced with the reality that they may have to deflower an animal during pledge week. Honestly, just the stench inside of a frat house says something about their social habits. Something good, clearly.

Frats will undeniably shape your college experience. Where else will you have an opportunity to display your slutty mixer outfits, obtain formal invitations, and day drink while pretending to know guys who like you for your personality? If you play your cards right, you might even start dating a bro who has pledges who are not only his bitches but also yours by default. Just remember to never make the mistake of dating a bro while he himself is pledging—their concentration isn't where it should be: your G-spot.

A true betch is something of a frat celebrity, but try not to take this too far, because bros talk shit. A lot. Almost as much as you do. The frat star superslut always ends up either (A) wifed up after she gets bored of being a slut, or (B) a chlamydia-carrying whore.

There are few things more quintessentially college to a betch than waking up in a disgusting frat house, maneuvering your way around beer cans and bongs, and "borrowing" a never-to-be-returned fraternity sweatshirt as a memento of your hottest and easiest years. Memories fade, but your closet of frat letters is forever.

Athletes: What Their Sport Says about Their Game

While they may not be the sharpest scissors on Edward's hands, athletes usually have sick game due to having been especially good-looking and athletic since middle school and never needing to try that hard with girls. But before you anxiously hop into bed with the captain of the badminton team, take note: Not all athletes are created equal.

We've taken the liberty of breaking down the athletic bros you're sure to encounter in your betchy college existence, but keep in mind that these types hold true for postcollege life as well.

Lacrosse: Biggest douchebags in America. (See: Duke University scandal.) Still, the lax bro is always hot and usually rich, because poor people don't play lacrosse. He clearly plays a sport in college for the sake of his reputation, because there is no such thing as professional lacrosse in America. If you dispute this, try finding five people who can name the lacrosse equivalent of the Super Bowl.

Football: He's a meathead and probably got into college because of his football skills. He will never touch a book because his university-provided tutors and jersey-chasing bitches will do everything for him.

Baseball: Hot all-American types. That or probs Latino.

Soccer: A slightly more European-looking—but equally douchey version—of the lax bro. There's something about a shin guard that makes me want to take my shirt off.

Tennis: They're hot but their bodies cannot be described as anything but long. Their screen names in middle school were probably Federerlover88 or IamnotaDjokovic314. The only two things being on the tennis team has gotten them is a stronger serve and the misguided idea that their balls are the size of the ones they slice.

TENETS OF TAILGATING

If you go to a college where football is a thing, and you're not willing to wake up at seven A.M. to drink yourself stupid every fall Saturday, you're committing social suicide.

You're ready to drink at any time of day. A true betch will be fine setting her alarm for 7:05 after getting home at five A.M. if it means she'll be getting drunk again.

Proper attire is essential. In the north it's all about rocking school colors and accessories like necklaces, tattoos, knee-high socks, sunglasses, and face paint. You need a new out-fit for every weekend, so set up your bursar account at the school store. In the south, it's considered a serious offense to be caught not wearing your nicest frock. If you don't look like you own a plantation, consider yourself an outcast.

This is the only time you're allowed to eat. You want to avoid vomming before noon, so be sure to at least share a bagel with the garbage.

Always pre-pregame. You wouldn't go to a nighttime pre-game without getting wasted first, would you?

Rally for Saturday night. If you can't handle it, transfer.

Basketball: See *Keeping Up with the Kardashians* for merits of a swoon-worthy Kris Humphries type. The basketball athlete is an idiot, and likely from the hood, but great for the tall betch. He thinks he's the shit, especially if his team is in March Mad-ness. He will walk around like he's above everyone else, because like he physically is. He's usually a boob guy because he can see down everyone's shirts, and he has been known to hook up with a fat girl or two, because he can't see her stomach from way up there.

Hockey: Canadian.

Squash: These WASP types pick up their skills at the country club and are usually pretentious as fuck. Why can't you just play tennis like everyone else?

Golf: Another country club sport, so you know he's rich. However, he's usually under the impression it's socially acceptable to wear a polo shirt at all times of the day. You'll often find this prick bragging about all the famous courses he's played on in Scotland and Greenland, while trying to repress his urge to sodomize himself with a nine iron. Save it for when you're too fat to play a real sport, like our dads.

Crew: You're a Winklevii.

Track: They're like nobody's type.

(Water) Polo: Went to Newport Harbor High School, got rejected by Oxford, and—due to being a closeted homosexual—gets turned on by horse boners.

Swimming: He shaves a greater percentage of his body than you do. So . . . .

Wrestling: Has a chode, severely repressed anger issues, and quite possibly a Napoleon complex. Wishes he were taller so he could've been a basketball star. Instead, he's stuck performing what seems like a homoerotic mating dance on a mat every day, while attempting to conceal his boner. He may or may not have some sort of skin issues due to rolling around on smelly mats. (See also: your high school gym teacher.)

So, betches, if you encounter an athlete, play it cool. There's something about great physical game that hints at a scintillating mind game. *Basketball Wives* showed us that athletes are as dickish as they come, and they often have a hard time growing up. He might not go pro, but he'll always be a bro.

Reliving Prom Every Semester

Date functions and Greek formals are the proms that never end. Except instead of being chaperoned by your high school teachers and strapping a fucking petunia to your wrist, you get dressed up, fucked up, and bussed to a venue where it's considered socially acceptable to vomit in the bathroom . . . or hallway. It's like going on a date, except better. Why? Because getting completely plastered is mandatory and free. Plus you can get too drunk with your besties to even notice all the bad highlights and tragic dresses with ruffles going on in the room. *Gross.*

> "Formals can give people hope. They give povo people something to live for."
> —Ja'mie King

Though you should never confuse a formal invite with an actual date, formals are a great excuse for pretending you were taken on one. It's better than a date, because if things go sour, you can always ditch your bro for the open bar. If you really don't like him, feel free to attempt a date swap. Extra points if your "swap" lands him with nobody.

Any college betch knows there's nothing formal about a formal. If we wanted to be classy and proper while getting drunk we'd go to like a wedding or something. If you didn't get the memo that your parents just paid your sorority $150 a head so that you could bounce as soon as the open bar runs out, consider yourself informally fucked.

GRADUATION:
A SURVIVAL GUIDE

There comes a time in every betch's life when she has to say goodbye. After four years of spending your time getting wasted and not doing anything of significance, suddenly that magical May weekend is upon you.

It's of utmost importance that you milk graduation weekend for all it's worth. This is the last time, other than your birthday and wedding, that you can reasonably ask for whatever the fuck you want. This applies not only to your immediate family but also your fifth cousin twice removed, whom you haven't seen since her baptism in 1997. Remember, this is a weekend to celebrate your favorite thing: yourself. Your parents are so proud of you right now, they won't even care that your summer plans are centered on taking Klonopin while tanning. So, guard your credit card with your life and hit Shopbop hard before you're kicked off the money train.

If the thought of graduating makes you want to slit your wrists, chill out, Suicidal Sally. This is only the beginning. True, you're moving on to the "real world," where it suddenly becomes way less acceptable to do things like selling textbooks back to your university for drug money, but don't panic. Postgrad life isn't going to be so bad.

Remember how fun it was to be a freshman in college? Now you get to be a freshman of an entire fucking city! Graduated betches make a mass exodus from all sorts of bumblefuck states to major cities, where it's no longer creepy to interact with a "local." You're opened up to a whole world full of new clubs, new bars, and, best of all, new people who haven't seen your outfit rotation a million times.

Graduating college marks the start of a new era. Bros will no longer have the mentality that they can fuck you without buying you so much as a drink, let alone dinner. Forget well-paying jobs and alumni networking, diplomas give us the right to say that guys who want to get laid are going to have to empty their fucking wallets.

So when you're stressing over the travesty that is graduation, just take a moment to relax and reflect on the major accomplishment of graduating college. After all, no matter how many classes you never went to, or how many nights a week you blacked out, your future employers will never have any clue. You see, the diploma you're handed at graduation is just as valuable as the one given to the nicegirl who had the privilege of spending her Friday nights writing your papers while you were out getting your BS in how to BS your way through life.

Dear Betch,

I went home for Thanksgiving break and I got it—the Turkey Dump. I guess he just couldn't handle my betchiness. He was constantly complaining about how I was in a sorority, which, according to him, automatically makes me a raging slut. I am now faced with the dilemma of returning home to a small suburb in Masshole with no one to fuck. I have a boy on call who is willing to let me be a home wrecker and I am considering, because what can possibly be betchier than that?

Help a betch out,
Proless

Dear Proless,

Everything is betchier than being a home wrecker. We don't wreck homes, we rule them. Though it may seem like we are down for cheating because we don't promote being nice, cheating is not cool. When you say, "willing to let me be a home wrecker," you sound like a pathetic slutty loser. A betch doesn't need to hook up with other girls' boyfriends, because she can get her own. But since you seem to think that cheating is betchy (meaning you probably have the morality of a syphilitic hooker), try working on yourself for a little.

Sincerely,
The Betches

PS. Being in a sorority doesn't make you a raging slut, desperately seeking dick on the four days of Thanksgiving break makes you a raging slut.

"Career"

A Word We Use Loosely

Women in the Workforce: A Short History of Misery

Back in the day, betches had it made. No one expected anything of us, and all we had to do was look hot, birth some sons, and order around ~~our indentured servants~~ the poor girls. But as women started gaining more rights, the expectations of their societal roles also grew. This really began to get intense around one hundred years ago when we got the right to vote. Voting is one of those things similar to your back-burner bro or like a coupon. You want to have access to it, even if you know you might never actually use it.

Once we were allowed to vote, everything went downhill from there. People actually took this as a sign that women should get involved in the workforce. They got their first taste of how much work sucks during the world wars, when all the bros went away and there was nothing to do. Fortunately, we went sake bombing with the Japanese, so betches got to take the '50s and '60s off from work, and they went back to chilling hard and hosting Tupperware parties.

Some time after that, shit got really weird. Some angry women decided they weren't happy wearing pearls and heels and went on a major power trip. They even decided to burn their bras. And they wonder why they didn't get into our sorority. Ever since then, it's been a struggle against the Hillary Clintons of the world, who try to get us to dress manly and recycle.

We'll admit that we appreciate the feminist movement for making sure that if we wanted, we could have everything in the world. Even if it's just the right to pretend to work for a few minutes before we have a baby. So thanks for all your hard work, Sandra Day. But like no thanks, I'm in the middle of my tennis lesson.

Laziness: A Defense

Living in a country that prides itself on the idea that with enough hard work, anyone can become extremely successful, it's no surprise that "hard work" has such a place in the American value system. It's ingrained in us from the time we're in kindergarten, when we're given gold stars for doing stupid shit like spelling our names right or feeding the class guinea pig the correct number of pellets.

Without proper guidance, it's easy to get lost in the idea that working hard will get you everything you want in life. Next thing you know, you're up until 3 A.M. and it has nothing to do with cocaine. You find yourself doing things like studying on weekends and "working overtime."

> "My mum used to say to me, 'You can't have fun all the time,' and I used to say, 'Why not? Why the fuck can't I have fun all the time?'"
> —Kate Moss

We're about to let you in on a little secret that the president and the puritans have been trying to hide from you for years. If you're young, hot, and at least moderately intelligent, there's really no need for you to work hard. Ever. The American dream is for your Slovenian housekeeper and ugly people who never got the memo that the best way to get shit done is to get other people to do it for you.

There's only so much time in a day, so why spend it being bitched around by a workaholic boss? If they were so competent to be promoted to boss, they should be competent enough to get things done without your time and mental energy. What happened to specialization of tasks? Like, sue us for being particularly skillful at sitting there and looking gorgeous, while interjecting an occasional "Ugh, what I'd do for an iced coffee right now. Spreadsheets are like so random."

CAREER PATHS:
PICKING THE LEAST TOXIC POISON

When college comes to its sudden and disastrous end, it's inevitably time to move on to the real world . . . that is, after spending your summer wasted, while claiming to plan your next postgraduation step. During college there's no question more perturbing than "What do you want to do after you graduate?" Confusingly enough, our natural response garners little respect. Many people even think we're joking when we reveal our plans to marry rich ASAP so we never have to stop having a good time. It's unnerving how much this answer bothers people . . . we thought honesty was the best policy.

Avoiding work may be the only life plan you've actually planned for, but trust us when we say it's not

"The most important career decision you're going to make is whether or not you have a life partner and who that partner is."
—Sheryl Sandberg

nearly that simple. Aside from the fact that most people can't afford to do that, if you want to avoid being labeled as lazy and mentally unstable, it's necessary to accept that we need to do *something* that involves making an income to occupy the greater part of our twenties. Being financially dependent on your parents at age twenty-five exposes you to a lot of shit-talking . . . and while you and your besties are allowed to make fun of how bad you are at working, no one else fucking should.

> "I always wanted to be some kind of writer or newspaper reporter. But after college . . . I did other things."
> —Jackie Kennedy, First Housewife

Other than the rare, exceptional person who decides she wants to be a power betch and run her own company or something similarly stressful and time-consuming, most of you will fit into one of the following postgrad categories. If you're unsure which career path is right for you, it probably means that none of them are and you should definitely go back to school until one of your additional degrees helps you figure it out.

Public Relations/Fashion/Marketing/ Advertising/Entertainment and Media Jobs: Because Work Should Always Be a Party

These are the jobs that involve going to work but not really working. Kind of like being a club promoter, working in these industries offers the illusion of having a grown-up job, while really being paid to glorify our lifestyle of indulgence. The downside is that the salary fucking sucks. So this type of job is ideal if you have a backup source of income (read: trust fund) and you want people to think you're really pretty and glamorous, or you're Heidi Montag. While they probably pay child sweatshop workers in Malaysia more money than an entry-level fashion girl, there are definitely some great perks. From products to parties to celebrities, it's a great way to surround yourself with people that matter.

We love this line of work because it involves one of our favorite things: manipulating people into believing that which is exaggerated or not true. Think about it logically. No, Beyoncé does not *really* use Wet n Wild mascara like that article in *Glamour* said she did. She has actual money, remember? But the boring, uninformed public doesn't have to know that. And that's the beauty of PR.

That's not to say these aren't insanely important jobs. Like, pivotal for shaping the thoughts of stupid people. Let's look at a historical anecdote that demonstrates the necessity of public relations. Nixon had a shitty PR rep who let him go on national television looking like a greaseball. No one wanted to vote for a gross, sweaty old man, when they could daydream about fucking a hot, confident JFK for four years. And there you have it, he lost the election, got a makeover, won the next election, and opened a recording studio at a chic hotel.

Whether your job is to tweet how delicious the restaurant you're promoting is or to harass an editor at *People,* these jobs are just not that hard. And if all your dad said was that you needed to get a job or else he wouldn't pay your rent, why not do something that makes you happy until you find a husband to start picking up the tab? Betches in these fields will inevitably get married and start doing "freelance PR," also known as making three calls a week and using this as an excuse to hire a full-time nanny, because they're "working."

So if you don't have to rely on your salary for stupid things like rent or spending money, PR/Fashion/Marketing/Advertising/Entertainment and Media is definitely the path for you.

Finance/Consulting/Real Estate/Sales Jobs: Excel Is Hell

Obviously, none of us have ever come close to an Excel document, but we're pretty sure that's what goes down in the underworld. All we know is that our friends in finance want to fucking shoot themselves. Typically, the betch who finds herself working at a bank was a hard-working type from a top school who was attracted to finance because of the "status," high salary, and good potential for meeting pros. What you don't realize is how horrible it is to work sixty hours a week and that those pros are actually more likely to use a work trip to try to sleep with you than they are to take you out for a fancy dinner. But look on the bright side . . . I mean, if you're working at all times, at least you're not eating.

Working for Dad: The Key to Job Security

Working in any sort of family business capacity is ideal, because no matter how much you fuck up, you probably won't be fired. However, if you're lucky enough to be in this position, we don't recommend acting like a complete asshole. Fucking up your family's company just means your inheritance will be smaller. If your coworkers are resentful of the nepotism that landed you in the cubicle next to them, just get them to believe that you really wanted this job and are super worried about people judging you for being related to the boss. *So what if my grandma is one of three references on my resume, she thinks I'm like really sweet! And it's not my fault my dad is keeping you off welfare!*

Our one caveat is that you should be cautious how you advertise your profession—if your dad does something totally embarrassing, be discreet. Just know that no one is impressed when you say you work for a company that manufactures geriatric wheelchairs. Except maybe old people.

Law School: What, Like It's Hard?

When one accidentally sells her soul to law school, nine times out of ten it was based on the misguided assumption that she was signing up for three years of postcollege partying and putting off deciding what she actually wants to do. This could not be more false.

> "*Law school is for people who are boring, ugly, and serious.*"
> —Elle Woods's dad

Few people actually *want* to be a lawyer. The only thing uglier than law textbooks are the professors who teach from them. But when faced with having to reveal your "true passions" (aka husband hunting and texting), lots of betches will choose the road more traveled: a law degree.

Unless you're a betch who is smart enough to know that she's probably too ugly to land a husband to support her, it's best to steer clear of law school. Seriously, your dad's money could find a better home somewhere else, like your line of credit at Saks.

Although attending sporadic lectures and having one test per semester may sound more appealing than working a nine-to-five job, earth to Minkus: it's not. Like when all your friends are going to happy hour after their joke PR jobs, where their main responsibility is to tweet all day, you will be trying to convince competitive nerds to send you their case briefs for the final. *Yes, I know there's a fucking curve, maybe if you didn't have so many, you might be interested in collaborating.* We can promise you, it only gets more competitive when you're an actual lawyer with, you know, trials and shit.

However if you're actually interested in law, like you enjoy arguing with people and sounding smart, the best way to do law school is obviously to do nothing at all. While all the nicegirls will spend orientation week getting acquainted with professors and scheduling office hours appointments, your job is to meet the naturally smartest and most relaxed friend you can. This is the person who broke 170 on their LSAT and went to a mediocre but expensive school for rich people. This winning combination suggests that he didn't care about getting into a good college (read: likes to do drugs) but is definitely intelligent and can excel without trying. In other words, this person will be very similar to you, but it's best if he's a guy. He will be responsible for doing all of your work throughout law school, in exchange for being associated with you.

Once you find this legal-minded mensch, it's best not to fuck him. Keep it casual. Turning this symbiotic relationship into a sexual one will only get you one place: alone, in your 1L dorm, angry as fuck because it's apparently really hard to understand the difference between malum in se and malum prohibitum when you're really high.

Of course, there are some benefits to law school. Like for the rest of your life, when your air conditioner breaks down or your mom is being annoying, you can shout out legal jargon to sound scary. There obvs has to be someone in each bestie group to inform the cashier at Starbucks that credit card minimums are illegal, just like her outfit should be.

The Career Student: The Path to Never Working

The career student is the girl who realizes that if she just keeps studying, she'll never have to work a day in her life at a "real" job. Enrolling in a grad program of almost any kind is the vastly preferable version of going to law school. That is, it's shorter, less time-consuming and competitive, and much more pointless. Seriously, unless you're going to use your PhD for something logical, like becoming a professor or a social worker (and why would you?), then grad school is not at all necessary.

But don't let that stop you from going! In fact, grad school is the favored path among postgraduate betches who don't want a job and are looking to kill time while waiting to get married. The most manipulative among us are capable of convincing our parents to support us while we get three to five diplomas certifying our concentration in color theory and Native American folklore. Our one caveat is that you definitely need some family money to support yourself while you're completing your third dual-degree in Advanced Adolescent Cyberbullying and Art Therapy.

Med School: Leave It to Overachievers

Just when you thought there could be no postgraduate school more torturous than law school, don't forget the place where fun goes to die: medical school. Reasons not to go down this path are basically infinite, but this list sums it up pretty well.

✦ To apply to med school, you need to be premed in college. Clearly this doesn't make the list of betch-approved majors.

✦ Med school is competitive to get into and is even more competitive once you're in. Basically, you should aim to get involved in academic competition in the same way you would get involved in sex with an AIDS patient.

✦ When embarking on the path of the aspiring doctor, you're committing yourself not just to four years of casual schooling, but to twelve years of grueling work and the fugliest outfits imaginable. I mean, the coroner's garb is cuter than a fucking doctor's. Point-blank, by the time you finish your residency, you could've lived an epic poem.

✦ Sure, you may be on the hunt for a hot doctor husband, but why the fuck do you need a hot doctor husband when you yourself are a doctor? Truth. Bomb.

✦ If you choose to go med, go plastics. The people are usually good-looking and unlike nicegirl shit like pediatrics, you'll actually make money.

Remember, leave the science to the scientists, and stick to what you're good at. No one likes the bitch doctor friend reminding us of our impending liver failure as a result of mixing vodka and Xanii. You might think the road to your MD will be paved with hot Shakespearean tragedies à la *Grey's Anatomy,* but if that show taught us anything, it's that everyone in the OR ends up either dead or related.

HOW TO APPLY FOR A JOB LIKE YOU GIVE A SHIT

Once you've figured out which career path you're going to reluctantly pursue, applying for a job like a betch is similar to how normal people apply for jobs, except for us it involves being pretty. It's a statistical fact that attractive people are more likely to get hired, all other shit being equal. But unlike all other areas of your life, being hot won't get you the job automatically. First you'll need to know how to pretend you're a legit

> "A career is wonderful, but you can't curl up with it on a cold night."
> —Marilyn Monroe

person for the thirty minutes it will take to convince a high-level corporate person that you have ambitions beyond blacking out and getting cast on the *Real Housewives.*

Though we can't tell you the secret to landing every job, we can give you a few simple guidelines that should at least imply basic competence. After that, it's all on you and how well you pull off business-casual chic. It's a style, look into it.

Rule 1: Don't Be Hungover

This is perhaps the most important rule because it's difficult to be as manipulative as necessary when you're not at your best. You'll also probably look like a crypt keeper and care less about what anyone's saying than you usually do . . . and that's like really hard. You might also accidentally curse without realizing. This is a little talked-about side effect of drinking. "What are your weaknesses?" *Shit . . . I can't even think of one.*

To avoid the dilemma of your job hunt interfering with your busy schedule of barhopping five nights a week, it's best to plan your interviews on Mondays or Tuesdays so your work won't interrupt your weekend. Besides, you didn't even get the job yet and they're already asking you to come in on a Blackout Wednesday? Anyone who works in HR can list the many benefits of work-life balance for you, but every true betch knows that you should never let your job interfere with your drinking.

Rule 2: Pretend You Give a Fuck about Company X

The key to any good manipulation is understanding your target inside and out. That being said, all you have to do is remember two distinct things about the company and talk about how much you love them. *Hmm, let's see, why do I want to work at Google? Well, I love how you guys change your little logo for important holidays; I have many good ideas for that . . . maybe we can make the whole page brown, you know, for Kwanza. Also, let's be real, Bing is for fuglies . . . and like, have you seen me?*

Every once in a while, a betch will find herself in a job interview that she applied for as a joke in an industry she's clueless about. Your best bet here is to just look good and channel your freshman-year econ professor: as in, your rhetoric should be far above your level of actual understanding. Don't know what private equity is? Your interviewer should be as aware of this as he is of your plans to quit as soon as you're out of the disgusting limbo between being financially supported by your dad and your husband.

Rule 3: Have Common Sense

Do: Look hot and pray for a male interviewer.

Don't: Forget to ask someone else to proofread your cover letter. Not only will you not get the job with a fucked-up cover letter, but everyone will laugh freely at you for writing that you'd "enjoy the possibility of a full-time position with insert company name here."

Do: Wear a forgiving button-down if you have a C cup or bigger. You might think your interviewer wants to see your cleavage—and he does—which is okay if it'll get you the job . . . but wait, your button just popped off and hit him in the eye.

Don't: Get a spray tan right before. Your interviewer will think you're having your period down your neck. Just ask Xtina to give you a spray-by-spray of her bronze-menses debacle.

Do: Hop yourself up on Red Bull and iced coffee. Sure you don't give a shit about this job, but with these tools, your fake maniacal excitement will have everyone thinking you're hot and ambitious.

Don't: Actually do any work once you get hired. Find a nicegirl to do it for you. Fucking duh.

SO NOW YOU HAVE A JOB: HOW TO NEVER DO WORK AT WORK

Once you've secured yourself the easiest possible job with the highest possible salary, it's an art to figure out the balance between doing too much work and doing so little work that you're about as useful as Paris Hilton in a vegetative state.

> "All paid jobs absorb and degrade the mind."
> —Aristotle

So what's the secret? These strategies require you to not be a completely incompetent asshole and to have a great deal of people skills. After all, this is about getting people to do things for you, and our version of success involves larger goals than getting the most desirable shift at Jamba Juice.

The double exchange: This is the same as the work exchange you used in college, just applied to office tasks instead of term papers.

SIDE NOTE

You might be saying, "But, betches, you're hypocrites, you wrote a book!" Normally we would agree with you, but in this case you're just wrong. Sure we'd so much rather be rewatching all four seasons of *The OC* all day long, but we're not completely useless. Besides, we're not exactly waking up at six A.M., taking a subway, and talking about shit like projections and yearly reports. The only time we'll use "excel" in a sentence is when the other words are "we" and "at life."

The holdout: This goes under our Threshold Theory, which goes as follows: The person who cares the most will give in first. When working on a project with a group of people, the key is to hold out long enough for someone to eventually do the work for you. During this process, it's important to be constantly telling the nicegirl in your group (who will inevitability give in first) how amazing all the work she's doing is, even though you probably have no fucking clue what's going on. As a result, she will feel more motivated and less angry about doing your part in addition to her own. This strategy will also serve to remind her that she would probably do a much better job than you would anyway, and since the team will be judged as a whole, why would she want to risk a bad evaluation? It helps to mention an upcoming party you're hosting soon, and that you'd love it if she came. *I would finish the project, but I just don't know if that would leave me any time to get the chasers!*

Getting bros to do your work: Look around you. Are there men in the group? There's no harm in playing the ditz card and telling them that they're guys and so they'll probably do *such* a better job than you would. *But I brought sustenance!* Accept no less than a completed PowerPoint presentation in exchange for each minute they're allowed to stare at your cleavage. In a group project, a nice guy who wants to fuck you is a one-way ticket to the boss's good graces with no effort whatsoever.

Always keep in mind, telling someone they're the best at something and that there's no way you could possibly do it better will usually have them yearning to prove you right. It's not that we want to take advantage of people who are in love with us, but when you're so desired, it's almost harder not to. *Matt is obviously dying to win my approval somehow. What better way to give him the opportunity than allowing him to run my Q3 figures?*

If you've tried all these and failed, paying someone to do your work for you or popping an Adderall are your best bets. That is, unless you've managed to avoid ever being assigned work at all because your boss wants to fuck you. If that's the case, cheers to you.

Manipulating the Boss: Master This Line of Work, and You Won't Have to Do Any

The most effective way to get out of actually having to do work while maintaining job security is obviously to manipulate your superiors. Believe it or not, this is actually easier than manipulating your coworkers.

Only work for males: Just like girls hate one another in sororities, they also hate one another in the workplace. Based on statistics we haven't read, we know that the majority of women in executive jobs are angry, lonely workaholics. Therefore, you'll most likely be subconsciously deemed a threat if you're too competent. Older women live in constant, paralyzing fear they will be replaced by younger women, both in their marriages and in their jobs. This problem has an easy solution, just avoid working for women. Men will probably be easier to look at, and will definitely be easier to manipulate.

Understand the office atmosphere: Working in a modern office requires feeling out the intensity level of your coworkers. If you glance over at your coworker's computer screen and notice that she's consistently on Facebook and online shopping, this is usually a cue that it's fine for you to do the same. You both will enter into an unspoken agreement to not mention the fact that you're getting paid to assess this week's sales at Michael Kors.

However, if you're in an industry where everyone is running around doing things like saving lives or chasing down the latest copy of *Harry Potter* for the boss's twins, it's best to keep these procrastinating tendencies under wraps until you can finally quit this miz place.

Become the office favorite: Becoming the office favorite involves doing zero actual work whatsoever, while putting a lot of effort into frivolous and fun activities. The truth is that you're probably never going to become the office favorite by doing your actual job, because no one wants to see a hot girl compete and come out on top. Trust us, they would prefer that you spend your time sending funny articles over Gchat or staging only-cool-people-invited happy hours because that probably means they'll be promoted over you. And when that eventually happens, and they become your new boss, they'll remember how much they loved working with you and, in turn, will be even easier to manipulate. It's a vicious but effective cycle in which everyone wins!

Don't worry about people calling you lazy or unproductive; they will be so overwhelmed by all the positive energy you add to the group that before you know it, you're employee of the month for a year running.

Sexual harassment: This tactic is limited if you're working for a woman, but we've found that merely using the words "hostile work environment" in a sentence together will leave your boss afraid to go anywhere near you for at least a week or two. God, the justice system is like sooo gullible. Fucking your boss to get to the top is frowned upon, unless this leads to him wifing you up, eliminating that pesky "work" thing anyway.

HOW TO ASK FOR AN UNDESERVED RAISE

So apparently there's all this research showing a huge salary gap between men and women. According to our dads, women make something like eightyish cents for every dollar men do. While men would say this is due to their greater skill set, the alleged "real" reason is because women don't negotiate their salaries when they're hired or ask for raises, which sounds ridiculous to us. If you're going to pretend to work for a few years, you should be doing it for as much money as possible. Just remember, whatever raises you get, you shouldn't tell your parents about them. Best to let them think you're still living off some absurdly povo entry-level salary and you need them to continue paying your cell phone bill.

Do something really well and then ask: They say timing is everything in life. At no point will your boss be more open to giving you more money than immediately after a big money-making accomplishment or after hearing whispers that his girlfriend finally put anal on the table. It's also best if your achievements reflect positively on your boss as well as you. Seriously, even if you haven't done anything for months, your supervisor will quickly forget this as soon as he or she receives a lot of positive recognition thanks to you, and therefore will be in the mood to pay you more.

Ask for a promotion: While a promotion is unpleasant because it involves getting more responsibility, asking for one is actually a shady gateway to getting more money without doing more work. When you ask to be promoted, most likely this won't be possible. Either there are no open positions, you're not trained to do something else, or your boss doesn't want to train someone new to do your job, because you're like really good at it. Who else could pull off a professional-looking miniskirt like you? Exactly.

To prevent you from leaving the job they think you've been doing for the past year, it's likely that they will offer you a raise in place of a promotion, which is really a win-win for everyone.

Bring up your upcoming meeting with HR about your prospects at the company: When your boss hears this, he or she will automatically start to think of themselves and what illegal shit they might have done to you in the past few months. Follow this with a tactful comment about how you're moving to a really expensive apartment soon, and you're hoping to buy that just-skinned-yesterday zebra rug for your new living room. This will leave your boss both sympathetic and afraid of what you'll say to HR about him or her. This is the perfect recipe for a glowing recommendation to Travis in payroll.

Hint that you may leave: This is essentially the back-burner bro theory applied to your career path. Basically, you just apply for another job on the side (or pretend like you did), and when you receive an offer (or pretend like you did), you tell your boss that you're leaving unless they can match the hypothetical salary of this other job. Cha fucking ching. If they call your bluff and you're left unemployed, best to just marry your actual back-burner bro.

Summary

When it comes to working and developing a career, an untold secret is that most women don't really want to be in charge or work endless hours to be the ultimate best in their field. We'd prefer to do something that gives us a balance of feeling somewhat useful and productive, while still having time to go out for group dinners with our friends. In other words, in an ideal world we would plan our work around our vacations, not the other way around. The best way to achieve this is to be aware of the work culture around you, pick the job that best suits your desire to not work, and manipulate others into doing your work for you. If you do these things effectively, you should be able to get the maximum benefits of a job with a minimum amount of effort. And that, girls, is the path to a fulfilling career.

Dear Betch,

Okay, so I've got a problem. Due to the economy, my parents have practically lost everything. Though we still have the luxury cars and properties (that we're hanging on to by a thread), my indulgences have been cut. Hence, no crazy spring break trip to Ibiza this year. As a true betch from birth, it is an inborn characteristic to take Daddy's credit card and really have no limits. Now I can't do this, and it's really depressing. I'm sure you understand. Like, this is poverty to me.

So this is the problem: My girlfriends don't really understand. I've told them multiple times of my embarrassing situation and they really can't comprehend why I can't be the indulgent girl that I've always been. I'm def not stingy, but, you know, I've got my limits now.

What do I do (besides getting a job)?

Thanks for your time, betches.

Love,
Poor Little Rich Betch

Dear Poor Little Rich Betch,

Being a betch is not about how much shit you have or how many fancy vacations you go on. Sure, those things help, but at its core it's about manipulating the way the world sees you and letting everyone think that you control your lifestyle, rather than the other way around.

Of course it's hard to go out and rage when you have no money. But here's the secret: you only have to spend money when you go out if you're ugly or a guy. So use your hotness to your advantage and get a lot of free shit. Clearly getting a job is a surefire way to have money, but this doesn't mean you necessarily have to do work. Try for a job for which you need to be attractive, because those rarely require thought or real work. Being a promotional bottle girl for alcohol companies lets you go out while getting paid for it! If this doesn't work, just get a boyfriend—or at least a guy who really wants to fuck you—and make him pay for shit.

Being poor sucks, but you can figure out how to work it anyway. Look at Madonna for inspiration. She came to New York with thirty-five dollars in her pocket, but after a few minutes wearing a slutty corset and singing a song about loving diamonds, voilà . . . self-fulfilling prophecy.

Keep your head up high and remember, it's better to be sort of poor than completely ugly.

Sincerely,
The Betches

Sex

As women it's important for us to understand how our actions and inactions affect not only ourselves but also the image we project to others. This is never more evident than in the age-old power play over sex. Many of you rip your hair out trying to discern things like, *When should I do it? Have I done it too soon? Will he think I'm a slut and do this all the time? Should I have made him take me on a real date first? Been more of a bitch? Taken out my tampon?*

These are often the thoughts that go through any rational girl's head after sleeping with a guy with whom she's not clearly in a monogamous relationship. With that, we begin our stance on "to fuck or not to fuck" with a little inspirational anecdote, based on a true story.

It's two A.M. and you're hanging outside the bar trying to think of ways to distract yourself from eating. That's when you see him, standing across the street: the bro.

The bro's goal for the night is to fuck the hottest girl around. He motions for you to come over. You scream that if he wants to talk to you, he can cross the fucking street.

The two of you start talking when he mentions that he has weed. This entices you enough to go back to his place, smoke, and watch Hugo.

After a few hits, you announce that Martin Scorsese looks like your grandpa. The bro takes this proclamation as a sign that you're down to hook up. Mid-make-out sesh, you feel drunk/high enough that you're actually considering having sex with him. At least it'll be a workout!

He starts to put his hand down your pants. An ass-cheek squeeze later, you snap out of it and realize who you are. It will take more than a blunt and a compliment to conquer this shit. While bros may rule the world, betches have the power to not have sex with them. As he tries to put his hand down your pants again, you yawn and say that you've got a super early group meeting. You're like sooo sorry and so thankful for the blunt, but you really have to go. Bye.

See, the difference between a betch and the average slut is that the former doesn't just use her hotness to get laid, she uses it to manipulate the bros who think they're in charge. This is not to say girls don't love having sex, but, unlike bros, our vaginas aren't attached to our brains.

The Theorem: Not Having Sex with Bros (Sometimes)

While men are allowed to approach sex mindlessly and are praised for the amount of meaningless sex they have, women are led to think that giving in to their sexual desires without question will leave them pathetic, alone, and with the reputation of the village bicycle. Sad as we are to admit it, people who idolize Tucker Max and Charlie Sheen are correct

> "Women need a reason to have sex. Men just need a place."
> —Billy Crystal

HISTORICAL BETCH ROLE MODEL: ANNE BOLEYN

Known for her quick wit and vocal opinions, there were like dozens of guys trying to get it in. She kept her eye on the prize, though, and by not having sex with King Henry VIII until he made her queen, she not only secured herself a position of power and luxury, but she also got the guy to denounce the entire Catholic religion and risk eternal damnation. Talk about thinking with your dick. Okay, so she eventually lost her head. Happens to the best of us.

about this double standard. But if you're smart, you can manipulate this unfortunate truth to your advantage.

If the biology tutor our parents hired in high school taught us anything worth remembering, it was that no matter the species, males are always looking to spread their seed to as many ~~hot~~ women as possible. Women, on the other hand, are supposed to be more selective. *Who is going to show up to my cousin's wedding with me, make all of my friends jealous, and make a great father to my future kids? And who's going to want to be the one to invest an entire life of resources and time to make sure this child not only survives but also gets into Dalton?*

Lesson learned: If you're screwing a poor bartender/actor on the first date for the sake of getting laid, you're really just fucking yourself. This guy will not have any of the durable attributes—wealth, stability, and status—that are integral to the survival of your superior genetic code. The facts don't lie, and neither do we.

It may seem counterintuitive that the most desirable betches are the ones who also deny bros the most often. It's important to realize that it's not just appearance that men find attractive, but also how selective you are with your sexual partners. Ever heard a bro's boring story about his hunting trip? Did any of these stories end up with him saying, "Yeah, that deer just ran into a tree and I picked it up and felt like *the man*." *No,* that would make him feel like shit because killing that deer was *easy,* and who the fuck places value on things that are easy?

The fun is in the chase. Even when the bro finally kills the extraordinarily elusive deer, he still treasures it because he knows that he worked hard for it. It would have been really difficult, if not impossible, for anyone else to do it. Thus you hold a secret that no bro will tell you, but every bro knows: He wants to feel special. He wants to feel like you'll do shit for him that you wouldn't do for others. And that is why men crave women who project self-respect and self-control, and who are particular about what they put in their body and with whom they spend their time. If a bro knows that you'd just as easily hook up with his short, chubby, B-team friend as you would with him, you're very quickly putting yourself in a bad place. You can be sure he has no interest in putting his dick in the same place as a second-tier bro.

Having sex with you is a prize for which bros should work. If you're giving away the music for free, no one's going to buy the album. It happened with Napster, it will happen to you. Being a strong, independent, and powerful woman is about understanding this fact and using it to dominate in a world where men believe they have the upper hand.

So next time you find yourself having sex with a guy you just met at a bar or on the first date, realize that the only shots he'll be getting you from now on are the kind that are about to come out of his penis.

Knowing Your Number:
The Importance of Being Organized

Most girls, at minimum, keep track of the names and quantity of their sexual partners. As a betch, you should definitely know the last name of everyone you've had sex with before having sex with them, or at the very least, after. If you can't keep track (within a two-person range of the true number), your number's too high.

If you are currently in college, you're most likely within three degrees of hookup separation with any given person at the bar. Being aware of who's on your list will help you avoid confrontations as well as the guys who will have sex with anything with two legs and a pulse.

As you get older, tracking your sexual encounters is more like a parenting style. You should know where your kids are, but it doesn't mean you have to attach a fucking tracking bracelet to their wrists.

Now we're declining to name an appropriate number of sexual servants before you get engaged, because it really depends on a lot of factors. It is totally important to gain sexual experience so that you

> ### *AMERICAN PIE 2:* A NOTE ON THE RULE OF THREE
>
> STIFLER: When a girl tells you how many guys she's slept with, multiply it by three and that's the real number. Didn't you fuckers learn anything in college?
>
> JESSICA: If a guy tells you how many girls he's hooked up with, it's not even close to that. You take that number and divide it by three, then you get the real total. So if Kevin is saying it's been three girls it's more like one or none.
>
> VICKY: None?
>
> JESSICA: The rule of three. It's an exact science. Consistent as gravity.

can learn about your body and what turns you on and off. You may have had more or fewer sexual partners, depending on how old you are when you get married, how much of a serial dater you are, and how many dinners and presents it takes for you to put out. The important thing to remember is that it's not about your actual number; it's about your standards. There is no formula, or "right" amount, just a number indicating that you're hard to get into yet not a Mormon.

PS. Your future husband doesn't necessarily have to know about the guys with whom you've drunkenly played "just the tip." Like the fact that you've farted in your lifetime or that you once ate at IHOP, certain things are better left unsaid.

When Desperation Needs to Go to Rehab: Being TGF

While you shouldn't beat yourself up over the occasional blackout slip-up (think of it as a scrimmage before the big game), there is absolutely nothing more unacceptable than being the girl that is outwardly and obviously Trying to Get Fucked (TGF).

THE LITTLE MERMAID

Ariel was a princess, but she wouldn't shut the fuck up about how she needed to get her legs done. Although Prince Eric was a total pro, it's really desperate and losery to sell your voice to an evil octopus to get ~~legs~~ laid. She is a great example of how any girl can be really pretty, rich, and chill, but if she doesn't have enough self-esteem and gives up everything for a guy, she winds up with no girlfriends and chasing after a guy who has no idea who the fuck she is.

You and everybody else know exactly who she is. She's the girl eye-fucking everyone in sight, she's the one lingering around the bar trying to take advantage of the drunkest guy there, the guy who's too drunk to realize how annoying and/ or ugly she is. She is undeniably TGF.

> **TGF IN THE BIBLE**
>
> *"Yet she became more and more promiscuous as she recalled the days of her youth, when she was a prostitute in Egypt. There she lusted after lovers, whose genitals were like those of donkeys and whose emission was like that of horses."*
> —Ezekiel 23:19

Now every normal person who's not a home-schooled jungle freak or has witnessed pop culture in the past five years knows what being DTF[4] is, and frankly there's nothing wrong with that. We totally respect every girl's choice to be a slut if she so chooses. After all, it's 2013 and it can be tiring to continuously reject the massive amount of bros vying for your attention. In fact, empowered girls do have sex with guys, but while making sure to maintain control of the situation.

TGF, by contrast, is simply unacceptable. Being DTF is being open to the idea of having sex if it presents itself. Being TGF is projecting an oozing vibe of desperation for ~~someone~~ anyone to have sex with you. When a bitch is TGF, you may not always see it, but you can definitely feel it—like the wind or a trust fund.

However, while having sex with bros is okay, and even encouraged in some circumstances, trying to fuck anything with a penis is sad. If people don't hate you, they will inevitably feel pity and wonder what your daddy issues are.

---

4   You really don't know? Down to Fuck

If you notice that one of your besties has come down with a case of TGF, you should sit her down and knock some sense into her. No one is going to buy the cow if said cow is spraying milk all over the fucking bar. It's a sign of low-quality produce. So if you find yourself taking home the guy all your friends have rejected, or lingering at the bar until every last viable option has gone home, or texting every bro in your phone, make an emergency appointment with your therapist, bitch, because you're fucking infected.

NAVIGATING THE BEDROOM: IT'S HARDER THAN YOU THINK

In the instances when you've decided to bestow the gift of hooking up upon a worthy suitor, what actually happens in bed is an entirely new world of ~~pleasure~~ manipulation tactics. Obviously your approach to having sex is just as important as how you behave before and after. You definitely don't want to be a sexual bore, but at the same time, you're not looking to draw comparisons to a Vegas hooker. It's a fine line, betches. You should approach your sexual game like you would any game: keep it mysterious and breezy, and allocate sexual favors like you would compliments—sparingly and only when extremely deserved.

Penises: What to Do When They're Softer than a Nicegirl's Heart

Unlike Silly Putty, a dick is supposed to get hard when handled. But in some unnatural cases, it just won't. If you thought a hard dick was ugly, Putty P is like something straight out of *Saw IV*.

If you're hooking up with a guy and he can't get hard, your only and immediate reaction should be to laugh hard—to compensate for the fact that he isn't. Best done directly in his face. Under no circumstance should you "try to help him out." As a betch, you are by default hot and amazing, and even if this guy was in a coma, you should always be enough to raise his interests.

> "Hey, just so you know: It's not *that common, it* doesn't happen to every guy, and it is *a big deal!"*
> —Rachel Green

Let's back up a little and talk about what Carrie Bradshaw might call "the twentysomething ED era." Although we're not doctors or shrinks, we can easily say that unless you have mucus dripping all over your face from the eight ball you split earlier, it's not you, it's him. No exceptions. There are various types of ED, and some are clearly more disastrous and alarming than others. Let's discuss the two most common:

The teenager: This is what most would consider the most benign/acute form of ED and probably what 50 percent or so of young guys have experienced at one point or another, usually as a result of drinking too much and doing too many drugs. If you're hooking up with a guy and have to question his hardness, this is a clear sign that the only thing that will be getting up is you, off his bed.

What we're describing here is the teenager. It is not a baby, but not quite adult-size, and may or may not be suffering from pacne. With some encouragement, it could develop into its full potential, but then again, you also run the risk of having a mouth full of mush.

The noodle: The noodle is a more severe form of the teenager and could potentially indicate a physical or psychological disorder. There is no doubt in your mind that this guy is not hard, and even if you endured enough Botox to have the mouth of Uma Thurman, there's no way this thing is budging.

This can be the most annoying kind of ED because frequently the guy may try to compensate for his "short-comings" and attempt to:

1. Aggressively dry-hump you while naked and fully soft, continuously thrusting and growling some form of, "I want to fuck the shit out of you!" Cringe. Or:
2. If he wasn't raised in the jungle, he will softly cuddle you and rub his soft penis around in circles, a term which we often refer to as "noodling." So don't fucking lie there and pretend it's normal, because it's not. Like those terrorist announcements on the subway, if you see something, say something. Noodling is creepy, and betches don't do carbs.

And then there's ED's perverted cousin, the premature ejaculator. There are few things worse than the minute man who's delusional enough to think he's actually good in bed. This guy's even worse than the embarrassed bro who comes immediately at the touch of your hand.

All these guys will complain about being too drunk, too tired, too stoned, blah, blah, blah, but the fact of the matter is that it's nine A.M. and the only thing they have put in their system since one A.M. is your saliva. Be it fear of shitty performance, the fact that the sight of your amazing boobs makes him come in fifteen seconds, or that you're his unsuccessful beard for the night, it's not your fucking problem.

When presented with any of these nonsticky situations, it's best to move on right away and focus on guys who are on your level. Even prissy WASP Charlotte York MacDougal was not down to deal with a guy's inability to get it up, and he had a Park Avenue apartment.

Blow Jobs: Your Charitable Donation

When hooking up with a guy, you'll often arrive at a night-altering decision: to blow or not to blow. That is the fucking question. Though it seems counterintuitive, giving head can sometimes be a bigger deal than having sex. As Chelsea Handler once said, this is one of the rare times that you're doing something truly selfless. But does it have to be?

First we'll say this: If a guy ever actually takes your head and pushes it toward his penis, do not fucking do it. Would you take a guy's credit card and nudge it toward the bartender?

Let's not underestimate the manipulative power of fellatio. Head can be the gift that gives back later. We're pretty sure wars have been fought over a good BJ. Just ask Marc Antony or anyone else who let their dick run their country.

There are many factors to consider when deciding what to do in that awkward moment when a guy is pushing your head down with his eyes. You'll probably consider a variation of the following: *Is it losing if I do it now? What if he takes like forever? What if his penis is one of the scary ones?*

But, bros, take note: Even if we decide to bestow this gift upon you, don't be mistaken. Given the right circumstances, this is not a sign of submission. A betch clearly knows how to use head to fuck with yours.

Whether or not you decide to give the guy a BJ should depend on three things: if you've had sex before, how much you give a shit about him as a person, and whether or not your goal is to get a boyfriend.

If you've had sex with him already, there's no reason to play suck and blow unless you'll definitely gain something later, like an

> "I may not have been the greatest president, but I've had the most fun eight years."
> —Bill Clinton

orgasm. If you haven't had sex with him and it's your intention to date, it's best to use your BJs as a tool to get him to come back for more. It may sound prude, but waiting for sex is always the way to go . . . but not for *that* long. Trust us, a guy would rather date a pseudo-prude than Courtney Love, whose mouth is just as loose as her vagina.

On the other hand, if you have only lukewarm feelings toward a guy, you might have sex to avoid giving him head. For instance, you might wind up having sex with a back-burner bro because on your three dates he's spent upwards of five hundred dollars on you. Though you're not a hooker, you're pretty sure the line of basic human decency is about to be crossed. As in, how many more nights can you make out with him and maybe allow him to go down on you? Because you're not that physically attracted to him, having sex—as opposed to giving head—allows you to gain more while giving less. The anxiety over feeling obligated to "return the favor," as opposed to feeling general lust for a bro, is how you know you have encountered a true BBB, therefore a BJ is unwarranted, because you're not trying to make him your boyfriend so there is no reason to postpone sex.

The fact remains, however, not every girl is down to go down. So the question is: Is it betchy to give head? When and to whom?

The dickaphobe: Maybe you're terrible at it, maybe your gag reflex is just really sensitive due to your bulimia, but this is the girl who's more likely to buzz her grandpa's inner ear hair than go anywhere near a guy's dick. The phobe might also just be terrified of the penis, possibly due to past-penis trauma. Like Cam Diaz in *The Sweetest Thing,* you never know what's on the other side of the wall in a public bathroom.

The just because: This girl will usually give head to a guy the first time they hook up, maybe because she thinks she's good at it.

Maybe she is. Congrats. What does a guy think when you give him head on the first date? That you will give any guy head on the first date, which is probably true. No one would want a Birkin if they were giving them away for free. But be aware that once you've set the hookup bar this high, you can't just go back to casual OTPHJs.[5]

> "My mother told me that life isn't always about pleasing yourself and that sometimes you have to do things for the sole benefit of another human being. I completely agreed with her, but reminded her that that was what blow jobs were for."
> —Chelsea Handler

This might also be the girl who would rather give head than have sex, but only if it's a one-night stand in order to keep her number down. When it comes to a guy she actually likes, she's down there faster than an Asian valedictorian running home to practice the violin.

The classic conditioner: This is the best method of allocating BJs. This is the girl who uses head as a manipulative tool to get what she wants. Since we're smart, we know that any worker will perform better when the rewards are great and given only in exchange for a job well done. But whether it's for a particularly good performance on you, a surprisingly lovely gift, or flowers at work so that everyone can be jealous of your amazing boyfriend, the recipient of the Pavlovian beej knows that he's being rewarded, and he will be motivated to keep up the good work.

The BJ extraordinaire: Above and beyond the "just because," this girl just fucking looooooves cock, plain and simple, wants to eat it for breakfast, lunch, and dinner—in lieu of her normal meals (air and Diet Coke). Or she's just fishing for compliments. You know, that

---

5 Over the Pants Hand Jobs

special type of compliment, the kind you can buy things with? Modern society refers to these women as prostitutes.

So it's clear that the BJ question is different for everyone. Sometimes sex and head hang out, sometimes sex brings head to the pregame and bounces before the party, and for some girls, head is the friend they put on their shit list years ago. But please, once you've made your decision, follow through with it. Half-assing a BJ is like a guy taking you on vacation to a dude ranch or buying you dinner and letting you pay the tip.

Orgasms: They Play Hard to Get

Every betch has a different relationship with her orgasm. Maybe she's your best friend and you see her every time the lights go out, maybe she's your frenemy and only shows up when you're with the shadiest of bros. Maybe you've never even met her, and she's a legend whose amazingness is only known to you through your besties' tales and HBO.

But no matter how tight you and Big O are, there are very few betches who don't wish their relationship was as strong as the Svedka in their vodka sodas.

Let's explore the pivotal role that orgasms, both real and pretend, play in your sex and dating life. At the end of the day, would a betch rather be wined and dined by a rich pro at Per Se or go home with a shady asshole who can make her scream louder than a tween at a Bieber concert?

Ideally, the guy you're dating is hot, rich, funny, not a complete douchebag, and ridiculous in bed. But let's get real, this bro is fucking hard to come by. Unlike males, who give more thought to the time and place of their next ejaculation than Obama put into Osama bin Laden's elimination, girls often prioritize other things before the 'gasm. Such as the quality of presents, wardrobe, and mind games. I mean, you can't introduce a vibrator to your parents at Thanksgiving.

Faking it is stupid. Pretty much every betch has faked it at one point in her life. From the skillful passive "Yesssss" to an overdone performance that would be right at home in a scene from fucking *Glee*, this shit is frowned upon. We're used to faking emotion, but only

> "Remember, sex is like a Chinese dinner. It ain't over till you both get your cookie."
> —Alec Baldwin

when it benefits us—utilizing our fake smiles and faux-down-to-earth demeanor to lock in a promotion or a new car from our dad.

Faking an orgasm involves a level of kindness that makes us want to vomit, and not in the eating mac and cheese kind of way. Why? Because usually we fake it to make a bro feel better about not being able to get the job done, or because he's taking too fucking long, and we have other shit to do.

Though the importance of the orgasm is different for everyone and further complicated by feelings about the guy's other qualities, the one thing we will say is that it's time to stop faking it. You'll never get off that way and honestly, who gives a shit about anyone's feelings but your own, right? Fake an orgasm, and the next white lie you'll be telling this bro that it's "totally okay" he bought you a Coach bag.

Being a betch means having the best, whether it's friends, guys, clothes, or sex. Heed the words of legendary slut Samantha Jones: "Who we are in bed is who we are in life. I never met a man who was bad in bed who was good at life." So keep in mind that if a guy can't kiss, he sure as hell can't fuck. Letting a bad kisser slide

ANAL: THE FINAL FRONTIER

Though we're sure women have been taking it from the back end since Adam found a way around Eve's leaf G-string, the answer should usually be no fucking way. Contrary to popular belief, the vagina isn't the most sacred orifice, the asshole is. Here's the key: Of all things to save for marriage (or the end of time), it should definitely be anal penetration. There's nothing more degrading and revolting than knowing the guy you hooked up with last night is potentially telling his friends, "Yo, this bitch let me do it in her butt last night." The only circumstance in which your ass should be an option is for a long-term boyfriend with whom you mutually want to experiment with this act. Think of it this way, if regular sex were the fox-trot, anal would be the wolf that beats the shit out of that fucking fox. So let it out of its cage at your discretion.

Let them work for it, and even then, you should only consider saying yes if this work consisted of dating you for a year and buying you a lot of shit. And if he can't wait that long, like he *really* wants to do it, give him directions to the apartment of your Gay BFF because it's clear your bro's not only looking to be the pitcher.

his way from a third date to inside of you is like volunteering at a homeless shelter or eating dinner, a huge fucking waste of time.

One-Night Stands:
Fun For When You Can't Stand

We all fuck up and make bad decisions, and one-night stands are a great example. While the occasional slip-up is forgivable, you should make sure these don't become a habit. No one wants to earn the nickname "Sleepy the Mattress Professional."

If you're going to have sex with a guy just one time (and this is excusable only in certain instances, such as spring break or immediately following a hard breakup), you should make sure you'll never have to see him again and that he doesn't know anyone that you know. An ideal one-night stand is with a hot stranger who doesn't plan on telling any of your acquaintances details of your time together or that you put out so easily.

While in theory the ONS sounds erotic and exciting, in reality it's kind of sad and lonely. They're really lose-lose situations. If the sex sucked, you just put out for a complete stranger and have nothing to show for it. If the sex was great, you won't ever see this guy again, and you'll probably develop irrational feelings of affection toward him. Either way, it's best to avoid, if you want to maintain a healthy mind-set and a normal pap test.

POSTCOITAL CONDUCT: LEARNING TO TAKE A HINT

If betches know anything about the inner workings of a bro's mind, it's that how he treats you before you have sex with him doesn't mean shit. Any guy will be really nice to you, tell you how amazing and beautiful you are, and text you up a storm in order to get you to have sex with him. What matters are the events that follow. Here's how to navigate the postcoital predicament, in order to come out on top.

Obviously this is easiest when the guy you're seeing comes over to your place, seeing as he can leave whenever he wants, and you have the power to throw out one of the following: "Oh, I'm so tired/I have drunk brunch with my besties in twenty minutes/Why are you still here?"

Obviously, if you like this guy, you want to him to stay. But if he's putting his pants on like it's a fucking timed Olympic event, he's clearly not into you.

When you wind up at his place, determining the next move gets trickier. It's all about interpreting the hints, like you're Nancy Drew . . . if she had just gotten fucked.

Learning How to Take a Hint

He wants you to stay if...	He wants you to leave if...
He says he loves morning sex.	He says he has to wake up early.
He asks you to stay over.	"So like . . . are you gonna stay over tonight? Or, um like what are you thinking?"
He starts telling you family stories.	He starts telling you about his ex-girlfriend or delves into the seriousness of the dump he just took.
He gets back into bed to spoon with you.	After peeing, he comes back and immediately puts on pants and starts looking at his phone.
He asks what you like to eat for breakfast.	He comes and then throws your bra, which had landed on his side of the bed, at you.

So, betches, if you hook up with a guy who gives you clear signs he's not interested in hanging out after he comes, be aware that you are 100 percent in fuck-buddy territory and it would probably take a miracle or a nose job to move you into mainland dating territory. Unless this is what you want, move on. No one likes a stage-5 clinger.

After you leave do not:

Text him first after you part ways.

Seem too into him or too clingy.

Text him things like *Thinking about you* or *Last night was fun.*

Tell him you can't hang out next weekend because you'll be menstruating and the first few days are when your flow is heaviest.

SEXTING: GETTING FUCKED IN 4G

Sexting has become something of a controversial issue, with antisexting shit like MTV's A Thin Line campaign, which urges teens to reconsider sending naked pictures of themselves and saying sexual stuff to each other. Yeah fucking right. Where's MTV when it's 2 A.M. on a Friday night and I don't remember where I pregamed?

Although sexting seems like a great idea in theory—what better way to accomplish your conflicting desires to be shady and simultaneously not fuck bros than by putting out with only your words—sexting is a very slippery slope.

As Anthony Weiner and Blake Lively taught us, the things you send out in cyberspace will follow you for the rest of your life. And you can bet any bro to whom you send sexually explicit shit is sharing those messages with all his friends. I mean, if he wasn't an asshole, you probably wouldn't be sexting him in the first place.

Then again, there's a fine line between telling someone you're DTF and sending them a picture of your entire body. We may promote dressing like a slut, but we definitely don't promote being on youjizz.com.

However, the entertainment that sexting provides, when you are the sextee and not the sexter, is the ultimate form of comedy. There's no situation that could match the hilarity resulting from showing your bestie the weekly sext you got from your creepy high school friend only to find out he sent her the same thing. *Victim of the mass sext.* Honestly don't even pretend like you're so repelled by sexually disturbing texts from your guy friends, you know you're wholly amused. (And again, there's no such thing as guy friends anyway.)

The best thing to do when a bro you're hooking up with initiates sexting is react the way an asshole would when you recommend he take you on a date. "I want to fuck you" should be replied to with "If you say so." If you're too fucked up to use this tactic, you can take advantage of being drunk out of your mind and allow yourself to misspell everything, as if you're absolving yourself of having made a conscious choice to send these messages. (You're not, this excuse exists only in your mind.)

You may think that having a boyfriend gives you a free pass on the sex-via-text thing, but you never know what kind of blowout breakup you might have with this guy later. So unless you have an equally embarrassing anecdote or picture of his unfortunately sized dick, we'd steer clear of this option as well.

Remember that cyberspace makes the world a lot smaller, and there's nothing that says "losing" more than your evil ex sending a topless picture of you to your grandma. So save your dirty talk for the bedroom. Your future kids don't need to be tormented by a naked pic they found on the Internet, no matter how hot you used to be.

BIRTH CONTROL:
MANIPULATING YOUR PERIOD
AS IF IT WERE A MAN

Your body is a wonderland, and you should know it inside and out. Knowing things like the type of skin, hair, and metabolism you have enables you to tend to them with the care and expensive products they deserve.

Every betch knows when her birthday, anniversary, and holiday breaks are, but many fail to fully comprehend the most important cycle of all: her period. If rhythm is a dancer, then your period is the lead ballerina in the fucking *Nutcracker*. If she's off, the whole show that is your life is dunzo. So you need to make your period your bitch by picking the right form of birth control.

The issue of BC has been a heated one, ever since the ancient Egyptians used gynecological papyrus to ward off fun-sucking babies (we kid you not). But history aside, modern birth control has to be one of the greatest inventions to hit the world since the corset.

First, know this: It is an absolute necessity to avoid premature motherhood. Anyone who appears on *Teen Mom* or has a bastard baby before the age of twenty-five is not someone you should aspire to be. Why? Because we have better things to do with our time and futures than raise some

> "If you're going to have sex, use a condom."
> —Dennis Rodman

expensive, whiny child who demands we be sensitive to their problems and not drink ourselves to oblivion. We have our little dogs for when we want to hold something cute and cuddly. Plus it's considered socially unacceptable to leash your baby.

When choosing the right form of contraception, it's important to consider your own personal tastes, whether or not you're an irresponsible fuckup, and just how much you care about not having to call that guy you accidentally had sex with last week to take you to the clinic.

The condom: For the girl who can't take pills or is going through a depressingly long dry spell, the condom is your method. Also, one thing the condom has going over the pill is that it also protects you from STDs. No one wants to fuck the girl with genital herpes, let alone the dying AIDS girl. So if you ever want to like get married or live to fifty, tell your bro that if he doesn't wrap it you won't . . . fuck it.

Let's not even get started on condomless sex unless you're 100 percent positive your guy isn't having sex with anyone else on the side. Jamie Lynn Spears or any public school idiot can tell you that pulling out is a shit method and lands you a ticket to the delivery room.

The pill: Invented by some genius back in the sixties, this is the most common among unmarried girls. In addition to making sure your skin is as clear as the day you were born, the pill allows you to know pretty much exactly what day Aunt Overflow is coming to town. This allows you to strategically schedule things like dates, spring break, and time spent with the more irritating members of your family.

Occasionally a betch will state that she's not on the pill because she has a fear of getting fat. Unless you insist on taking your daily dose with a pint of fucking ice cream, the only girls who get fat from BC probs had an eating disorder already. Besides, you know what *might* make you gain five pounds? Hormonal changes from the pill. You know what will *definitely* make you gain fifty? A fucking baby.

Side note: We all know the girl who's horrible at remembering to take her pill. She'll usually remember one day of the week and take five at a time, resulting in an excess flow of estrogen which causes her, unfortunately for you, to continuously cry or to punch someone in the face later that night. You should recommend the following to her:

The NuvaRing: For the forgetful betch. Although we don't really like the idea of getting fingered without a date or at least some foreplay, some say it's less stressful than enduring the Marimba jingle once a day. The only downside is that we know many a betch who's either got it stuck or had to deal with the embarrassment of knowing that it's still in the guy's bed from the night before.

> "Before you die, you see the NuvaRing."
> —The Betches

The injection/the IUD/the diaphragm: Okay, Mom, you can go back to fucking rando divorced dads now. Quite frankly these are for old people who are stuck in an episode of *Seinfeld*. (Side note: There are some psychos out there who swear by the IUD, but we have never met one in our lives.)

Plan B: This can be used in the event that you fuck up any of the previously mentioned methods. However, Plan B is NOT an appropriate birth control method in itself. It's expensive and embarrassing to take it frequently. Nothing is more shameful than the CVS pharmacist nicknaming you "Plan B," or worse, "that whore who comes here on Sundays."

Abortion: Try really, really hard not to need one of these, as too many can fuck up your future fertility (and make you feel like shit for aborting something with your very own genes). Duh, no one wants to marry a sterile bitch.

If you don't have access to any of the above, use **Plan A**, also known as **Plan Keep Your Fucking Legs Closed**. Remember, it's really hard to host excessive pregames and go out clubbing when you have a little party foul following you 24-7. Plus Plan A requires zero effort or planning—you just refrain from letting anyone enter you.

Summary

So as this chapter demonstrates, sex is a major part of our lives. It's therefore pivotal to approach it in the correct way, to ensure you maintain power not just emotionally but also physically.

Here are a few take-home points to consider at the end of that crucial third date or a wild evening at the bar with a hot guy.

✦ You should be selective about *everything* that you put in your body, from regular soda to penises that are attached to assholes.

✦ People by nature enjoy things that don't come easy to them, so the longer you wait, the bigger prize you become.

✦ Once you do wait for the appropriate amount of time and gain enough respect from a guy, be safe about it.

✦ Sex is by far our favorite workout. And with the right guy and good game, it can be one of the most fulfilling—pun intended—times of your life.

Dear Betches,

Lately I've been having trouble with my pro boyfriend of a year and half. We have sex a lot and it's great, but he's never gone down on me. I know, as a betch, if this is any problem at all he should be forgotten faster than you can say, "Boo, you whore," but I don't want to end our relationship just because of this. He says it's one thing that really grosses him out and he would never be able to do it with anyone, but I want it. How do I get him to go down on me without pressuring him too much?

Love,
The (lack of) Head Betch

Dear Lack of Head Betch,

Your pro sounds pretty selfish and is clearly not treating you well. He's grossed out by eating you out!? What does he think his dick is, fucking calorie-free froyo? If he's so repulsed by a vagina, he should go fuck another guy.

To clarify, based on the spectrum of sexual orientation, you are attracted to the genitals of the opposite sex, therefore you are willing to put them in your mouth. Like, are you grossed out by other girls' vaginas? Probably. Ask yourself, are you sure your boyfriend would think twice about mouthing the peen?

We all do shit we don't want to do for the people we really like, so if your boyfriend's not even *trying* to please you (or at least compensating by buying you so much nice shit that you forget about the issue), and if he's not gay, it means he's just not that into you. A guy will go down for a girl who asks for it if he likes her, no matter how much he doesn't want to. But don't try to convince him of this. Who wants to get something when the giver isn't putting forth all his effort? It'll suck.

So unless you plan on marrying this guy and having shitty sex for the rest of your life, move on. His lack of giving head is a symbol of greater selfishness to come.

Sincerely,
The Betches

The Game, Dating, and Love

"What is sexual is what gives a man an erection. . . . If there is no inequality, no violation, no dominance, no force, there is no sexual arousal."

—Catharine MacKinnon,
Toward a Feminist Theory of the State

This quote is taken from the book *The Game* by Neil Strauss, which essentially shows men how to pick up women by being an asshole. While the quote explains a lot about why men approach dating in the way they do, the author readily admits that all pickup artists are essentially scared of women and the assholery is their way of reacting to it. This is great to keep in mind as you navigate the dating world. Any guy who is mean to you or tries to throw your game back at you is inherently scared shitless. As always, the important thing to remember is to care less, because nothing terrifies a guy more than the thought that no one cares about him.

THE GAME: LOVING SHADY ASSHOLES AND HATING NICE GUYS

As an overall superior being, people whom you allow into your life will naturally be those who have proven their value to you. Whether they've proven worthy via literal favors or by simply providing you with amusement or anecdotes for your memoirs, everyone you surround yourself with is there to help you pursue your own interests in some way, even if it's subconscious. Even Freud said so. Because your subconscious always wants you to be looking out for yourself, it's totally okay and entirely expected that you only give a shit about your own needs. The importance of this is never more evident than in your relationships with the opposite sex.

When it comes to guys, the goal is to find the ideal balance between a bro who subtly puts you in your place and a bro who has a nauseating tendency to tell you how perfect you are. Why don't we want the latter guy, the one who puts us on a golden pedestal, no questions asked? Because you know you're special, so rather than date someone who's clearly overwhelmed by your awesomeness, those you date shouldn't be shocked by it. They should be worth it, like L'Oréal if it weren't sold at Walgreens.

> "I have been a selfish being all my life, in practice, though not in principle."
> —Jane Austen

Here's why a strong betch craves a power struggle with someone whose game is on par with her own. There's a psychological concept called "flow," which describes an ideal level of engagement in an activity as being fully immersed in a feeling of energized focus, full involvement, and success in the process of the activity. In flow, the emotions are not just channeled toward the object of your attention, but are positive, energized, and aligned with the task at hand.

Normally flow is used to describe a person who is really good at boring shit, like Yo-Yo Ma with music or Michael Jordan with basketball. But let's apply that concept to the art of a relationship. Your ideal guy is going to challenge you, and his game will be on the same level as yours. That is your ideal match:

"*What is the point of dating without games? How do you know if you're winning or losing?*"
—Seinfeld

someone who can take your shit and give it right back to you. You'd rather play the game with a worthy opponent who provides a challenge rather than an entirely callous asshole or a complete pushover, right? You want someone on your level. This, betches, is the essence of the game.

The simple fact is that the opposite sex drives almost everything we do. Are you working out to look hotter to impress other girls? Are you blacking out to make it easier to charm other girls (other than at sorority rush)? If the answer is yes, then guess what, you're a lesbian. (Not that there's anything wrong with that, you're welcome for helping you find yourself.)

The nonlesbians among us know that most things women do are in the pursuit of a guy. Sex is a primal urge, and there's no underestimating its importance in the grand scheme of things. Biologically, we're wired to reproduce, and so a huge part of our childbearing years are spent searching for that special someone who will provide our children with the BMWs they need to survive in this world.

So why is maintaining the upper hand with guys so important? Ever gone shopping for shoes and had your desire for that mediocre pair skyrocket when you discovered they were sold out? Ever been monstrously disappointed when your boss said you could have the afternoon off but then decided there was simply too much work for you to leave? It's human nature to want what we can't have, even more so things that seem just within your grasp but you can't completely have. This is what you should try to project. Appearing alluringly unattainable lets you dominate in your social life, at work, and—most important—in love.

> "It's only a game, Focker!!!"
> —Robert De Niro

Guys like to date girls who are independent and not needy. However, there is a balance. Men have an innate need to be the dominant one, so on a scale of one to Christian Grey you should aim for the bro who refuses to let you pay for anything yet still permits eye contact. In other words, let him do shit for you to make him feel like the big man, but continue to lead your life in a way that suggests you could also live without him. Winning in this context is the successful execution of giving off that vibe.

When a girl thinks of herself as a prize to be won, she knows that the guys she dates are lucky to have her and winning becomes easier. Showing a guy that you have a lot of shit to do and that he's not your number one priority will send the memo that he has to work for your attention and you are not just another ~~notch on their bedpost~~ girl he fucked on a Wednesday night. This is why it doesn't matter how long it takes to respond to texts from friends or bosses, but when a guy you went on a date with texts you, it's necessary to pretend you have such a very active and busy lifestyle that you don't see your phone immediately.

> "She was pleased to have him come and never sorry to see him go."
> —Dorothy Parker

People naturally like people who don't like them back. Some might call this "low self-esteem." We call it the "necessary push and pull of love."

Encountering a Nice Guy:
Lessons in Drying Up Faster than the Sahara

It seems counterintuitive to dislike someone described as "nice." After all, "nice" was the number one adjective you were bombarded with growing up. Your best friend was "so nice," these drapes are "very nice," your new Lexus is "really, really nice." So why do we hate things associated with this adjective? Like we said before, because it's fucking boring. Who wants to be nice? Nice is bland; nice is comfortable; nice is never going to be anything better than that. It is the opposite of a challenge. It is settling. It is easy. So when it comes to guys, it's easy to understand why the thought of being with someone "nice" is extremely underwhelming at best and depressing at worst.

SIGNS YOU'VE ENCOUNTERED A NICE GUY

1. He refuses to play mind games.

2. He tells you how he feels far too soon.

3. He talks to his mom several times a day.

4. He's president of the Academic Integrity Hearing Board at your university.

5. He constantly goes on beer runs and offers to DD.

6. He continues to contact you after you've stood him up four times.

7. He says you should take things slow . . . sexually.

8. He listens to what you have to say and *actually references* it in later conversations. Ew.

The nice guy has a certain lack of confidence that makes us want to vomit. Don't be flattered if a nice guy asks you out. He's the kind of tool who's been on the prowl since he broke up with his last lame girlfriend, which was probably less than a month ago. If you're a nice guy, it is virtually impossible to attain even ugly-hot status (see: Ugly-Hot, page 241). And sometimes, even if he is hot, being a kind and overly affectionate person will end with him getting fucked . . . and we don't mean on the kitchen table.

Granted, bros don't have to be sadistic or mean for betches to like them, although it does help. But beware: There's a very thin line between being a slight challenge and being someone's bitch. Sometimes nice guys are hard to spot during the initial flirtation, and we don't realize it until they've already been around awhile.

If you find yourself entangled with a sweet and boring guy, don't panic. There are a few courses of action you can take. First, you can either ride this one out for fun to see how long he'll keep coming back, no matter how many times you tell him his wardrobe is repulsive and that you hate kids and small animals. If you have a softer side, you might tell him you're just not that into him. Or, you could "wrong text" him something explicitly sexual using another bro's name. Either way, you should wait until after your birthday to end things, just in case he has a cool gift lined up. We wouldn't want anyone to waste their money, especially not on us.

You might even decide to keep him around on the off chance that he suddenly decides to become an asshole (*yay!*) and starts to ignore you. (See also: back-burner bro.) Then it's only a matter of days before you're in love with him and you can't figure out why. Seeing him hook up with someone else usually does the trick. *I don't want you, but you're certainly not fucking allowed to want anyone else!*

Not to sound like haters, it's just that we're very intriguing and complicated people. Nice guys don't fuck with our heads enough to keep us interested. We won't be won over with flowers, candy, or disgustingly emotive handwritten love letters. Instead, the key to our hearts is to strategically ignore the fact that we're hot shit and subtly insult us, at least until we're in a real relationship. Everyone knows the only thing hotter than a good actual fuck is a quality mind fuck.

Shadiness: The Less You Know the Better the Sex

So if being showered in excessive compliments and lavish gifts doesn't do it for us, what will? Let's talk about the shade factor. No, we don't mean relief from the sun. We're talking about every betch's relief from dealing with nice guys. The shady asshole bro. Some may wonder why we would ever deal with the extreme mind games that accompany shady guys, but the truth is that even the most empowered women among us have sought shade from the toxic rays of endearment and guys who long to meet our mothers. Although enjoyable at first, such nice guy attributes can send you over the edge if they go on for too long.

Sex and the City is the perfect demonstration of the shady asshole. Mr. Big is the ultimate Shady McShadester, stringing Carrie along for all six seasons of the show, doing

> **SEX AND THE CITY:**
> **A LESSON IN SHADY**
> **LINGUISTICS**
>
> CARRIE: So you and me . . .
>   then maybe this is for real?
> MR. BIG: Could be . . . .
> **TRANSLATION:** I'm shady and
>   agreeing with you without
>   actually agreeing with you,
>   so you can't hold it against
>   me later when I prove
>   extremely emotionally
>   unavailable.

douchey things like not telling her he loves her and watching basketball instead of meeting her friends. The whole idea that Big, *after ten years,* would decide to marry the delusional yet narcissistic Carrie is totally fucking ridiculous. This would *never* happen, and if it did, he would cheat on her constantly.

SIGNS YOU'VE ENCOUNTERED A SHADY ASSHOLE BRO:

1. He texts you while you're in the same room.

2. He texts more than one girl in the same room.

3. When asked if he has a girlfriend, he says, "Not really."

4. He asks you to go for a "drive."

5. He sends you videochat requests after midnight.

6. He is a late-night sexter.

7. He whispers, "Let's keep this our fun little secret" right before you hook up.

8. Response when he sees your eyes gaze over to his iPhone screen: "Oh, I call everyone baby."

9. He's consistently on Facebook chat so as to see who's available at that moment.

10. Hides his Facebook pictures *and* wall. There's something he doesn't want you to see.

11. He answers your questions with "If you say so" or "It is what it is." Fucking run.

But shadiness is one of the best forms of mind games. For a bro, possessing the shadiness gene is the gift that keeps on giving, because regardless of how long he's been whipped by some lame-ass girlfriend, his naturally shady vibe continues to work its magic. He raises an eyebrow toward a crowd and has girls in frenzies, because they each think he's trying to send them a subtle personal signal.

But while some smart bros can learn how to play the shady card strategically, there are others who just can't control their need to be fucking at least five different girls at a time. If you actually fall for the latter guy, you will find yourself being fucked emotionally twice as much as you will be physically. . . . Well, five times as much, to be accurate.

And shadiness is not limited to men. If you're sneaking off to hook up with the asshole who everyone knows will just screw you over, you know you're doing something shady. Not uncommon, not abnormal, but still shady.

WHEN YOUR BESTIE COMES DOWN WITH SHADY ASSHOLE SYNDROME

When your best betch tells you about the new tall, mysterious man in her life, what this really means is that he's probably got a lot to fucking hide. She won't buy this, though, so the only thing you can do is tell her the exact thing she wants to hear. "Yeah, he's probably just fucking you in his car because his apartment is getting redecorated . . . totally only seeing you." Or, "It makes sense that he has a lot of early meetings . . . he's like a really big deal!"

What you're really thinking is, *Okay, so he's not technically cheating on you because he never said you were exclusive. But don't worry, I'm sure he would be, if you were actually dating!*

But after having been around the block a few times, getting with the shady asshole can become tiring for a true betch. She will slowly realize that these guys are and will always be liars and cheaters, and she will move on. Let's be real, this won't happen for a really long time, like when she's looking to get married (aka realizing she's never going to have a "career").

But typically women come to this realization around the same time that males begin to see settling down as a possibility, so it all works out.

Male Evolution: From Bro to Pro

Generally speaking, whenever we reference "bros" what we're referring to is the male gender in general. This is just a facet of our chill approach to speaking, kind of like referring to all our Mexican bartenders on vacay as Pedro.

Let's first visit what the term "bro" means to us. The relationship between a betch and a bro is complicated. We're not talking about the actual romantic relationship. No, the complex part lies in how we feel about the "bro." In college, we just can't help but love their douchey behavior and excessive drinking, and we totally think it's hot when they do noble things like beg the university's president not to kick their frat off campus for hospitalizing five pledges. These guys are a great time, we love the mind games they play, and there's nothing like being able to brag to your besties that you woke up to the harmonious sounds of your bro's frat dog vomming.

The dark side of the bro is where they get their reputation.

> **INSPIRATIONAL SCENE FROM**
> **DANGEROUS LIAISONS**
>
> VICOMTE DE VALMONT: Why do you suppose we only feel compelled to chase the ones who run away?
> MARQUISE DE MERTEUIL: Immaturity?

Assuming you didn't get wifed up during freshman orientation week, chances are you can point to at least one instance when a guy treated you like shit, hooked up with another girl in your sorority, or refused to call you his girlfriend even though you were "exclusive."

These games, charming as they may be, start to go out of style when you decide you're over the days of crying in bar restrooms. As a betch matures, she begins to realize the waning appeal of the crush-a-beer-can-on-his-forehead frat-trastic bro.

A NOTE ON GOLD DIGGING

The difference between desiring a man who has a lot of money and being a gold digger is a very fine line. In general, it's okay to have a certain standard of means for a man you're willing to date, although by doing this you might miss out on the chiller, more artsy creative and interesting types in favor of the douchey Wall Street i-bankers. However, there's nothing wrong if that's just your cup of Earl Gray tea at the Plaza. However, it is unacceptable to be with a man for the sole reason that he has money. If everything else sucks or he's extremely hideous or has a really shitty personality and the only reason you're staying with him is that he keeps you in a certain lifestyle, that make you a gold digger and that's more disgusting to most guys than a fat girl. As Adam from *Girls* says right after he talks about getting eight hundred dollars a week from his grandma, "You should never be anybody's fucking slave." While it's true that everyone gets boring but rich people get boring slower, spending your nights cringing next to a repulsive man in Egyptian sheets is far less desirable than enjoying the company of a moderately well off guy whose texts still make you jitter.

Enter the pro. The pro is like the evolved bro, a guy who has "being nice" in his repertoire of capabilities, but he isn't a nice guy. The pro has morphed into an older, more subtle bro. His best qualities were always people skills, networking, and creativity, but he no longer uses them to avoid arrest for public urination or to market an eco-friendly bong. Now pros are granted positions in the business and banking world by friends of their dads and/or delusional people in HR, who actually believe that these bros don't do drugs. Ha fucking ha.

Pros are ideal for twentysomething betches because they still maintain their aura of being a dickhead, without overtly being one. The pro still parties hard and remains hot, except now they pay for VIP tables with their own salary rather than their dads'. There's nothing a mature betch would rather hear on a date than a pro complaining about how he has to wake up at five A.M. or how he secured a coveted slot on his boss's lunch schedule. These topics cause the mind to wander directly to sex second homes.

He's still a bro if...	You've found a pro if...
He had a job offer but lost it after failing his drug test.	He's six months away from his second promotion.
He gives you his number.	He gives you his business card and takes your number.
He goes to frat events every weekend.	He goes to black-tie events every weekend.
He wants to eat takeout in your apartment.	He picks you up at your apartment before taking you out to dinner.
He lives with his parents.	He takes you on his parents' boat.
He buys you cocaine.	He buys you jewelry.
He introduces himself to people by his last name.	He introduces himself to people by his full name.

So from now on, pros over bros, betches. Don't let yourself be twenty-five and still dating a bro. Remember, guys are five years behind betches in maturity, so a twenty-two-year-old girl dating a twenty-two-year-old bro would be considered borderline pedophilia. Just ask Britney Spears how much fun it is to get knocked up by an unemployed, backup-dancing loser bro.

	BRO	PRO
SHADY ASSHOLE	**Shady Asshole Bro** *Justin Bobby* *Chuck Bass* *Hank Moody*	**Shady Asshole Pro** *Bill Clinton* *Tiger Woods* *Mr. Big*
NICE GUY	**Library Wedding GDI** *Dan Humphrey* *Dwight Schrute* *Kenneth the NBC Page*	**"I will get fucked because I have a lot of money" Nerd** *Bill Gates* *Mark Zuckerberg* *Jeremy Lin*

Douchiness/Game ability ↑

← *Maturity Level* →

Betchy and the Beast: When It's Okay to Fuck Someone Ugly-Hot

A betch is very aware of her own beauty and charm, but what about the appearance of those whom she dates? Obviously, there will always be tons of hot guys who are trying to have sex with you and/or be your boyfriend. Even after you've snagged a hot pro, most of us will let his occasional weight gain or lazy beard slide for a guy who's confident. However, this does not work the other way around—a girl getting fat in a relationship is issuing herself an express ticket to a breakup. This is because men are visual creatures. While they're happy you have a good personality, they're happier that you're a size 2. Having a boyfriend or a husband with a prenup is never an excuse for you to let yourself go. Once you gain weight, your guy—and the rest of the male population—will notice. Being sexually desired and simultaneously fat is impossible for women (unless you snag a chubchaser and can somehow live with yourself).

We realize that everything we just said promotes a significant double standard, but instead of crying about it, you need to deal this reality. Ever been perplexed by that bro from high school who had a string of gorgeous girlfriends even though he vaguely resembled Hagrid? Or that guy who has fucked almost every girl you know, despite that fact that his greasy dark hair makes him look like Tim Burton? This is because this bro possesses *something*. He is ugly-hot.

An ugly-hot guy is not classically good looking. In fact, many people on the street might look at you and wonder why you're with that guy who's clearly well below your attractiveness level. However, he still retains that certain redeeming quality that keeps you interested. Most often he's hysterical, insanely cool, thinks he's hot shit (and he *actually* is), and generally just oozes self-confidence that comes from real-world success. Suddenly, it becomes easier to ignore his crooked nose/weak chin/chubby body/weird sideburns, because you're mesmerized by his ugly-hot vibe.

> "*A man can be short and dumpy and getting bald but if he has fire, women will like him.*"
> —Mae West
> See, even Mae West said so. Who is she? I don't know.

You may be wondering why it's okay for the guy you're dating to skip the gym or go bald, but it's not okay for you. The reason lies in science. Also in who's paying for your couple's retreat to Aruba.

A guy with great game and a winning personality can and will get you to like him, even if he's not drop dead gorgeous. This is because girls are more attracted to attributes that predict future support of their kids, like money and a sharp mind. Men are mainly attracted to women who look fertile, namely girls with 36:24 hip-to-waist ratios and big boobs.

Since we're making an exception for ugly guys, let's be clear. Ugly-hot is not your ex-boyfriend's delusional, 290-pound dad who thinks that his twenty-two-year-old model girlfriend wants him for anything other than his money. Ugly-hot is not about appearance; it has to do with the attitude with which a guy carries himself and, most importantly, his game. *Why am I so attracted to this bro whose facial hair is merging with his chest hair?* Definite musings of a girl who's stumbled upon ugly-hot.

Look at the royal family. Every betch you ask will tell you that Prince William is hot, but really he's just a balding Brit with bad teeth. Princely titles go a long way. Meanwhile, there are few guys lining up to fuck Adele.

Ugly-hot game can be, and often is by necessity, superior to regular-hot game. Maybe it's his badass attitude, maybe it's his funny nature, maybe it's that you just don't get why he wouldn't return a phone call from someone so much better looking than he is. Whatever his game may be, ugly-hot can be kind of a nice change. As a woman,

> "Men are only as faithful as their options."
> —Chris Rock

it's a good idea to try to date someone equally, if not slightly less, good looking because guys naturally have more of a wandering eye. What we mean by this is that a guy is more likely to be lured to the hottest thing around. It'll be easier for you if all he has to do to find the most attractive woman around is look next to him. Ugly-hot gives you that security, on top of a whole lot more stimulating conversation.

The bottom line is simple. For ugly fat girls, no matter how funny or smart you are (due to the years you spent developing your personality because you're ugly/fat), a bro probably won't even talk to you long enough to unearth these qualities. But as a girl, if you're lucky enough to snag yourself the male counterpart, an ugly-hot gem, hold on to him. He'll prove much better than a guy with a six-pack who makes you feel suicidal every time he speaks. As Evan Rachel Wood will tell you, there's something immeasurably sexy about a guy who doesn't give a fuck.

Tiny Douchebag Syndrome

Now that we've touched upon the topic of general unattractiveness, let's talk about the male's equivalent to a female's weight: height. If you ask most girls to describe their perfect guy, "tall" is usually one of the top two things on the list. Yet, who among you has not found herself in the following situation:

You're at a bar with your friends when you see some hot bros sitting at a nearby table. They signal the bartender and buy your friends a round of shots, so, naturally, you go over to thank them. You wind up sitting there for a little and hit it

> **TDS: TINY DOUCHEBAG STATUS**
>
> **Noun:** A guy below the height threshold. He manages to act like such an asshole that you ignore the fact that he's extremely short. A guy is said to have TDS if he's below 5'9" and acts like a big enough ass-hole that he can trick everyone into thinking he's much hotter and cooler (and therefore taller) than he is.

off with one of them. He's dropping just the right amount of sarcastic insults and hints about New York real estate to seem like a great catch.

You're already counting this guy's winning qualities on two hands when he gets up to go to the bathroom. At this point you're pretty much wasted, but wait, are you hallucinating? This guy is well under 5'10". You do a double take. Yup, you just spent a half hour of your night cozying up to Tiny DeVito.

Your buzz is slaughtered, and now all you can think about is how to make a quick escape before Mini-Me returns.

While this situation sucks, it is part of reality. Short guys do exist, unfortunately. And for taller girls, it's probably a deal breaker you encounter constantly. It's inevitable that bros of all shapes, sizes, and game will be interested in you. It's something you just have to get used to, like people hating you because you're pretty.

HOT HISTORICAL BRO

Former Emperor of France and a bunch of other places, Napoleon Bonaparte measured in at 5'6". Needless to say, he is a role model for short bros everywhere who want to rule the world. Psychologist Alfred Adler used him as an example to describe bros with inferiority complexes, in which short guys become overly aggressive (read: develop TDS) in order to compensate for their lack of height so they can date hot betches like Napoleon's wife, Josephine.

Fun Fact: There are no recorded portraits of N & J standing next to each other, only sitting. Draw your own conclusions.

Keep in mind that the height requirement for every girl always varies based on her own height and standards. Like, if you're 5'6" and a guy is 5'9", that means you'll be taller than him when wearing

Side note: Asking a guy his height is kind of like asking a girl her weight. If this question is even dignified with a response, you can always be sure of one thing. It's a fucking lie.

Take the stated height and subtract at least two inches. Also note, any guy who claims to be six feet is 5'11" at the most.

heels (aka always). Even though he's naturally taller than you, this is still a problem.

In general, height commands power, and taller is almost always better. That is, of course, unless this guy is like 6'9" and not in the NBA. *Yes, you and your besties all remember the incident of Jane and the Giant Freak.* Be reasonable.

But before we automatically disqualify every man under six feet, we'll admit that there are nuances in judging guys' heights, and as Albert Einstein or Rumer Willis illustrate, there are ways to overcome genetic misfortune.

The first question you must ask yourself is: How short is too short? Let's discuss:

The Height Threshold

The Height Threshold is basically a way of judging if a guy is too short to date, without considering any other factors about his personality. When debating a guy's merits solely based on height, you can refer to him as being above or below the Threshold.

For girls who are average height (like, not a midget and not an Amazon), the shortest potentially acceptable height is around 5'9", assuming the guy isn't like a scrawny nerd.

Once a bro is judged as below Threshold height, he's more dunzo than Mel Gibson at Passover. That is, UNLESS he possesses the one redeeming loophole that will get you a vacation to Munchkin Land: Tiny Douchebag Status. Think about the confident 5'7" bro who dicks around girls as he pleases, versus the guy who's 5'7" and offers to cook you dinner and holds your purse. We all know who's the first in line to the friend zone.

A bro with TDS is kind of like a girl with chubby arms. Her skinny arm pose doesn't always come through in group pictures, but if she knows how to skillfully screen texts and make bros jealous, guys will still want to fuck her instead of nicknaming her "Chunky Arms Amy." So, guys, acquire the necessary case of TDS, and we might even wear shorter heels for you (but not flats, don't be insane).

Bottom line, you shouldn't always dismiss a guy because you think he's not hot or tall enough. You should at least give him the time it takes to buy you a drink before you judge whether his physical inferiorities can be overcome. It's okay, and even encouraged, to get to know someone before you reject him. Unless, of course he's like poor.

The Maybe Gay Bro

Yes, you know who we're talking about. It's the guy with the chiseled abs whose summer polos perfectly match his boat shoes. The one who hooks up with girls, yet doesn't ever try to get past second. The guy whose dad has a voice that's just a little too soprano for comfort. He's the maybe gay bro and, well, he may be gay.

We're not talking about the guy who is so fabulously homosexual that his adeptness for Gaga sing-alongs, combined with his gorgeous gay face, confirms everything he hasn't announced. In contrast, the MGB wouldn't be caught dead at a Britney Spears concert or wearing a denim jacket, but he usually showcases things that excite us, like puffer vests, a home address on a major shopping street, and ambitious dance moves.

Don't be embarrassed if you've made out with him, you're not the only one. In fact, many of us have had awkward sexual encounters with the MGB, because this bro's sexuality is more perplexing than those buttons on the laundry machine. The MGB will often confuse a betch by doing lot of typical manly shit, like talking about how much weight he can lift, playing a sport, and spending quality time drinking with his bros. Spotting him is often harder than navigating an LF Sale.

The MGB is more mysterious than a model who doesn't do coke. When talking shit with your besties, the conversation will always at one point or another lead back to the pivotal question, "Well, is he or isn't he!? I don't get it, like can he just come out already???" Unlike our out and fabulous gay BFFs, the maybe gay bro has something to hide and secrets he'll never tell. That, or you've convinced yourself he's just like super metro with an unusual affinity for passion fruitinis. If you're the girl who's brainwashed herself into believing this, you are probably dating a gay dude. There's even the girl who hooks up with him for his amazing apartment and wouldn't think twice about continuing to date him upon hearing he bats for the other team. Undoubtedly, this is your friend who hates sex and whose husband will likely have a "best friend" in the pool house.

That's not to say that the MGB can't be straight. After all, there's a sexual spectrum, and maybe this guy has the kind of sweet sensitive heart that allows him to have twenty minutes of platonic hand holding with his female friends, who will keep him in the loop and publicly defend his sexuality. And hey, there's a part of you that even hopes you'll never find out, in the interest of maintaining intrigue and conversation points.

Though he may seem like the perfect combo between the shady asshole bro and the gay BFF, the MGB isn't someone betches actively seek out for the purposes of hooking up or dating. Often a well-meaning sorority sister set us up with him, because "you'd look good together," or we drunkenly met him postmidnight at the club, and our vodka sodas told us his velvet loafers were totally legit.

When debating whether to actually date the MGB, the decision is simpler than a trust-fund baby. Betches don't need to be a sexuality weathervane, and for an ego boost, we simply look in the mirror. Unsubscribe. While he's great for a sushi date or making straight bros jealous, the MGB is potentially playing a game that we could lose by default, and no one wants to be a guy's beard.

WINNING THE GAME: THE SCIENTIFIC METHOD OF CONQUERING ANY MALE

So it all comes down to how to win the game. Because betches don't have actual feelings, winning the game is not about the fulfillment of any sort of need for love and affection. Nor do we actually give a shit about anyone. Caring about others is for Jesus. Caring is the opposite of winning, and winning scores the ultimate prize: power and control. There's nothing more important to a betch than being on top.

For a bro, winning is fucking a girl and never calling her again. For a betch, it's receiving a triple text at two P.M. from the guy who thinks he's hot shit, desperately pleading for her to accept his date invitation.

So how can you win at the game of love and affection power and control? We've devised a handy points system for those clingy girls out there who don't naturally possess our superior analytical skills and innate fuck-off vibe.

Winning by Points

+2	Don't fuck him.
+5	Take his drugs and then don't fuck him.
+2	Let him buy you a drink, say you have to go to the bathroom, and never return.
+3	Let him go down on you, then "pass out."
+1	Casual flirting with another guy while he's looking (-1 for being obvious . . . -5 for plastering your face to this other guy's. This makes you a skank, not a winner).
+1	Wait two hours to respond to his text. Another +2 if you don't respond at all.
+6	Make a bro your bitch. You've scored these points if he holds your purse while you're in the bathroom.
+1	Invite him over, be elsewhere.
+3	Cut to the morning after. "Why are you still here?"
+2	The next girl he hooks up with is uglier than you. +3 if she's fat.
+3	He leaves a voice mail. Game over.
+2	Laugh when he tries to confront you for doing any of the above. +3 if he cries. +4 if it's in public.

Losing by Points

-2	Initiate drunk sexting.
-2	Show emotion.
-4	Stalking, in cyberspace and/or in real life.
-3	Call him. (*Never call.* If you have to dial a phone, he's just not that into you.)
-1	Friend him on Facebook.
-10	Use the word "boyfriend" in any sentence with his name just because you've hooked up three times. You're done, just quit the game.
-10	Crying. Betches don't cry, it causes wrinkles.

Disclaimer: The irony of the game, which most people refuse to acknowledge, is that you lose simply by participating. The object of the game is to be the one who cares the least, and you both still care enough to play, so you both lose. That being said, what else are we going to do with our time?

At the end of the day, winning is really about the quality and skill of your manipulation. Always watch your game, because it only takes one public display of tears (and yes, the bathroom at a party counts as "public") to be labeled a psycho and lose the game forever. Betches always get what they want and never show emotion. Remember, nice guys finish last . . . nicegirls don't finish.

The Back-Burner Bro

Truthfully, you should always have your pick of guys to date, ignore, or have sex with. Be this your fuck buddy, a shady asshole bro, or a pro, all of these men vie for your affection and bring a different kind of mind game to the table. What if, however, you're aware that a guy with great dating credentials really likes you, and so technically you should like him back, but for some reason he's just not hitting the spot?

Enter the back-burner bro. You could say that the BBB is like the opposite of the ugly-hot guy. Instead of being perplexed by your attraction to someone you normally wouldn't be attracted to, you're mystified by your ambivalence toward a guy who has all the qualities you're looking for.

All BBBs share certain nonredeeming qualities. They're not exactly nice guys, nor are they ever mean to you, but for some, the thought of having sex with him is more revolting than drinking an entire bottle of ranch dressing. Maybe he's like Ryan Seacrest: technically attractive, but you're not just physically into him. Or maybe he's like Mitt Romney, too good on paper to just throw away but like ew, Mitt Romney.

In theory, you should like the BBB, so there's really no reason to ignore him or be rude to him. But he's the kind of guy who you don't want to hang out with one-on-one. You might, however, want to meet out at a bar or club with his friends, if only so you could drink at his table. Maybe if you were drunk and/or bored enough, you'd hook up with him.

The BBB is the guy you went on the second date with, just to see if maybe something was just off the first time. By the end of the second date, you've made out with him and realize you have no desire to do that again unless extremely drunk.

WHO'S THE BBB IN YOUR LIFE?
READ THESE SIGNS AND FIGURE IT OUT.

You know that knot in your stomach when you're hanging at the top of a roller coaster or about to jump out of a plane in Interlaken? Yeah, not only is that the furthest thing from the feeling you get when he texts you but also the moment before he tries to kiss you you're usually thinking about how proud you are of yourself for not eating today.

He's the guy you text when you're in the mood to hear flattering shit about yourself and are on temporary hiatus from wanting a shady bro to call you out on your bullshit.

He's the Kevin Connolly to your Scarlett Johansson in *He's Just Not That Into You.*

He's the guy who, if you were thirty-five and for some pathetic reason, still single, you'd just marry him . . . if he were making enough money.

Like ~~Robert Frost~~ Britney Spears once said, you're at a cross-roads. Rejecting him for a third date would be like throwing out those killer shoes that aren't really in anymore, but you'll probably never wear again. You just can't bring yourself to do it, because there's this part of you that's convinced you might one day wear them again. But really? Fat chance.

How to Use Your BBB to Sign the MVP

Honestly, the back-burner bro would not even merit discussion if he weren't somehow useful to you. Everyone and everything should be a means to some end. Machiavelli was a pro who knew what was up.

Back-burner bros are like the alternates for when your star MVP is out of commission (read: acting especially shady). And we don't actually know if our sports reference makes sense, just go with it.

Because your BBB is so great on paper and good-looking, he can easily be used to make the guy you're really interested in jealous, which is always beneficial. If a guy who you really like is dragging his feet to tell you he loves you or make you his girlfriend, a smart move would be to invite your BBB to the bar for five minutes of obligatory in-his-face flirting. This will usually get the guy you really want moving. He will see how desired you are, how obviously you could potentially be happy with someone else, and how easily he could fuck this up.

The BBB can also be used to annoy your enemies, be it an ex-boyfriend, frenemy, or arch nemesis. This is because just like one man's trash is another man's treasure, one girl's BBB is usually another girl's shady asshole

"After all, isn't settling about having no opinions at all? About taking something because it's better than nothing?"
—Emily Giffin

bro. Sure you think he's lame, but to some girl that he has luke-warm feelings toward, he's just the asshole she's looking for. Just as Mariah said to her BBB Eminem, "Why you so obsessed with me?" Meanwhile, getting wifed up by Nick Cannon. If you're bored, flirting with or dating a BBB might stir up some drama among your group, or it could be a perfect opportunity to annoy a girl who has fucked with you in the past.

One caveat: Don't get too complacent, as you might be surprised how quickly a BBB can turn the tables. If you see your BBB with another girl, it might make you think you're truly into him, especially if the girl in question is your equal in appearance or coolness. If you find yourself in this situation, the important thing to remember is that the original attraction was never there. Even though you may be fooled into thinking you're into him, this probably won't last. Don't give in to your urges to settle for a guy who you think you should be into. Every moment spent with someone you think is "just okay" is a waste of your time (and his, we guess).

A girl's standards speak infinitely of her self-esteem. Being gorgeous and amazing, there will be plenty of first-rate guys who will always come along. So remember not to settle. Betches always get the best and most desirable accessories—including boyfriends and husbands. Plus, it's pretty much a fact of life that if something's easy to get, it usually fucking sucks.

The Best of Both Worlds: The Fuck Buddy

As a betch, you'll likely struggle between a desire to have a boyfriend and the desire to take advantage of your youth by meeting new people and experimenting sexually. Although boyfriends are nice for the moments you're not raging and for family functions, they also come with a lot of annoying shit. A girl in a relationship is usually a much lamer version of herself. Why waste your late teens and early twenties being tied down to one guy who you probably won't marry? Having a fuck buddy is really the best of both worlds. It allows you to be your truest, most amazing self, while getting laid on a regular basis—without having to deal with some miserable boyfriend around telling you that your crop top looks slutty.

There are some times in life when a girl can't be tied down, because there are just too many people out there who want to hook up with her. She can go out and rage, do whatever drugs she wants, and not have to answer to anyone. But while *American Pie* taught us that guys can get off with no more than a warm, fruit-filled pastry, a girl has a much better time when a guy knows what he's doing.

> " *I need more sex, okay? Before I die, I wanna taste everyone in the world."*
> —Angelina Jolie

While there are a lot of dicks out there, some are better than others. We like everything in our lives to be special and exclusive, especially the things that go in us. But since we're not about to date anyone, your established fuck buddies become very important penises (VIPs).

A VIP is just like an investment (*thanks for teaching us about the stock market, Dad*). You should do a lot of research and select carefully for the best return. Ideally, we're thinking tall, has a penis on the larger side, and knows what the fuck he's doing. We're not trying to devirginize anyone here. No need to worry about details like personality, since the two of you won't be doing much conversing. Sometimes several investments will go great for you, so you can choose which you want at any given time.

Every Wall Street asshole understands the importance of a diversified portfolio, and so does a betch. Diversification allows women the freedom to explore multiple options, while still having consistent sex and minimizing her number. Also, helpfully, it takes the pressure off talking to other guys who you might actually want to date. You don't need them for anything, so you're free to be your carefree self instead of an annoying TGF loser. One might call them a friend with benefits, but unlike *actual* friends, who you'd be there for in times of sickness and trouble, the only reason to text a VIP when he's ill would be to see if he's going to make it out tonight. Remember: He's not *really* your friend. Maybe you talk occasionally, but if not for the sex, there would probably be little-to-no contact at all—and you should keep it that way.

It's important for girls to have a string of guys on the back burner, so you never have to rely too much on any one guy for your fun. Having a quality VIP allows you to go out and have an amazing time with your friends and then have something to do (instead of eat) when you're done with the bars for the night.

And remember, guys, if you secure a coveted spot on our VIP list, you should always RSVP in a timely fashion. Otherwise, you might not get in next time.

DATING: MORE THAN JUST FREE DINNER

With bros constantly trying to fuck you, it can be all too easy to waste time with guys who you know are not the "one." We get it. Just because you're not into someone right away is no reason to turn down free drinks and a chance to talk about yourself with an adoring male. This is perfectly normal. But once you realize you're over dating for kicks and want a relationship (read: you're either "over" hooking up, you're diagnosed with HPV, or you've reached the age of twenty-five), the time comes to be more selective.

While *Sex and the City* may have deluded a generation of women into believing that women can be happy and independently single in their thirties, we're going to do you a favor and call bullshit. No fate could be worse. If we found out we were going to be thirty-five, single, and childless, we'd probably kill ourselves right now. It's completely legitimate to declare your true aspiration is to be an ~~interior decorator, housewife~~ mom.

Once you decide you're through with the single life and realize you're over the intense heart palpitations that come with the feeling that your phone is vibrating and it could be that guy who's been ignoring you for a week, you should approach dating with a new clarity. You're not in this for the thrill of the game anymore. Gone are the days of wasting your time sifting through anyone under the highest tax bracket or six feet, just for the story.

> "If you kiss on the first date and it's not right, then there will be no second date. Sometimes it's better to hold out and not kiss for a long time. I am a strong believer in kissing being very intimate, and the minute you kiss, the floodgates open for everything else."
> —Jennifer Lopez

Usually you go on a date with a guy you met recently, so it's okay if you aren't completely sure what he looks like, especially if you met him at a club while blacked the fuck out. Fear not, that's what the predate cocktail is for. While getting ready, feel free to have a glass of wine, but stay away from pounding shots. No one's trying to go on a second date with Wasted Wanda who can't be semisober for like five minutes.

Now let's look at the bro and the numerous ways he can fuck up. While we can't choose a guy for you, we can definitely tell you who's not for you. Here's our guide to dating deal breakers and how to know when you've encountered them.

First-Impression Deal Breakers

First-impression deal breakers are the small, but bothersome, qualities that you notice right upon meeting someone. If you notice these issues now, you should consider yourself lucky that you didn't waste more of your time uncovering his other shitty qualities.

His appearance and/or style: Most normal, straight guys will tell you that they never notice or care what girls are wearing, as long as they're hot. We're going to assume that this blasé attitude toward style is why guys think it's acceptable to look like shit. But they could not be more wrong. First impressions are extremely important, and the number of opportunities a bro has to fuck up is terribly underrated. Let's picture the task of getting it in as a mountain he has to climb. (You're obviously the top of the mountain.) If he starts the hike in the wrong shoes, he's going to have a much harder time getting to the top.

Making a judgment based on what a guy is wearing is kind of like assuming fat people are lazy: substantiated and very fucking accurate. Judging guys by their appearance is easier than a girl who's TGF on Blackout Wednesday. Although men are more visual creatures, girls are more fashionable. What you wear will let us know very quickly things like your wealth, power, and general ick factor. Let's break it down.

Clothes: They say it all, but generally this is a taste thing. Preppy look, frat bro look, fake hipster look, surfer look, blah,

---

CLOTHING DEAL BREAKERS

✦ Cargo pants
✦ Excessive bling
✦ Any amount of Ed Hardy
or Hollister
✦ Crocs
✦ Tevas
✦ Rings . . . on any finger

blah. It's all up to you, as long as he looks presentable in whatever way he's going for. You know the brands you want to see.

If you overlook blatant mishaps in wardrobe like the short-sleeved shirt over a long-sleeved shirt, we guarantee that, eventually, he'll be asking if you mind wearing elf ears while fucking to the *Lord of the Rings* sound track.

Shoes: A picture is worth a thousand words, but a guy's shoes can write a fucking novel. The effort one puts into the details of his footwear will be synonymous with the details he will attribute to your birthday present. If a guy doesn't give a shit about his shoes, why should you give a shit about him?

> **INSPIRATIONAL SCENE FROM *THE DICTATOR***
>
> ALADEEN: What's wrong with Crocs?
> NADAL: They're the universe's symbol of a man who's given up hope!

Elitist shoes: A betch will rarely reject a Sperry, unless the guy who's wearing them is particularly heinous. Loafers are cool, like he's definitely wealthy, but be wary of how much time he spends with his mom. Sure his Berlutis may say he's loaded, but remember gay guys can be rich too.

Flip-flops: If it's summer and the guy is wearing flip-flops, that's totally normal. But if he's wearing them during the winter, he's a fucking weirdo and will most likely work up to walking around completely barefoot by next year.

Sneakers: Reebok and Adidas are poor, Nike is legit. A guy who wears weird/old-ass running sneakers day and night is not to be spoken to. And if you stumble upon a guy wearing bright white sneakers it's safe to assume that he's a volunteer firefighter or straight from the ghetto. Tell this guy to go back to *8 Mile* and take his flat-brimmed hat with him.

Streetwear or collectible dunks can be cool, if a guy is rich and can pull off the faux-hipster vibe . . . like if he collects Les Pauls or is trying to start a clothing line called Crisp.

Hair: As with most aspects of style, standards go according to taste. Long hair, short hair, blond or brunette. Any combination of these can go so right or so fucking wrong. If the guy's hair is longer, he can either be dirty hot or just plain dirty, depending on the rest of his outfit and, you know, his face. Like, if he's rocking an oversize dark green coat and cutout-finger gloves, he's either homeless or Justin Bobby on an off day. When it comes to short hair, as long as he's not bald, we're down. As the saying goes: if he's not a skinhead, you can give him head.

Accessories: Regarding those certain guys who wear religious necklaces, like a cross or Star of David—the bigger the pendant, the smaller the penis. In general, it's best for men to accessorize minimally, as in, wear a nice watch and call it day.

His pickup lines: Once you're past the initial evaluation of his outer appearance and decide his clothes are inoffensive enough, you can now leave him an opening for the pickup line. To get a guy to try and pick you up, if you're pretty, all you have to do is smile or start a conversation with his friend. Also, making fun of him is a great subtle way of saying, "I'm not entirely opposed to fucking you at some point." A pickup line can tell you a lot about a guy. Here are a few scenarios, and how you should approach them:

"Why don't you have a drink in your hand?" [6] We will pretty much take a drink from any guy with two legs and a pulse . . . fine,

---

6 Variations include: "Hey, can I buy you a drink?" Less than thirty seconds of conversation will follow his offer, in addition to awkward conversation between his friend and yours, before he buys her a drink so shit's not awkward.

one leg and a pulse. It's simply poor form to reject an opportunity to get more fucked up. Nothing kills your libido more than having to reach for your wallet at the bar. Assuming the guy isn't on the list of local sex offenders, you should accept his offer. You may now allot him the time it takes for the bartender to hand you a drink, giving him the chance to impress you enough that he'll be around for its consumption.

"You're so beautiful." [7] This line and its variations are relatively nauseating and definitely one of our least favorites. Yes, it will work for the insecure gals. But the truly hot betch already knows she's gorg, and his statement of the obvious does not earn him any insight points. Would a journalist write an exposé about the grass being green?

"Why do you look so miserable?" [8] This could go one of two ways. If you're actually pissed off, you'll either roll your eyes or spit out a rude comment. *Why the fuck are you talking to me?* If, on the other hand, this is just your natural fuck-off vibe working its magic, he has just started a discussion about one of your favorite topics. This guy has your attention, until he begins to talk about himself. Stay tuned to find out how lucrative his job is.

Side note: In pickup artist terms, this is known as a "neg." A neg is used to subtly insult a girl to get her more interested in the guy. While these can sometimes be alluring, the guys who use negs are probably saying this shit to like fifteen other girls. It's important to watch your own game very closely. Hold out as long as possible before doing anything sexual with the guy who approaches you with the neg. You can be sure his strategy is well-rehearsed, and

---

7   Variations include: "Your eyes are so beautiful." "You're the hottest girl in this club/bar/supermarket/elevator."

8   Variations include: "You look like you're having a great time." "Things aren't so terrible." "Rough night?"

you should beware of a bro whose game is so artificial he needs to practice his pickup lines before he goes out.

"I'm like a Rubik's Cube, the more you play with me the harder I get." [9] Walk away, even if he's joking. Just . . . no.

"Hey." [10] Let the mind games begin. *He said hello, but he didn't ask how I was! Do you think he's into me?!* This one is pretty simple; either he's convinced that his looks will suffice, or he is actually incapable of maintaining a conversation. The betch is intrigued. *Oh, the mystery!* Bro has just earned another ninety seconds of your time.

What to do if a guy gives you his number: If you meet a guy, talk to him, and he offers you his number without taking yours, the only thing you should ever consider doing with that would be a fun prank call with your besties. This is how you show him how much we love to make the first move. Same goes for business cards. That's code for "I'm a douchebag with a job."

If you respond to this move that means you're contacting him first. This means you start off losing, which is a pretty bad sign for the rest of the game. This isn't the Special fucking Olympics, there's no reason to start any game with a handicap.

Secondary Deal Breakers

Secondary deal breakers only come to light once you're sober. He'll friend you on Facebook or ask you to dinner, and suddenly there's a whole new world of disgusting habits to discover and be repulsed by.

---

9 *"Am I dead, Angel? 'Cause this must be heaven!"* *"Your legs must be tired because you've been running through my mind all night."*
10 *"What's up?"* *"This bar kind of sucks, right?"*

He's poor and/or cheap: Nothing puts a bro in the friend zone faster than flashing a green Amex. *Ew, why don't you just pay with your food stamps?* It doesn't matter if he's good-looking, nice, and would probably treat us well. If we weren't superficial, we'd eat carbs.

And if a guy isn't poor but is still cheap, that's even worse.

He commits social media faux pas: Poke me once, shame on you. Poke me twice, shame on me. You should never, ever respond to Facebook poking; it's creepy and strictly reserved for pedophiles and people not from America. Bros should do the classy thing and Facebook chat us.

On the flip side, a bro who's too private on Facebook is a red flag. Hiding his photos is one thing, hiding both his photos and his wall means he has something to conceal (read: he's hooking up with many different girls, he's a former fatty, has no friends to take pictures of him, etc.).

Social media faux pas also include poor texting skills, such as the use of excessive emoticons or exclamation points. Curb your fucking enthusiasm, bro. Also, be wary of losers who use words like "homie," "dude," or "boo" even in the ironic sense.

> "Every time you date someone with an issue that you have to work to ignore, you're settling."
> —Andre Breton

He has bad date etiquette: This includes all aspects of going on an actual date. He should ask you out several days in advance and pick a restaurant that's diet-friendly. (Preferably some place that serves laxatives, ice chips, and thirty-dollar salads.) *If you want to eat man food, we know a fat girl who'd give her third chin to throw back a filet mignon with you.*

While on a date, it's a sign of insecurity if he talks about other girls. Be it be his mom, ex-girlfriend, or some girl who stained his sheets with her spray tan. We're not interested. This isn't because we're jealous (well, maybe a little), but because we're not happy unless we're talking about ourselves.

Sexual etiquette: On a date, any postdate make-out sesh should be respectful and classy in the gentlemanly sense. He might think this is a chance to show you all you're missing and more by not sleeping with him tonight, but hints of S and M while making out are aggressive and not hot. We're all for a playful bite here and there, but drawing blood on the first kiss is a major turnoff. *We know you're excited. Tone it down, Eric Northman.*

Hidden Deal Breakers

They say you can never really know a person, but hidden deal breakers are the closest you're going to get. Many guys you date won't even make it to the point that you know them intimately enough to understand psychological things about them. But if a bro can make it past the first stages without being rejected, this is when you'll discover the ugly truth. To be clear, the potential deal breakers at this stage are truly infinite, but here are a few common ones.

He has a reputation as a cheater: Shady assholes were great in college, but the postgrad betch is over it. If watching *Friends* reruns reminds us of anything, it's "once a cheater always a cheater." Date a reputed cheater, and you'll find yourself permanently *on a break.*

He's bad in bed: This encompasses all sexual dysfunction (crooked penis, ED, premature ejaculator). If he can't get it up now, you'll be feeding him his nightly Viagra before age forty. In addition, things like sexual selfishness make for shitty sex. If he's unwilling to go down on you or doesn't care if you have an orgasm, forget it. Would you want to spend the rest of your life (or any of it?) with a guy who doesn't seem sexually passionate about you?

Drunken rage issues: His aggression is so hot and masculine . . . until the night you discover he's an angry drunk. Then you'll see how truly unforgettable he is, as the hole he kicked in your door will remind you perpetually. Or worse, he's emotionally abusive. If we wanted to be verbally abused, we'd call our fucking dads to discuss our credit card bills.

He's obsessed with his mother: Whether this manifests itself through incestuous Facebook photos, couples' vacays with his mom, or erectile dysfunction due to mommy issues, you'll realize that Oedipus complex radar is kind of like having a sixth sense for guys with baby dicks. It's hard to explain, but you'll know it when you see it.

Drug addiction: It's all fun and games to date the coke bro in college, but what's called a "habit" in college is known as a "problem" in the world.

He has self-esteem, image, or weight problems: These go a little deeper, but you'll recognize this when he's eating even less than you. *Like, you're a guy! Stop ordering yogurt parfaits.*

How to Judge a Pro by His Job: Why Have a Good Job When You Can Marry Someone with One?

In college, it's pretty easy for girls to judge bros, as the best ones are either in the right fraternity or on the lacrosse team (assuming you have daddy issues/rape fantasies). Lucky for us, after decades of guys being able to pick us up without so much as buying us a single eighteen-dollar drink, we graduate college, and the standards for dating change.

That's right. Enter the real world. Bros have to get jobs.

Unfortunately for many of us, not doing work means we don't know shit about it. That means we can run the risk of being a vodka soda and some vague talk about "finance sounding things" away from waking up to some joker scurrying off to a job that requires a fucking nametag.

Let's take a look at which bros are worth granting the privilege of dating girls who are skinny enough to still shop in the Bloomingdale's juniors section.

Pros

These are the guys who make all but the most secure betch wonder if she's even good enough. If you land one of these, count yourself lucky (just don't let them know that).

Finance: This includes all the bros who work in investment banking, sales and trading, research, and private equity/hedge funds/venture capital. Because let's face it, we don't have the fucking attention span to learn the difference.

Why you want them: The dollars. Expect him to be as fashion-obsessed as a man can be without being gay and to take you to some classy places. Once finance has crushed his soul, he (rightfully) assumes that girls will only fuck him because he has money.

Why this job sucks: It turns out that no twenty-three-year-old bro,

> "If I really knew you, I know exactly what I'd find: instead of a brain a cash register, instead of a heart a bottom line."
> —*You've Got Mail*

no matter how good his education, is worth $180K per year, so they make them work the equivalent of three jobs. Also, keep your ears open for anyone who pronounces it "fin*nance*." If you hear this, congratulations, you're dating a real life Patrick fucking Bateman, and we don't mean a young Christian Bale.

Consulting: Consultants describe themselves as problem solvers who swoop in to help companies solve their greatest business challenges. What they really mean is that their liberal arts degrees prevented them from getting into finance, and clients hope that paying their firm to come in and work as really expensive interns will bump up their stock price a few eighths of a point.

Why you want them: Ah, the life of a consultant. Jetting off to exotic locales (or Bumblefuck, Nebraska), having all of your expenses paid, and making your clients feel like idiots on a regular basis. Plus, all that travel adds up to a shit ton of frequent flier miles that he can use to take you on trips, which marks the first and only time that paying with a coupon legitimately passes as a status symbol.

Why this job sucks: The nature of his job means he's almost never in the same city you are. If he's got the goods to get your attention, odds are he literally has hoes in different area codes.

The Low-Hanging Fruit

These are the guys you often settle for because they're great on paper. Having a job where someone knows what you do when you say the name usually means you'll never reach billionaire status, but still, at least they had to go to college (we think).

Law: Self-explanatory. Often sheisters of guys who wanted to make money by doing exactly what their mom told them to.

> **INSPIRATIONAL SCENE FROM _PRETTY WOMAN_**
>
> VIVIAN: That would make you a . . . lawyer.
> EDWARD LEWIS: What makes you think I'm a lawyer?
> VIVIAN: You have that sharp, useless look about you.

Why you want them: To be fair, big-time corporate lawyers can make a lot of money. Bankers and consultants love their lawyers, because they exist to rubber-stamp whatever bullshit they try to pass off as work on their clients. Never mind that three years of law school means he's pushing thirty and working first-year banker hours for less money. But at least the next time you get a public intoxication charge, you know who to call.

Why this job sucks: Two words: Public defender. Welcome to dating a guy with crushing debt, no income, and an unflappable belief that poor people deserve a voice. If you're having trouble adapting to bulimia, this ought to help.

Medicine: Thanks to the near impossibility of getting into med school these days, the guy who's on the track to becoming a doctor or actually is one is guaranteed to be pretty fucking brilliant, although probs extremely nerdy.

Why you want them: When in doubt, opt for the plastic surgeon. These guys are the coolest of the nerds, which doesn't say much. But when it comes to picking someone with a job with actual family utility, your saggy breasts will thank you later.

Why this job sucks: Long hours and it takes them fifteen years to make any real money, anyway. Best to only date these guys when they're done with all their residencies and shit, or else you'll be dating this guy in name only. A _Grey's Anatomy_ fantasy is one thing, but the only reason Meredith got to fuck McDreamy was because they were in the same building for 95 percent of the show.

Accounting: Accounting is the bottom rung of the professional services world. They neither work enough hours to feel entitled nor enjoy enough perks to flippantly fly down to Argentina for a weekend.

Why you want them: Ummm . . . we really don't know. If I wanted to hang out with people who stood over my shoulder checking my arithmetic all day, I'd go back to the third grade.

Why this job sucks: Other than "There's no accounting for how my dick is so large, given that I'm white," not once has a sentence using the word "accounting" gotten even the most desperate betch to lie about being on the pill. Here's a tip, girls: If a guy works in a field that your dad can hire on an hourly basis (be it law, accounting, or fucking gardening), he's not worth wasting an OTC Plan B on.

The Untouchable Caste

Guys in this category don't deserve a fucking breakdown, because you'd need to have one to even consider fucking them. Still, we'll give you a little cheat sheet to keep in the back pocket of your J-Brands:

Anyone in customer service: Like being a public defender, without the law school pedigree.

Actor/musician/artist/writer: All euphemisms for unemployed.

Working "in industry": A fifty-fifty shot. His dad's an oil/telecom/media mogul? Welcome to the Lucky-Sperm Club. He had to interview for his job? Welcome to fucking an accountant who couldn't even cut it at an accounting firm.

Construction/mechanic or any other manual labor: Exception—if you just got dumped by a pro with an office job and want a guy who will make him feel like less of a man.

> "I'm just a poor boy, nobody loves me."
> —Queen

So remember, when it comes to jobs, the only way you should judge a pro is by his business card.

THE GROUPIES AND
HOW TO GET RID OF THEM

Congratulations, you've realized that the man you've been seeing is a total whack-job. Now, how do you end things? Pick your poison:

The phase out: A betch with an eighth of a soul will choose this method. It involves being "busy" when asked for follow-up dates, a gradual nonreturn of texts (never underestimate the one-word reply), and the hope that he will get the hint.

The dead out: His deal breaker was so obviously offensive that he doesn't even merit an *nm u*. You treat this guy as if he has died and you wouldn't waste a black skirt on attending his funeral. Whenever someone brings him up, you sigh and state that he's DTM—Dead to Me.

The Truth: Awkz. This is a last ditch effort to get this guy to stop harassing you. He's left you various creepy voice mails asking you—with a shrill laugh—why you haven't returned his calls and asking you to "call me . . . or not." In this scenario, you're now sure you've dodged a bullet, but want to make sure this psycho doesn't burn your house down. So you send him a text describing his offense and letting him know the truth—that you're not that into him. Try and let him down easy, with something like "I think you're great, just not for me." (This is the truth-ish.) This is usually the only lie it takes to get this stage 5 off your ass.

At the end of the day, it's important to always remember that how a guy acts in the beginning of a relationship sets the tone of how he'll act for the rest of it. Hence the reasons for deal breakers at every stage of the game. So, if he's a cheap, poorly dressed, bacne-ridden bastard before the one month mark, chances are in three he'll be a McDonald's-date-taking, Proactiv-using, hemp-necklace-wearing douchebag.

THE ART OF GETTING TO THE SECOND DATE

The art of dating is a delicate one, filled with rules and complications that are difficult to follow. It's almost like a face-off, with each party wanting different things. You want a potential boyfriend, free dinners, and expensive gifts and maybe eventually sex, once the guy deserves it. The guy wants to fuck you and *maybe* all that other shit you want, once he feels you deserve it. This is why it's so important to have a plan for the face-off, and the first step to getting a second date is starting the first date right.

Even though betches have it all together at all times, every girl knows that as soon as we step into our apartments, the sweatpants come on faster than an *American Idol* runner-up is forgotten. When we're alone or around our closest besties, we have no shame picking the strawberries out of the Special K box or dipping into the weed brownie pan with our hands. But when we're on a date, shit changes. Even though a guy may claim that there's nothing sexier than a girl with her hair up and in sweats, we know that the last thing he's trying to fuck is the female version of Bruce Bogtrotter. What guys think they should want and what they actually want are two very different things. Guys *think* they should want a girl who wears sweats and no makeup because she's "chill." No guy actually wants this. Believing this is like being on the train to Lonelyville, population: you, "being chill" all by yourself, on a Friday night.

No matter how great your first date went, the real accomplishment of going out with a guy is getting asked out for round two. But since we're in the business of manipulating people and getting our way, we're going to take you through the do's and don'ts of dating like a betch.

Don't: Accept dates from guys who ask you out via Facebook message. Asking for your number via a Facebook message should be the *most* you're willing to put up with, but that should automatically put him two points behind (for lacking creativity). Asking someone out via Facebook is easy and therefore unimpressive. The next acceptable way to be asked out is via text. This is okay, but you can be sure that a guy who actually calls you has real balls and the kind of confidence that will prove itself hot in future situations.

Do: Reject the first date he suggests, because you "have something else going on that night." Then give him two dates that you would be available, even if you're free all fucking month. These choices should also be during the week and not the weekend. Even if you don't have plans, he better not know that, or you're a hop, skip, and a jump away from the booty call zone. You may be a loser with absolutely nothing going on, but he doesn't have to know that.

Regardless of the situation, when you get asked out on a date, it's poor etiquette to say no. Assuming the guy isn't heinous, you should say yes. Betches are really good people at heart, and we wouldn't want to deprive someone else of getting acquainted with the best person we know.

What to wear: While we usually preach that dressing like a slut is the only way to go, what you should wear on a date is different. We call the look you should strive for "slutty-chic." You want the guy to imagine what you'll look like with your clothes off, not be scared of how you will appear at family functions. Your goal is to look stylish, classy, and with just the perfect amount of cleavage to accomplish "speaking without speaking."

What to discuss: When out for drinks, keep the conversation light yet intriguing. In other words: about you. No, this does not mean you should explore in detail your parents' divorce and unbearable menstrual cramps. Bond over how overrated the Vatican is or the uniqueness of your first name. You should also be asking him questions about himself, but please limit this to important qualities like his income potential and the spot on the Amalfi Coast where he's planning on building his dream house.

What to order: In movies, they're always like, "I like a girl who orders a hamburger instead of a salad on a first date." Those of you who are stupid enough to believe this (and aren't fat on the outside) are fat on the inside. For the rest of us, a salad will do. Don't get anything with onions, or making out with you will taste like cheesesteak.

How to reach for the check: It's always a nice gesture to fumble through your wallet, or reach through your bag looking for your credit card, but this should always only be a gesture. If the guy actually allows you to split—or worse, pay—this guy is a cheap-ass bro, or he just wasn't that into you. There is no excuse for a guy to let you pay unless (A) you're married, and (B) it's his money in the account. A guy letting you pay for dinner before he has even had sex with you is an absolute, no holds barred deal breaker.

How it ends: There are several ways in which a date can end. Here are two.

Scenario A: If after five drinks you realize he's not that attractive, and you can't stop focusing on the disproportionate size of his ears, or if he uses nauseating terms of endearment like "beautiful" (I know how hot I am, you don't need to keep telling me), you tell him it was really nice to meet him and give him a kiss on the cheek, and head out to meet your friends at a club. It's always best to accept a date with a backup plan for later.

Scenario B: If, however, he's kind of an asshole and gives off the vibe that he might not call you back, you immediately make moves to prolong the date. As he walks you to a cab, you play coy but accept his invitation to go to another bar or chill at his apartment. This is usually followed by a lengthy make-out sesh, after which you get home and await his call one to three days later. The more unsure you are of this impending call, the hotter he gets, and the more you build up a relationship in your head, envisioning drama and hot makeup sex.

> "Christian said he'd call the next day, but in boy time that meant Thursday."
> —Cher Horowitz

Even if this guy is the douchiest shithead at the frat house, or like an actual celebrity, you should never have sex with him on the first date. It's the cardinal rule. If you put out, he'll forever only want to have sex with you, if even that. For those of you who think this isn't a big deal, that's chill, but you're also a slut. Even Kate Bosworth didn't fuck Tad Hamilton in that godforsaken movie, and he fell in love with her. The movie was very fucking stupid, but it proved a point. You could be the biggest good-looking loser from a bumblefuck town and still end up with the celebrity, as long as you *don't fuck him on the first date.*

Side note: Remember that you should leave him wanting more. It's best not to spend the entire night with a guy you just went on a date with because he'll have had his fill of you by the time the night is over. Leave at the peak of your encounter, and the guy will not be able to think of anything else but the next time he's seeing you.

Also, *don't* contact him after the date is over. That is his job. He should be thinking about you, and the knowledge that you're thinking about him will leave him feeling ambiguous toward you at best and turned off at worst. Keep the mystery alive, and don't text him. Remember: She who texts first loses.

DELUSIONAL DATING: THE GUIDE TO DATING A GUY WHO DOESN'T KNOW IT

Before we delve into the mind of the delusional dater, the word "delusional" should sound an alarm. This is not a guide to succeeding at having an imaginary boyfriend. Rather, this is a lesson in what *not* to do.

We use the term "dating" loosely here, because anyone who seriously believes they're in a real-world relationship when they aren't isn't someone we would know. When we say dating, we're talking about a situation in which a girl is so delusional about her relationships with guys that she exaggerates them to the point that she has genuinely convinced herself of untruths.

Delusional dating, like HPV, is unfortunate but widespread. Although you should never strive to be a DD, you probably have at least one friend who fits this description to a degree. Why? The DD is a constant source of hilarity, because although she's completely clueless as to the true nature of her ~~relationships~~ booty calls, everybody else knows exactly what the fuck is going on. The DD teaches us that with enough creativity, you too can twist every conversation to make it sound like you're just months away from an engagement ring. But she also serves as a reminder to live in the reality that the rest of us can see.

> "His name is . . . Glass . . . George Glass."
> —Delusional dating floser of the Brady family. Jan Brady

How to spot the delusional dater:

✦ She's the girl who tries like way too hard to be friends with his friends. This is for two reasons: to get them to say nice things to him about her, and to stalk him without *stalking* him. She will actively pursue any avenue—no matter how insane it appears—if it will get her foot in the door with this bro.

✦ The way she *talks* about guys. "So Scott and I were texting about like what he had for lunch. He's totally going to ask me to meet his parents soon, I know it!" Dead fucking giveaway.

✦ She somehow manages to turn every mention of his name into a twenty-five-minute discussion. Complete with certain specific details that she saw on Facebook. "OMG, Bryan is going to Ultra this weekend, too!" Yeah, that's not exactly a fucking secret. We all saw him write it on that girl's wall. We also didn't fail to notice how you "liked" one of your mutual friends' statuses who also posted about Ultra. We know you did this so he would see that you also like house music. We're not amateurs, and neither is he, if he even cared enough to notice.

Now let's examine why delusional dating exists in the first place. The "delusional" part usually doesn't come from anything that bros do. Every bro is going to lead women on for one obvious reason (though it evidently continues to elude some): sex, fucking duh. A girl who never recognizes this reality of the male gender is the one who positions herself for a life of delusional dating, and a future of marrying her closeted gay friend. Delusional dating is entirely about the girl and the way she wishes male-female interactions could be. It's like when you're a kid and you watch movies about Santa Claus and convince yourself that he's real. Except in this case, Santa is the guy you want to marry and you're a sad twenty-four-year-old.

So for anyone reading this, if you have the sneaking suspicion that you yourself might be a DD or even just occasionally exhibit some symptoms, listen the fuck up. If a guy is trying to date you, he will be clear about it. Obviously bros play games, but if one wants to be your boyfriend, you'll get the fucking memo.

ON THE IMPORTANCE OF BEING SINGLE

We all know these types of people. They're the ones who haven't been single since they were twelve, and if they have been, it was for about three months until they found someone new to attach to their hip.

For girls, the serial dater is a complex entity within the bestie group. Assuming she's not the UGH, meaning you still see her out at night and not just at the library or graduation, the serial dater (SD) can be an asset to any crew. Depending on what type of SD she is, she brings different things to the table.

The serial six-monther: The serial six-monther is always dating someone but the relationship never lasts longer than six months. It always ends badly and is filled with countless dramatic stories and nauseating tears. This is because the SSM models her next boyfriend after her ex. This almost always means she is with essentially the same SAB over and over again, the only difference being the guys' last name and his taste in boat shoes.

This friend will often still party hard, if only because she's going out to check on her boyfriend to make sure he's not cheating on her, or to find some bro to flirt with in hopes that someone will tell her boyfriend about it later.

> "I really don't know anything about being single yet, really. I was with someone from the time I was eighteen, so I've never been forced to take care of myself. I've always had someone doing that for me."
> —Megan Fox, not a role model

This girl is great for when you're bored and have run out of TV shows to watch. Like when you have the choice of listening to the SSM bitch about her boyfriend or watching *Grimm,* you'll choose the former, because at least it'll make you feel better about your love life. On the plus side, listening to her bitch will give you some insight on how to strategically avoid dating douchebags with no soul.

You know you're an SSM when you:

✦ Have had more than one boyfriend with the same first name.

✦ People constantly introduce you as "Jenny, she used to date Brad" or "Brad's ex-girlfriend."

✦ Have found yourself crying in a bar bathroom more than once a semester.

✦ Track your boyfriend's whereabouts more precisely than NASA tracks a meteor about to hit Earth.

The long-term relationshipper: This girl is also always in a relationship, but these relationships tend to last years. Marriage may be mentioned or, in some extreme cases, planned. While she also hasn't been single since she hit puberty, this is usually because she's been with the same one or two guys since fucking forever, usually with stints of long distance relationships (LDRs).

This friend is great because her love life is pretty much drama-free, and she's like nauseatingly happy. Because of this, she has more than enough time to listen to you talk about yourself, your dating issues, and why various guys fucking suck, without adding in her own two cents about herself. Although she's great to hash out your problems with, beware that she tells everything to her boyfriend. You can bet your ass he knows more about your sexual history than your gynecologist.

The caveat to this betch is that she's usually boring as fuck. Usually, when she's not Skyping with her BF, you'll find her sober-driving her besties to the bars or wearing a turtleneck long-sleeve dress to clubs. She makes an effort to still go out and have a good time, but fear not, she will always be ~~having less fun~~ more sober than you.

Now that we've established who this girl is, we're going to pose the question that boggles our beautiful minds: Is she boring because she's constantly in a relationship, or is she constantly in a relationship because she's boring? The world may never know, or give enough of a shit to think about it after this paragraph.

Now let's explore the elusive, yet interesting, constantly wifed-up bro. With guys, there are two types of serial daters. You should know how to spot them, in case one of them chooses you as their next special project.

The David Duchovny: The guys who constantly have girlfriends and constantly cheat on them, probably because of an undiagnosed sex addiction. They keep these girlfriends around so they can have consistent sex in an LDR, yet they still go out nightly with their bros, in attempt to enter anything with a pulse. The best part is how their girlfriend is either oblivious (dumb as shit) or pathetic (afraid that she won't find a new boyfriend postbreakup). Most of the time, these guys like the idea of having a hot girlfriend who they can flaunt in public but never have any intention for this to be like a monogamous thing.

The ~~Hopeless Romantic~~ Potentially Gay Dude: Then there are the guys who date girls who are way out of their league, in order to lock them down and take them off the market. When they're not being called "pussy whipped" by their friends or reciting lines from *A Walk to Remember,* they're consistently being bitched around by these girlfriends, whom they worship. Meanwhile, the world marvels at how E was able to ~~date Sloane for six seasons~~ even hook up with Sloane.

So while we appreciate the serial dater's role in the bestie circle (and are disgusted by her inability to ever be alone), remember that she's seriously missing out by not experiencing the single life. Being a serial dater means you're either always stressed out, or more boring than the State of the Union. From time to time, serial dating can be great. But it will suck when you're thirty-five and discover you're Julia Roberts in *Runaway Bride,* but without Richard Gere to help you decide whether you actually prefer your eggs scrambled or nonexistent.

WHEN LOVE TAKES OVER

Haters will claim that winning isn't everything, that there's such a thing as being happy with one person for a lifetime. We'll admit that such relationships do exist (why else would Hallmark have cards?), but consider some divorce statistics and then try to argue that so-called true love is usually eternal and mutual. While your marriage fantasy may be, "I want a man who loves and cares about me, someone who will appreciate the *real me* for like ever," most guys' marriage fantasies involve a hot trophy wife half his age plus seven years.[11]

Obviously, we all hope to make it to our golden anniversary. The best way to achieve this is to be self-aware enough to know who's the right guy for you. Be comfortable with yourself, because it's the only way you'll ever be so with another person, long-term. You want your boyfriend/potential husband to understand and support you the way your besties do. Even after you've won so hard that you're in a relationship with a guy who's obsessed with you, it's necessary to actively keep this feeling alive. If you're a betch, it will be easy. If not, well . . . hence the divorce statistics.

Which brings us to the milestone that makes any true betch simultaneously the happiest she's ever been and also the most nauseated: the "I love yous."

When to say it: Everyone has heard the horror story of that girl who thought she had her game in the bag and initiated the unreturned *I love you*. Of all instances in life when it's best to learn from others' mistakes, this is situation number one. *Never* say "I love you" first. Never. The amount of losing that accompanies this is more depressing than watching a dried up old slut try to get laid at a road house. You should think of saying "I love you" first like volunteering to peel the carrots when your housekeeper makes dinner. Something no sane person would EVER FUCKING DO.

The drunken I love you: Long story short: It doesn't count, and you should not say it back, unless he says it when sober the next morn-

---

11 Even being a trophy wife is no guarantee, see: Grammer, Camille. And Kelsey is a bald fucking weirdo and he's, like, Frasier.

ing. Don't be fooled by the betch who claims, "OMG, he had fifteen tequila shots, vommed all over my toilet seat, and then swore he loved me as I fed him bread and water, right before he urinated in my bed! We're meant to be! I can't wait to tell our grandchildren about our first sober kiss!" Little does she know that this bro in his drunken stupor would probably proclaim love to an orangutan, if it promised to blow him.

He says, "I love you" sober, but you don't love him: As flattering as it is, this situation is mucho awkz. If a guy is saying he loves you, and you don't even want to mumble it back, you know there's something deeply wrong—like when your dad pulls out his reading glasses to review your credit card statement, or when your period is ten days late. But congrats, you've snagged yourself a back-burner boyfriend.

> "[You said] 'I love you'?
> My God, you are completely pussy whipped."
> —*Cruel Intentions*

It's awkward not to say "I love you" back, so we give you permission to tell this white lie. It's not worth hurting his feelings, especially if your birthday is coming up and you want some really good gifts. Also, who's to say you don't love this bro on some level? I mean, you love your besties and you love froyo, so can't you say the same for the guy who gives you jewelry and orgasms?

The line is drawn at the unnecessary embellishment. Don't say, "I'm in love with you," which is a very different story. "I love you" means "I actually care about you and want to continue hooking up with you." "I'm in love with you" means "I like you so much I'd give up Diet Coke or the life of my fat cousin for you . . . and I'll stab any bitch who I see talking to you at the bars."

Being "in love": This shit is deep. Though betches rarely ~~show~~ feel emotion or affection (other than when Mom surprises you with a spa getaway or you find out they're bringing back *The Hills* cast for a reunion . . . yay!), it's not betchy to be an old cat-loving spinster. The goal is, obviously, to find a bro whose company you appreciate and is still a good actual fuck after mind-fucking is out of the equation—and that's what betches call love.

So betches, *10 Things I Hate About You* taught us that while you can like your Skechers, true love is reserved for things like your Prada backpack and a bro who gets your stomach aflutter every time you smell his cashmere sweater. Feelings that make even the strongest betch feel out of control are usually frowned upon, but for love, we'll make an exception.

Love for a true betch means having someone to (sometimes) let your guard down around. It's someone who will hold your hair while you vomit, take care of you and your kids, and

A NOTE ON THE *SEX AND THE CITY* LOVE MYTH

Though some may stress the importance of doing it on your own, we say bullshit to women who like to call themselves "independent" and "modern" and claim they don't want to get married. Whatevski, though, more guys for us to choose from. It's really no secret that we want to get married. What *is* a secret is that we're shadily into romantic shit. *SATC* tried to portray a group of women who were thrilled to be thirty-five and single, carefree and living it up with their girlfriends, one Manolo Blahnik at a time. This, girls, is a lie. To be blunt, we don't really want to work that hard, and our dream is to fall in love with a man who will take care of us while we have a cushy job we truly love and kids we have the time to be around. There are so few female CEOs because women don't want to be CEOs. We want a balance of family and work. That's the true beauty of choice.

always put you before them. And for all you bros out there who can't help but shout it from the rooftops, we get it . . . if loving us were wrong, we wouldn't want to be right either.

How to Meet His Family

Being in a serious relationship means thinking about the future: marriage, your kids' names, and the most exclusive harbor for your yacht. When it comes to these familial topics, it's no secret that a guy's own family dynamic speaks volumes about why he turned out to be the way he is. What's slightly less obvious is that his relationship with his parents and siblings often determine what kind of husband he'll make later in life. When meeting your boyfriend's family, it's important to know what to do, what not to do, and what you should be looking for, as you judge them and, subsequently, him. Let's explore.

His dad: Dads are pretty easy. The hotter you are, the more likely your boyfriend's dad will like you. He'll be proud of his son, and you will remind him of his youth and all the young girls he's no longer getting with. As his father, he wants to know that he raised his son well and brought him up with good values: motivation, family, and hot girlfriends. As long as it's not obvious to his dad that you've got your boyfriend whipped, he'll be happy to have you in his home.

What his dad says about him: If your boyfriend happens to be somewhat rebellious and doesn't really care about what his parents think, this suggests his dad was probably really strict growing up. The same explanation applies if all your boyfriend wants to do is please his dad and grow up to be "just like him" (you often see this dynamic in all those stupid fucking rom-coms). Unless his dad used to beat him when he was younger, because then we doubt you'd be meeting his parents at all.

His siblings: It's important for a guy's brothers and/or sisters to like you, because if he's close with them, they'll have a lot of influence. For sisters, you can offer to lend her your clothes after she compliments them or suggest getting a manicure. If he has brothers, offer to set them up with your friends and joke around with them in a clearly nonsexual way. Again, if you're hot, it'll be easier to gain the brothers' approval.

His mother: A guy's mother is probably the most important member of his family that you will meet, and his relationship with her will say a lot about his relationship with women. Ideally, you'd like your guy to be respectful of his mom, but not too tight. If he's rude to her or hates her, he'll probably be rude to you or evil to women in general. There are few guys more douchey than those who were ignored or mistreated by their mothers as children. (See: Hitler, Adolf.) These types are usually commitment-phobes and are saddled with annoying mommy issues, so beware if a guy talks too much shit about his mom.

On the other side of the spectrum are the oedipal types who are in love with their moms, and it's just like fucking weird. This mother will be especially critical of you, as she views her son as her property, and no one will ever live up to the high expectations she's set for her little prick. Therefore she's the one whose approval may be a challenge. Because unlike his dad and siblings who will go with the flow as long as you're likable, there are some mothers out there who will find flaws you don't even have. Remember Charlotte York's first mother-in-law? Any psychologist will tell you that Trey's impotency issues were probably just a symptom of the fact that his mom probably jerked him off too much as a kid. A guy who's obsessed with his mother is also annoying, because he cares too much about what she thinks, and you'll probably never win if push comes to shove.

Either way, when meeting his family, you should try to curb your desire to dress like a slut. Attempt to look really pretty and mildly conservative. It's nice to bring flowers or wine, and at least offer to help clean up or serve dinner. This is clearly an empty gesture and if taken up is a whole different story, but whatever. Just the offer will help you feign just the right amount of nicegirlishness to avoid being dubbed a Vienna from season something of *The Bachelor* or a psycho rude bitch. Nice additional touches include pretending to love children and small animals, sending a thank you note in the form of an edible arrangement, or maybe just giving the mother a phone call. It's hard to justify hating someone when they've done all the formalities of being a nice person, even if this is just your "meet the parents" alter ego.

What to Do If They Hate You

A natural reaction to someone's family disliking you is to either try even harder to get them to like you, or to tell your boyfriend not to give a shit what they think. To be honest, the latter probably won't work, because forcing him to turn his back on his family will most likely backfire down the road. It's also somewhat disrespectful of his bond with his parents, and what does that suggest about *you* as a future mother? Therefore, if you've done everything you can to impress them without trying too annoyingly hard, and you're still just that pretty bitch who their brother/son is dating, the best manipulation tactic is the following:

Say something along the lines of: "You know, maybe your mom's right. I really couldn't be with someone whose family didn't approve of me. I understand that must be so difficult for you, so maybe we shouldn't see each other." This, of course, will have the opposite effect and make your boyfriend resent his annoying judgmental family and want you even more. Real betches don't beg for affection. It's thrown at us, because we don't give a shit about what other people think.

THE LONG-DISTANCE RELATIONSHIP: A RECIPE FOR TEARS

When it comes to relationships, the problems couples face are often trivial. They range from issues like *Whose family are we celebrating Thanksgiving with this year?* to *It's not my fault my ex-boyfriend is still in love with me!* However, there is one hurdle that can make or break a couple, and it's bigger than your boyfriend having ugly siblings. We're talking about the dreaded long-distance relationship.

If you're the lucky betch who has managed to avoid this type of moral dilemma, don't start cheering now. The LDR is like the chicken pox; if you haven't had to deal with it when you were younger, you'll probably come across it when you're older. But one thing's for sure, once you do it, you'll never go down that road again. Maybe you're headed to college and this guy was your high school boyfriend. Maybe it's the boyfriend you obtained while studying abroad, or maybe it's your boyfriend from college, and he just got a job across the country.

Whichever way you managed to get yourself into one of these relationships, brace yourself to be fucking irritated

> *"Absence makes the heart grow psychotic."*
> —Anonymous

90 percent of the time. The main problem with LDRs is that in order for them to survive, they take a lot of fucking work. Your goal in life should be to do as little work as possible while still reaping all the benefits. This is especially true regarding sex, something that presents itself to us as easily as jokes about fat people.

Honestly, though, what's the point of a relationship without being able to have sex on demand? It's like not being able to drive the cute little white Porsche convertible that your dad got you because you have a DUI.

Some girls may say that the anticipation of seeing your boyfriend every other weekend makes the sex all that much better. We say bullshit. Yeah the anticipation is great, but the last thing you want is your boyfriend *anticipating* fucking the girl who sits in the cubicle next to him. Sure she's probably fugly. But when he hasn't seen you in a month, there's very little he won't find sexy—even kitten heels and perfume by Justin Bieber.

So what's the best way to deal with the long-distance relationship? Don't fucking do it. There are so many problems associated with this type of relationship that in no world is it ever worth it. Even if you're dying of stage-4 breast cancer, you still need to have sex. The one loophole to this is if the long-distance part is short, let's say less than four months, and there's a serious possibility of you marrying this guy. So if it's your high school boyfriend and you've just gone to college, or it's some summer fling you think is "special," just fucking run. There's literally nothing we find more depressing than wasted youth. The following are reasons you'd have more fun in rehab than in a long-distance relationship:

Sexual impoverishment: The first and most cumbersome problem (to being a productive human being) is that when you become so deprived of sex, you will find yourself wanting every guy you see, like a fucking animal in heat, just because you can't have them. Betches get what they want; abstaining is for virgins and people who forgot to buy condoms. But paradoxically, betches don't cheat. It's hard to find a way to maneuver around this sexual roadblock. So now all you're left with is the fantasy of hooking up with the guy in your accounting class. *There's something about the way he speaks about cash flow that makes me want to give him head.*

Tedious convos about nothing: What's even worse about LDRs is having to speak on the phone all the time. You can't possibly sustain a relationship through text messages so both of you make it a point to call each other once a day. *How was your day? Good. How was your day? Good.* That shit gets boring fast. Next thing you know, you can't stand the sound of his voice, and the conversation is as scintillating as one with your grandma about her hip replacement.

However, when you do see each other, the only real options of things to do together are have sex and go out do dinner. And then you wonder how your ass got 50 fucking percent larger.

Jealousy: Sure, betches are confident people and should never display weakness. But there's something about the long-distance relationship that turns even the most chill girlfriend into a fucking psychopath. No matter how "stable" you claim your relationship may be, it is inevitable that you will schedule daily Facebook stalking sessions of your boyfriend's friends' pictures, looking for him in the background, no matter how busy you are. You know you've hit an all-time low when some variation of the following goes through your head: *OMG is that Ryan leaning on the refrigerator there? I totally recognize the back of his head. Who the FUCK is that streaky-highlighted whore he's talking to!?* It can only go downhill from here.

Soon you're left dating the bro's Facebook, and you suddenly regret being too cool to post your relationship status. Like we said, these thoughts are *crazy*.

Even worse are LDRs with a time difference. To win in this scenario would be to be the one in the earlier time zone, but even so, these relationships are shorter lived than ones working in the same hour. Think about the TV and movies. Turtle and Jamie-Lynn Sigler, Mena Suvari and Chris "Oz" Klein, Justin Long and Drew Bar. Movies are supposed to glorify everything, and those relationships barely fucking worked. How do you suppose ones in real life would turn out?

Let's discuss the benefits. Okay, done. Seriously, though, the pros of long-distance relationships are slim, but they exist in winning over your guy friends. Having a boyfriend who isn't around is amazing in the sense that you have a free pass to flirt with your male friends, just as you would with your gay bestie, yet they can't act on it. Now you're that elusive girl that none of them can have, but all of them want. This will also be a setup for a really fun time when you and your boyfriend get into that insane fight when he visits, because he's sure you're having sex with one of them. *Not.*

Enter the open relationship. Nothing screams security more than being almost positively sure that the guy you're in love with is taking some fugly freshman on dates or to formals. *"But we have a rule! No below the belt!"* That's like telling a guy he's allowed to watch a basketball game but not the final quarter. Good fucking luck.

All in all, entering or sustaining a long-distance relationship is highly discouraged unless the long-distance part is temporary, and you think there's a significant chance that you'll marry him. Otherwise, there are few things more depressing to a girl than spending three years of college in a dramatic LDR with a guy, just to discover during senior week that she's "over it." No matter how good the phone sex is or how pretty he says you look via webcam, just . . . no.

MANIPULATING MEN

At every stage of the game, it's important to understand the male brain and what most of them value. Most men have a fear of marrying women who will be overly clingy, annoying, and take them away from things they love, like spending time with their friends and watching sports. Even if this is totally your plan, it's best to not let him know that right away. Wait until you've securely locked yourself into this relationship.

Pretending to Know About Sports

Pretending to know about sports is a cornerstone for dealing with the opposite sex. Bros like the idea that a girl has more going on in her head than clothes, this season's Essie colors, and celebrity gossip. A good way to do this is by honing your ability to pretend to know about sports. Although we don't give a shit about sports, guys seem to. And in order to run any machine, you should have some idea how it works.

So why not just take the time to actually learn about sports? Because what goes on in the world of sports

> **BETCHIEST ATHLETE AWARD GOES TO PRO BASKETBALL PLAYER SHAQUILLE O'NEAL**
>
> On whether he had visited the Parthenon during his visit to Greece: "I can't really remember the names of all the clubs that we went to."

changes hourly, and much like the news, this does not mesh well with our attention disorders. The best way to go about learning something about sports is to memorize a few key facts, so you can seem like you know what's going on. Just don't ask anyone if there's such a thing as a four-point conversion . . . we learned the hard way.

Don't get overwhelmed. You don't have to know much.

Guys like girls because they bring a feminine touch to life. If he wants to have a heated debate about how good LeBron James is at basketball or who the greatest football player of all time is, he'll turn to his bros, not to you. It's important to know cute, little, slightly wrong facts. You don't need an intense textbook of knowledge, because you have a vagina. Don't ever forget that. And sports "scandals" are a gimme, because you will see them on E!

Extra snaps to you if you can stomach a beer while doing any of the following (just one beer, let's not get fat):

Knowing how scores of various sports are distinguished: It's important to understand the distinction between a goal, a home run, and a touchdown. You might not be invited to the next football tailgate after you exclaim that the quarterback just made a

SPORTS PEOPLE YOU SHOULD KNOW

- ✦ Anyone who's had sex with the Kardashians
- ✦ Hank Baskett
- ✦ Derek Jeter/A-Rod
- ✦ LeBron James, Dwayne Wade
- ✦ Anna Kournikova, the Williams sisters
- ✦ Tiger Woods
- ✦ The Manning brothers, Tom Brady
- ✦ Tony Parker
- ✦ Michael Jordan, Shaq, Kobe Bryant
- ✦ Andre Agassi
- ✦ Federer, Nadal, Djokovic
- ✦ Michael Phelps, Ryan Lochte
- ✦ Tim Tebow
- ✦ Yao Ming, because he's tall as fuck

grand slam. And no, it is not okay to describe last night's game as an "epic match of red versus blue."

Know when to jump on the team-bashing bandwagon: This obviously depends on where you're from, and while betches generally don't care who wins, we definitely want our side to win. After all, we're the best, so our team should be champions.

Loving your boyfriend's favorite team and knowing his fantasy lineup: So when Aaron Rodgers gets 350 yards you'll know your boyfriend's in a good mood. A great time to suggest he take you out to sushi.

Who's Aaron Rodgers, you ask? Look it up. We did.

Be knowledgeable about sports films: Movies help us understand sports in an entertaining way, by adding in scenes about things we care about, like parties, sex, and rich people. Some notable and educational sports films include: *Rudy, Remember the Titans, The Blind Side, Moneyball, Wimbledon, Happy Gilmore, Bring It On.*

You've gone too far if: You know more than six players on any given team, you DVR actual games to watch when no males are around, or you're involved in intramural softball. Become too knowledgeable about sports and your strategy will backfire.

Finally, the NAACP is not an extension of the NCAA. Confusing, we know.

How to Pretend to Be Low-Maintenance

While most of us have many needs that must be fulfilled, a lot of guys can be intimidated by a task that seems too big for them at first. God forbid he might think you're shallow for wanting to be taken to dinner five nights a week and expecting flowers every

Friday. Think of your courtship with your bro like you're a car salesman, and he's the buyer. When selling the Mercedes, do you tell the bro all about the premium gas he'll need to fill it up with and the monthly car washes and repairs it will need? No, you let him discover that once he's already fallen in love. With that, we propose that you hide your true colors and pretend to be low-maintenance.

ANOTHER INSPIRATIONAL SCENE FROM *WHEN HARRY MET SALLY*

HARRY: There are two kinds of women—high-maintenance and low-maintenance.

SALLY: Which one am I?

HARRY: You're the worst kind. You're high-maintenance but you think you're low-maintenance.

SALLY: I don't see that.

HARRY: You don't see that? Waiter, I'll begin with a house salad, but I don't want the regular dressing. I'll have the balsamic vinegar and oil, but on the side. And then the salmon with the mustard sauce, but I want the mustard sauce on the side. "On the side" is a very big thing for you.

SALLY: Well, I just want it the way I want it.

HARRY: I know; high-maintenance.

Real estate: Although you'll likely live in an expensive and scene-y part of town, you should lightly make fun of yourself for choosing this location and make impromptu occasional proclamations of annoyance with "the scene."

Dates: It's important to pretend to enjoy at least one outdoor activity. Let's say you claim to love apple picking or trips to like a public beach or something. While disgusting, this will show your ability to "go with it" and get your J Brands dirty, if need be. This bro will think you're down for the long haul. Also, claiming you love manly foods, but never actually eating them, is a must. It's not that big of a stretch to say that you love foods that you've eaten once. Something like, "OMG I love steak so much. The rarer the better!" (In truth, you had it once at your grandpa's ninetieth birthday party at a steakhouse, and you didn't eat for a week afterward.)

Appearance: Make a *huge* deal out of the fact that sometimes you wear your hair curly, because "who has the time to always straighten their hair?" In reality, you did this once, and it was to pick up a dress from the dry cleaners.

Shopping: Claim that you love T.J. Maxx, when in reality you only went there the week your dad canceled your credit card. And you only bought gym socks.

Working out: Speaking of Lululemon, yoga just screams low-maintenance. Yoga has a very low-maintenance vibe. You appear chill, when in fact your favorite aspect of the activity is that it allows for an entire new wardrobe of expensive shit. "I love meditating. It's so Zen to be without my cell phone."

Once you've mastered the art of pretending to be low-maintenance, a man will start to picture you as a woman he could possibly marry. One who will not care if he leaves the seat up or is poor. Ha. Perfecting this art should lead to a ring, unless, of course, it doesn't. In which case, it's important to understand the following:

NOW THAT THE LOVE IS GONE: HOW TO GET OVER YOUR EX

Even for betches, life sometimes throws us hardships. We don't mean things like AIDS, poverty, or getting fat, so if you find a betch in serious distress, you can assume it's about a guy. But since we typically act in a manner that allows us to dominate males, if we're upset about a guy, it's most likely the result of a break-up.

While we'll make an exception and tolerate our besties crying (in private) during a breakup, there's nothing more perturbing to us than the girl who just doesn't quickly get the fuck over it. Popular culture tells us that you're allowed half the duration of the actual length of your relationship to get over it, but what they don't take into consideration is the entire ex-boyfriend life cycle.

This cycle applies to people who haven't found a new boyfriend or are unhappy with the new guy they're hooking up with. If you're fortunate enough to not be either of the above, it means you were probably over it for a large part towards the end of your ex-relationship, so skip to the last phase of the cycle. For the rest of you drama-seeking girls, here's what to expect when you're expecting too much.

The Ex-Boyfriend Life Cycle

New Boyfriend   The Breakup

WINNING TACTIC:
You don't actually wish this person ill. You don't care. As we've said before, the person who cares the least has the most power and is by default winning, but you're out of the game now. Winning is pointless when you've already won.

WINNING TACTIC:
Why would you revert to an earlier stage of your relationship where you still have to play games? You broke up for a reason. Be single. Why manipulate one guy when you can manipulate three? Fucking duh.

PHASE IV:

ACTUAL OVER IT

The rainbow after the storm. At this point, you might even give a smile and wave when you see him somewhere, possibly even a stop and chat. This is the greatest symbol of the Actual Over It Phase and is called the Winning Moratorium.

PHASE I:

WE STILL FUCK SOMETIMES BUT HE'S NOT MY BOYFRIEND

You're hooking up while always anxiously on edge about what he's doing and with whom. It's a mess. This never ends well, but on the slight chance that you get back together, it will probably be during this phase. We don't want to give you false hope that this will happen, so it's best to assume it won't and try to get out of this phase as soon as possible. Typically, unless you get back together, this phase ends when something happens to get you very angry at your ex.

PHASE III:

SILENCE

All communication with your ex is cut off and you've stopped cyberstalking him and talking about him. It's like counting the dead after a battle. Silent.

PHASE II:

OVER IT NOT OVER IT

You claim to be over it, but all you fucking talk about is how much he sucks and the whores he's fucking. For someone who's supposed to hate someone, you're checking for updates as frequently as one checks their Facebook or Twitter. Literally, by checking Facebook and Twitter.

WINNING TACTIC:
Eventually it becomes socially unacceptable to constantly talk only about your ex, so even if you're not fully ready for this phase, you better fucking pretend like you are.

WINNING TACTIC:
You have carefully calculated each and every move you make in order to make your ex jealous, angry, or upset. If you manage to accomplish all three, congrats, this is the ultimate in winning and greatest feeling of happiness in this phase. See the next section for a more detailed Winning Tactic.

The Postbreakup Betch and the ~~Over It~~ Not Over It Phase: How to Make Sure Your Ex Dies Alone

The only thing more fun than a betch with a boyfriend is a betch without one. This means that the postbreakup period is your time to shine. Your goal for this phase should be to appear not-psychotic and care as little about your ex as possible. Similar to the token crazy friend, the postbreakup betch is fond of diets, pharmaceuticals, and new bros. The newly single betch needs to show all those bros, especially that douchey guy who let her go, that she's single and over him.

While nicegirls may be heartbroken over a recent relationship and do horrible things like eat or cry in public, the smart betch focuses on his flaws, which never bothered her before, but looking back, she sees should've been total deal breakers.

You should repeat some form of the following mantra daily. *Whatever, his nose was crooked, he had a small penis, wasn't that rich, his hairline was receding, and he was too close with his mom.* No matter how upset you are, there's no need to drown your sorrows in Taco Bell or waste time making up revenge fantasies. Instead, remind yourself that you were better than him in every way, and there's another bro around every corner.

The postbreakup period consists of a series of events designed to rerelease you into the wild.

Step 1: The Breakup Diet. Some girls think a breakup gives them a free pass to stuff their faces with chocolate and ignore their workout routines. You will know otherwise. You will use this opportunity to become hotter, if that's even possible. The Breakup Diet is your basic, run-of-the-mill anorexia and exercise, assisted by a liberal intake of Adderall.

Step 2: Deleting your ex-bro from your contact list. This is critical, because you will avoid blacking out and texting him, which will almost certainly embarrass you.

Step 3: Being (or appearing to be) a ho fosho. Immediatcly following the breakup, wear your sluttiest outfits that border on nudity and prostitution. You already know you look good naked, now it's time for everyone else to know it too. This will also come in handy when posing with every bro at the bars while your friends snap pics. It goes without saying that your ex will be creepily lingering in a peripheral area, attempting to make eye contact while you shoot him a look that says, *I hope you die in a fiery car crash.* Extra points for embarrassing him publicly. Making him cry is the ultimate win.

> *"There's always a contest with an ex. It's called 'who will die miserable.'"*
> —Samantha Jones

Step 4: Torture via photos. This should be used to demonstrate to your ex how crazy your weekend was, with fifty-plus photos of you practically nude, surrounded by hotter, cooler guys.

When all is said and done, the not-over-it phase can be fun, if you're able to manipulate the situation so that you're always in control and never show any emotion. If done correctly, you will return to your former glory, while your ex unsuccessfully patrols the bars for a less hot version of you to take to his sister's wedding.

For the unfortunate guy who let a true betch slip away: Beware, you're not dealing with a nicegirl. She will make you more hated than Mel Gibson performing a Chris Brown song while wearing Ed Hardy at a Hitler Youth Convention.

Dear Betch,

I'm a classic betch and always have been. So after finding this site it has become my bible, nothing makes me feel better than reading a little betch.

So after almost a whole semester at college I finally met a bro I was into. We went on a date that was super cute and he ended up coming back to my room. We hooked up after watching a movie and it was totally awesome. He even texted me the next day saying what a great time he had and that he wanted to see me again. So we made informal plans for the next weekend. In the middle of the week he just stopped talking to me. The day we were supposed to hang out he texted me saying that he just didn't want anything serious.

I mean what? We only hooked up once and he initiated seeing each other again. We haven't spoken since and I know I should forget about him because he's being a jerk but for some reason I can't drop it. Should I try to talk to him or how should I handle this?

Sincerely,
I Want More

Dear I Want More,

If by "hooked up" you mean you had sex with this bro, the answer to why he's over you is clear. Clearly you suck at not fucking bros. As we mention countless times, if you have sex with a guy right away, he'll think that you have sex with every guy right away and therefore he's not special and you're kind of a slut. Of course he texted you saying he had a great time. But what he really meant is "I'm glad you put out. That was easy."

If you didn't have sex with him and just hooked up with him, you were probably being pretty clingy and annoying or showed that you were too into him. It's important to keep the mystery alive. Initially, a guy should always be unsure about whether or not you're into him and think that he can be easily replaced. Keep this in mind for the next bro, this one is a lost cause. Definitely do not try and talk to him. Get over it.

Sincerely,
The Betches

Dear Betches,

As a betch myself I can normally handle things, but I am coming to the queen betches for some much needed advice. Plain and simple I fell for my trainer (pretty hard) and he did, too, and in true betch fashion I scored months of free sessions.

Our weekly or sometimes twice-a-week sessions of cardio and weights that left me sweaty and better-looking were filled with long talks (leaving out any hint to his having a girlfriend) that turned to a very close friendship. We crossed the line over a night of sexting when we both confessed our feelings for each other. While it was everything I wanted to hear, I also feared the idea of anything happening and our relationship changing.

While we proceeded to have a total emotional relationship, nothing more physical than squats and deep stretching happened between us, other than a few hugs (which were the best ever. I know. Cheesy). I have since moved states away and receive *I miss you* texts on a regular basis, but I can't stop thinking about the "what if."

Please set me straight and back on my merry single non-hung-up-on-a-boy way.

Xo,
The "What If" Betch

Dear "What If" Betch,

This guy was never that into you. Let's explore just how we know that. You clearly gave him *many* signs that you were into it, from flirting to sexting to "deep hugs" to an *actual* confession of feelings (ew). Anyway, like we've said, guys are simple. If he wanted to hook up with you, he would've tried it by now. But he hasn't, so he clearly doesn't.

Maybe he's bored so he's texting you that he misses you. Maybe he's seeing someone else or has a girlfriend, but bottom line, if this guy wanted to fuck you and granted he's not a complete losery wimp, something would have happened by now. So it's time to move on and stop being a delusional dater.

Find a guy who's less concerned with deep stretching and more concerned with deep thrusting.

Sincerely,
The Betches

TYING UP THE LOOSE ENDS:
HOW TO GET RID OF THE
ONE WHO WON'T GO AWAY

We've all heard the songs and poems about the one who got away and, girls, if only singing a pop song while covering your nipples with Twizzler Pull n' Peels was the way to get this guy out of your head. You know that guy we're talking about, the one with whom you've convinced yourself you have a "special connection"? That guy who never does something so douchey that you'd cut him off forever, but he steadily maintains that just-under-the-radar asshol-ishness? If any of this is starting to sound familiar, you've encoun-tered a Won't Go Away (WGA).

Yeah, him. The WGA fucking sucks, but in a weirdly inexpli-cable way. It's kind of like trying to pinpoint one of the bullshit aromas that pretentious connoisseurs claim exist in wine. For some messed up reason, there's a part of you that's always drawn to him. Sure you tell him that you're busy and try to maintain an aura of not caring, yet he always seems to hold a certain place in your heart . . . well he would, if you had one.

WGA: WON'T GO AWAY

Noun: The guy who's been in your life for longer than two years, that you keep hooking up with yet you've never been in a serious relationship. You have a 40 percent chance of hearing from him on any given night, he's only "kind of an asshole," and he lingers in and around your life like a fucking dementor.

And worst of all, despite the large number of guys com-ing in and out of your life, this one is "different."

You could easily get over him, if he would just leave you the fuck alone, but why would he? He's made a point of sticking himself so firmly in your life that getting rid of him is harder than the diamonds on your Cartier watch.

Oh and when you casually mention him to your friends, they'll be wondering why you're still even thinking about this loser who has somehow managed to keep you intrigued for so long.

How To: Get Rid of the ~~One~~ Shithead Who Won't Go Away

Allowing a guy to keep you on his roll call while never actually making any serious commitments always leads to disaster. Not only it is a source of consistent anxiety, but also letting a guy jerk you around can take a toll on your self-esteem and can inhibit you from meeting other guys who will actually give you what you want. It's time to move on. So the question is, how?

❶ Stop the cycle. We're going to let you in on a little secret. The key to making a guy want to commit suicide is to ignore the shit out of him. Stop answering. Morning, night, mid-fucking-day. Whatever time you receive that seemingly innocent annoying ass *Hey, what's up?* text, it's time to just throw your phone back in your bag and forget about it. You snooze, you fucking lose. This guy has been given ample time to make his move and lock you down. Therefore we must conclude that either he's just

not that into you or has commitment issues. Either way, it's not
your problem.

❷ If you can't change him, change the
way you think about him. The key

> "A relationship isn't going
> to make me survive. It's
> the cherry on top."
> —Jennifer Aniston

to effectively ignoring him is the realization that the "connection" you feel is really just a very special kind of mind
game used by a very special and very sad kind of player.
He knows what he's doing, and what you're doing, for that
matter. Yes. He's completely aware that you take five minutes longer to respond back than he took to answer you.
And yes, he knows if you wait less, you're eager to speak to
him. You two have been doing this dance for a while, and
it's finally time to get the fuck off the dance floor.

So the next time you're tempted to reply to a text with
an aloof yet somewhat descriptive, *Just getting ready to
go out, u?*, remember that this guy thinks he's two steps
ahead of you. Be three steps ahead of him and repeat the
mantra that the WGA has G2G.

HAPPILY EVER AFTER
REQUIRES A PRENUP—
GETTING ENGAGED

Once you've been dating someone long enough, the obvious next
step is for him to propose to you. If you've been dating someone
for upwards of three years, and you're above the age of twenty-six,
the time for fucking around is dunzo. You need to make sure this
guy has plans to marry you, or you need to move the fuck on. Any
guy who says he doesn't believe in marriage winds up married two
years down the road—to a girl five years younger than you. If he

says this, it's not that he doesn't want to get married. It's that he doesn't want to marry *you*. If you want to get married, don't buy this bullshit. Instead, buy a vibrator and kick him the fuck out.

Assuming your boyfriend is in love with you and has decided to propose, you should definitely feel free to say yes assuming two things.

❶ You're not settling for a guy you're not that into, because you fear no one else will marry you. (This is a surefire way to wind up disappointed with your life.) Who you marry is a major decision, and if you're not totally in love with someone, you're bound to spend the rest of your life wondering what if you held out. Being single isn't the worst thing in the world, and those who are okay with being alone are more desirable anyway.

❷ That you're above the age of twenty-five. It's a scientific fact that the human brain doesn't fully develop until you're twenty-five years old. That means if you're twenty, you'll probably be a very different person when you're twenty-five. Why would you want to choose the person you're going to spend the rest of your life with when your brain could literally change at any minute? In addition to wasting your youth being married, you're missing out on key years in which to find yourself. You're holding a royal flush; don't fucking fold.

Important Things to Consider
When You Reach the Age of Twenty-six:

✦ If a guy has been with you for more than three years and he hasn't proposed, it's time to say something.

✦ Think seriously about a prenup. Divorce statistics are ridic. Make sure you get alimony in case this guy turns out to be a huge douchebag. (See: Law, Jude; Federline, Kevin; Brand, Russell.)

✦ If you're thirty and still single, don't panic. Join a dating site; you'll love the attention.

How to Plan Your Wedding Without Having all Your Friends Hate You

Congrats, you're finally engaged. Lost are the days of going to sleep in a sweaty panic that you're a ticking time bomb and your boyfriend is holding the switch to set you off (as soon as he tells you that he doesn't want to marry you). No longer must you sit through endless mimosa brunches hearing your besties' annoyingly excited voices bragging about how "he finally proposed!" Now you don't have to play another fucking game of pin the veil on the bride at the absurd bridal parties that the bride's sixteen-year-old sister planned. Go to enough of these and you almost wish that you could "accidentally" land the pin right in the bride's eyeball.

Now it's your turn. But take a deep breath; don't take this as a free pass to annoy the shit out of your friends, as they did you. You're above all this fluffy wedding crap. I mean, do you really want to go to another cake tasting, dress fitting, or small engagement brunch without any hard liquor with the fiancé's parents? Exactly. Our advice on planning your wedding is simple: say to yourself, "What would a nicegirl do?" And then do the exact opposite.

Rule 1: Talk about the wedding once a day.

If you bring anything up a noticeable number of times during a day, people will start to hate you. Like let's say you got a promotion. You'll tell your friends once, and that will be the end of it. No need to go on and talk about what you're going to buy with your upgraded salary. "OMG, guys, I think I'm going to buy new bedding, or like the iPhone 6 when it comes out. I totally deserve it, I mean hello? I got a promotion for a reason." The only thing your besties will wish you would buy is a new personality. The same applies to discussing your wedding: Speak when spoken to. You don't want to load too much detailed information to your besties too soon, or else the second you start asking them their opinions on how they think the chairs should be upholstered at the ceremony, we guarantee they're going to beg to be uninvited.

If you have bad taste, get a fucking wedding planner, or copy someone's board on Pinterest for all we care. Just don't be that annoying nicegirl who begs her friends to go synagogue-hopping to pick out "the perfect rabbi."

Rule 2: When it comes to bridesmaids' dresses,
say no to the Fritz Bernaise.

It has always bewildered us why people have the most hideous bridesmaids' dresses. It's your wedding, so as long as they're not wearing white, why would you ever want them to look bad? Yeah, like great, your friends look fat, and you look amazing, but your friends will never want to upload the pics from your wedding to Facebook because they will all look like shit. Are you happy now!? Think about it. Plus the uglier the dress, the more people will talk shit about you. You want to be in on the wedding shit-talking, not the subject.

So what should you do? Not be a fucking idiot, that's what. Pick a color, send friends options. Let them pick a dress that suits their bodies, and make sure you approve them. It's not hard, it's not rocket science, it's a fucking dress.

Rule 3: Don't become a bridal psychopath; you might end up in an asylum or worse, single.

There's no one more annoying than somebody who is stressed out. Yeah, sure, I feel bad for you, but only enough to throw you a Xanax and tell you to chill . . . not enough to sit here and rub your back while you're crying into your Balenciaga. If you're the type of person who needs a good sob, call a bestie who is married, your mom, or a suicide hotline. Don't put it on a single BFF or she'll immediately start texting others *Ugh, Amanda's crying and got mascara all over my white collarless shirt from Fred Segal, what a cunt.*

Planning a wedding should be an exciting time, and your fiancé should be involved. It's not normal for him to be like *IDC, you do it.* This is a bad sign for your future marriage, and you should definitely fight about it. You're not considered needy if you need help to plan your wedding; it's unfair that all the guy has to do is give you a marginally expensive ring and then it's on you to plan this entire party. You shouldn't stand for this. Let him know that he's going to get his ass off his swivel chair and go try fucking red velvet cake and interview various calligraphers with you on his lunch breaks, and he's going to fucking love it. It'll send a great message regarding your upcoming life together.

If this was too much to read, no biggie, we can summarize everything in four short words: Don't be *that* girl.

Summary

At the end of the day, dating is always a push and pull. The male-female dynamic has always been, and will continue to be, a power play. The winner is the person who is confident enough to know they'll be okay without the other person. We're not saying you shouldn't let your guard down ever, but always remember that you are the prize. The hottest thing about dating a betch is that she knows she's amazing, with or without a guy's affection. In the end, the best relationships are with yourself and, really, who could be hotter or more fun than you?

Dear Betch,

First of all, I've been a fucking betch for all twenty-three a-fucking-mazing years of my life, and your site is the best one I've been on yet (except for like *Cosmo*, so that's pretty fucking good). My problem is this: I've been dating a totally hot bro for like five years already. We went to different colleges and long distance totally fucking sucked. Somehow, I managed to get through four years of staying with him while remaining a total fucking queen betch and he should know that it was fucking hard. I mean I loved not fucking bros for four years and getting to be totally betchy to a ton of bros, but still, it was fucking annoying. Anyway, after five years, he doesn't want to get married yet. I'm fucking over it. My daddy's going to cut me off soon, and I'm relying on this bro to fund my Louis Vuitton habit that I totally refuse to kick. So my question is how do I get this bro to fucking propose without giving him an ultimatum?

Love,
I Want Fucking Carats

Dear I Want Fucking Carats,

We totally understand where you're coming from. We'd be anxious about this, too, but you're only twenty-three. We hope that writing to us helped you get this problem off your chest because a betch would *never* utter an ultimatum.

We know you're looking to avoid that, but we're glad you bring it up. We don't give ultimatums, and here's why. Giving an ultimatum is putting all your cards on the table. It's a losing tactic and smells of desperation. Also, why would you want a guy to marry you because he felt like he had to? The guy who you marry should be head-over-fucking-heels in love with you and anxious to lock you down. If he's not at this point now, skip to five years from now and he'll probably fucking hate you and resent you for forcing him to marry you.

Reality check: Most bros are not in any sort of rush to get married. Neither should you be. You might think you're ready now, but unless this bro is like six years older than you it could end badly. Bros are at least five years behind us in maturity level.

Also, why the fuck would you want to get married at twenty-three? Do you know how many years of raging and looking out for only yourself you're losing? Also, because we are smart we know that your brain doesn't fully develop until you're twenty-five, meaning you could be like a totally different person in two years than you are now. Suddenly two years down the line you're all grown up and decide that this bro's asshole remarks and constant clubbing aren't as charming as they originally were. Wait a while. Hopefully you're too cool to be locked down so early.

Since we don't know your boyfriend it's hard to give you really detailed advice, but we think it's obvious by now that your default strategy should be to play the game. Brush up on your tactics and you may have a chance at manipulating him into proposing.

Our last piece of advice is that whatever you do, make no mention of your desire to get married. Don't push too many timelines or milestones. And especially avoid doing things that may imply an ultimatum, like getting an apartment, getting a dog, or going off your birth control without telling him.

Sincerely,
The Betches

Conclusion

So now that you know that Nice is just a place in France, you should be able to go out and conquer pretty much anything you want—Everest, the mall, whatever. But just in case you're really lazy or have a short attention span due to all the drugs you've done, here's a summary.

+ Do as little as possible to get the most out of anything you want. If you have a job, it's important to manipulate others so it seems as if you've done a lot of work, while doing very little. This will free you up to enjoy the world and do things you really want to do, like tanning and keeping yourself from getting fat.

+ Speaking of fat, don't be it. It's simply never okay. Wearing stylish clothes and having the best, most expensive shit is great—but if you're fat, none of it really matters. Fat women in today's society are both consciously and subconsciously discriminated against on a daily basis. People will assume you're lazy, don't care about your appearance, and are undeserving of respect. Every celebrity, even the zaftig ones who claim to love their bodies, eventually do give in and lose weight. You can do it, too. Now stop reading, and get your fat ass to Equinox.

✦ Choose your friends wisely. Every friend has her purpose, and everyone should add value to you in some way, or else they're useless. Be good to your loyal friends and family; be bad to your arch nemeses. Everyone has his or her place in your race to the top, and not even you can do it alone. It's important to make sure you have a loyal, genuine crew with you, who can tell it like it is. Get rid of the shitty friends as early as possible. They're excess baggage and will probably stretch out your clothes. Make the most of your family, you're stuck with them for life.

✦ Use sex and dating to your advantage. Men and women are inherently different—it's a fact of life. Much as we hesitate to admit it, there are certain things our fellow women prefer and excel at. As women, sex is one of our most powerful weapons, and it dictates much of what we control in life. From the ability to bear children to the power to dominate men—a physically larger gender—your sex appeal is a major facet of who you are and where you're going in life.

✦ When it comes to love, don't let your guard down. Your lover may be the best person in the world, but he or she should always think that you are superior to them and that you, if necessary, could find someone new at any moment. Even if it's by a very, very small margin, you should maintain the upper hand in any relationship.

Finally, the driving point of this book is to tell you how to succeed as a woman in a man's world. It's to give you the tools you need to win at everything and the confidence and knowledge to rule the world. If you'd like to be nice, you already know you've come to the wrong place. But even after reading hundreds of pages that look down upon niceness and virtue, you still might ask yourself the following question: What is so fucking wrong with being nice? *What is so goddamn wrong with being nice?* Nothing.

Nothing is wrong with being nice. You could have a perfectly nice life with an okay body, a job where you fulfill all of your responsibilities, and a doormat husband who waits on you and respects you and who might never leave you for someone younger and hotter. You could have nice, low-key friends who support you through anything and are always complimentary. You could have a nice reputation, so others don't mind taking what they want from you, because they know you'll oblige them. This niceness is fine; the majority of the world is nice. And that is why it is average.

Nice will never get you to the top of any list, club, company, or dating pool. But you could still have a nice, happy life, if you decide to put this book down and tell it to go fuck itself.

No, you didn't misread, we said you could have a happy life by being nice. If there is anything this book is *not*, it's a guide to being happy. If you're

> "I've sold millions of books! I've had sex with hundreds, maybe thousands of women. . . . That shit didn't fill the hole, man. None of it did. I thought it did for a while, and it didn't. Because the hole was created by a different sort of pain, I thought this other stuff would make up for it. But that's not how it works. . . . You have to deal with those feelings directly. You can't deal with them in a bar. I wish you could, man! Because, if it was possible to cure your problems with pussy and drinking and book sales, I would have done it! I would have fuckin' done it, dude! I wish, man! I wish! But I couldn't. And neither can you."
> —Tucker Max, *Forbes*, 1.18.12

searching for happiness, search elsewhere. Take up religion, volunteering, knitting, whatever. No one said anything about being happy. In the musical *You're a Good Man, Charlie Brown,* there is a song that claims that happiness involves things like two scoops of ice cream, sharing a sandwich, and getting along. And you know what? That little fugly cartoon was probably right. Happiness is about all those things. It's about supporting others. It's about giving back to the world and being grateful for what you have. But this book isn't about being happy. This is about ruling your world. It's about being the most desired, powerful, manipulative woman you can be.

The most successful people in the world are not known for their happiness. Sure they enjoy themselves, but do you think our main betch Kate Moss is happy? No fucking way. You think Kim Kardashian wakes up every morning grateful for everything she has and setting out to make the world the best place it can be? No. She is probably fucking miserable, but we bet she's okay with that. This book is about success. Success does not guarantee happiness; it can only help you buy things in its pursuit.

This book is about being a leader, a revolutionary, about telling it how it is. You will make a lot of enemies along the way. Many people will hate you. Why wouldn't they? You only look out for yourself. You're hotter than them; you know you're better than them. Do they envy you for being happier? No. Because you're not—that's just not part of the fucking deal.

While Nice is just a place in France, happiness will always be a foreign state of mind. But fuck it. Let's rage.

Acknowledgments

We'd like to take a break from thinking about ourselves to thank the people who allowed us to embark on this glorious career that allows us to sleep late and write about the things we love.

First we have to express appreciation for our fans who share our posts, write absurd things to us, and interact with us every day. Your commitment and loyalty to spreading the shit we make up never fails to delight and flatter.

In terms of getting this book done, we'd like to thank our agent Alyssa for "getting it," making us focus, and inadvertently giving us notes for a very useful class in college, Country Club Management. Also, thank you, Kate, our editor. When we found you, you were a nicegirl who loved to read and had an embarrassing proclivity toward cats. You're still those things but now you also send us aggressive emails about comma placement so it's clear we've taught you to hold your own like a true betch. Oh and we can't forget to thank our editor-in-chief, Jen, and our publisher, Louise, and finally we can't forget to thank our other editor, Jeremie, for coming to that one meeting that one time.

In general we need to give many thanks to the Betches team, aka all the random people who've helped us survive this experience and listened to us bitch whenever we felt like it (all the time) . . .

namely the head pro, our interns, our lawyers, our agents at Paradigm, our betchy financier and everyone who tolerates us in the office building, and finally our tech team at War Against Work . . . a war we're clearly winning.

Additionally, we must thank our friends for constantly providing us with embarrassing yet empowering stories and for remembering their drunken party fouls the next morning, without which our lives would be way more boring and our book virtually nonexistent. We know it's been hard so thank you, really, for not throwing up (yet) upon any mention of the word *betch*, we really appreciate it. We'd also like to throw a half-assed thanks to all those guys we were mean to, the guys who were douchey to us, and everyone else whose life we exploited for our own personal gain.

Finally, we'd like to thank our families. We're so happy you don't cringe with embarrassment that your sisters and daughters write about sex, drugs, and blacking out, and instead embrace our ridiculous selves. Thanks for being there with us during every step of the way. Your support (read: money) does not go unnoticed.